RALPH ELLISON was born in Oklahoma in 1914. He is the author of the novel *Invisible Man* (1952), as well as numerous essays and short stories. He died in New York City in 1994. Random House published *Juneteenth*, the book-length excerpt from his unfinished second novel, posthumously in 1999.

ALBERT MURRAY was born in Alabama in 1916. A cultural critic, biographer, essayist, and novelist, he has taught at several colleges, including Colgate and Barnard, and his works include *The Omni-Americans, South to a Very Old Place, Train Whistle Guitar, The Blue Devils of Nada,* and *The Seven League Boots.* He lives in New York City.

JOHN F. CALLAHAN is Morgan S. Odell Professor of Humanities at Lewis and Clark College in Portland, Oregon. He is the editor of *Juneteenth* and *The Collected Essays of Ralph Ellison.* Callahan is the literary executor of Ralph Ellison's estate.

Trading Twelves

TRADING TWELVES

The Selected Letters of
Ralph Ellison and Albert Murray

EDITED BY

ALBERT MURRAY AND JOHN F. CALLAHAN

Introduction by John F. Callahan
Preface by Albert Murray

VINTAGE BOOKS
A DIVISION OF RANDOM HOUSE, INC.
NEW YORK

FIRST VINTAGE BOOKS EDITION, MAY 2001

The Library of Congress has cataloged the Modern Library edition as follows:
Ellison, Ralph.
Trading twelves: the selected letters of Ralph Ellison and Albert Murray / edited by
Albert Murray and John F. Callahan; introduction by John F. Callahan.
p.   cm.
Includes index.
Contents: Tuskegee and New York, 1950–1955—Rome, Casablanca, and New York,
1955–1958—Los Angeles and New York, 1958–1960.
ISBN 0-313-29424-0 (alk. paper)
1. Ellison, Ralph—Correspondence.   2. Murray, Albert—Correspondence.
3. Novelists, American—20th century—Correspondence.   4. Critics—United
States—Correspondence.   5. United States—Intellectual life—20th century.
I. Murray, Albert.   II. Title.
PS3555.L625 Z49   2000
818'.5409—dc21
[B]   99-054473

Vintage ISBN: 978-0-375-70805-3

www.vintagebooks.com

INTRODUCTION

In 1959, toward the end of his decade-long correspondence with Ralph Ellison, Air Force Captain Albert Murray writes wittily of judging a drill competition put on in Los Angeles by Negro Shriners. "Man," he tells Ellison, "I was hard put to maintain a solemn military calm watching some of the old middle-age Moses mixing all that old flatfooted, box-ankled, bunniontoed-bellhopping-headwaitering-pullmanportering stuff in there with West Point." Not to be outdone, Ellison replies from New York, in the second to last letter he wrote Murray, that during his boyhood in Oklahoma City, "no kid of a certain height was safe from [the] enthusiasm" of "old guys mad for drill." With his characteristic blend of comic description and analysis, Ellison remembers vividly the passion for drill and dance of the influential Negro adults back in Oklahoma. "Come to think of it, I probably embraced the difficult discipline of the trumpet just so that I could escape those cats." Nevertheless, young Ellison, as a member of the band at Douglass High School, accompanies the Elks drill team "as far as Denver" to the Western Convention where men and women "shuffled and ruffled and danced and pranced; some were tight and others were clowning and kidding the whole idea of what they were doing to a military form, discipline, pose, you name it—so that the occasion had everything: comedy and satire as well as the tension of tough competition. I can still see some of those tall, Watusi-looking Moses, wearing capes and fezzes and leaning on a pivot like a stagecoach taking a sharp curve, their shoulders touching, their faces skimming across a cymbal lightly.... I suppose there was the usual Negro yearning for ceremony and identification in it, and a feeling of potentiality and a threat—along with the joy in formalized, swinging movement. Whatever, I'm glad I lived through that phase and you brought it all back again."

Realizing that memories come and go and much that is precious about culture and tradition is summoned in conversation, then lost, Ellison floats an idea that suggests he is aware of the richness and depth of his and Murray's correspondence: "Why don't we do something along this line for publication, perhaps as an exchange of letters? I'm sure it would be taken by someone, especially if we pointed out the relationship to jazz. Think about it anyway." As things turned out, nothing comes of Ellison's trial balloon; in fact, as Albert Murray tells us, letters between them cease less than a year later. But the letters they did write constitute a remarkable correspondence between two American men of letters whose importance only grows as the twentieth century passes away, and a new century brings closer and closer that millennial nation of omni-Americans whose actuality and potential was recognized and described by both Murray and Ellison more than fifty years ago.

The letters between Ellison and Murray are the bounty of a rare and spontaneous friendship in which each taps into the deepest experience of the other. Spanning the fifties, their correspondence chronicles a friendship at the same time that it reveals the increasing, active visibility of the Negro who issued one unexpected challenge after another to the often desperate conformities and complacency of postwar America. Written while each man passed from youth into middle life (Ellison was thirty-five when the correspondence begins, Murray thirty-three), the letters have something of the unselfconscious, jaunty confidence and defiant attitude of the letters of Hemingway and Fitzgerald at comparable early stages in their writing lives. And although Ellison and Murray were friends on many levels, their correspondence is first and foremost a literary one in which literary aspiration is nourished by a parallel, almost proprietary interest in jazz. Indeed, like jazzmen, Murray and Ellison find their rhythm with each other and hit their stride on the page gradually. Two points of reference provide the initial bass line. The first is Tuskegee, where the two encountered each other in 1935, when Ellison was a junior and Murray a freshman. Because Murray is teaching at his alma mater when their correspondence begins, he whets Ellison's appetite for news with choice bits of gossip about who's in and who's out, as well as comments about the current character and direction of the place. Like many who leave their chosen college before graduation, Ellison has a love-hate relationship with Tuskegee about which he is much more honest in letters to Murray than in his more respectful public comments. The other tie that from the first binds Ellison and Murray is their literary ambition. When he begins writing to Murray, Ellison is obsessively yet good-naturedly in the last throes of work on *Invisible Man*, which, as late as January of 1950, he referred to as "The Invisible Man." While Ellison is finishing his novel, Murray, too, moves eagerly toward completion of his first, a manuscript that bears some resemblance to *Train Whistle Guitar*, the first novel he published in 1974, the initial volume of his Scooter trilogy. Ever the optimist, Ellison writes in his earliest letter to Murray: "Who knows, we might both have books published in 1950." Ellison, it should be remembered, had been a published writer since 1937. And although *Invisible Man* was very much in progress and still unfinished in 1950, Ellison's fiction and essays were increasingly in demand (Cyril Connolly chose the battle royal episode of *Invisible Man* for the 1947 issue of *Horizon*, which was devoted to art in America, and even as an excerpt, the chapter enjoyed a considerable succès d'estime). Murray had yet to publish any of his work, yet Ellison communicates with him as an equal in tones of easygoing fraternity.

As Ellison's star becomes ascendant after publication of *Invisible Man* and receipt of the National Book Award, and Murray takes his novel back to the drawing board for thoroughgoing revision slowed by strenuous commitments to teaching and the Air Force, one might expect the easeful, free quality of the correspondence to diminish or become a little awkward or self-conscious. But neither man lets this happen, and, best of all, neither seems to give the possibility even a passing thought. What modulations follow reflect exposure to a wider world of intellectual and cultural life, and both men's determination to bring their vernacular Negro American point of view to bear on that world. Clearly, Ellison thinks Murray is ready for and would profit from exposure on a bigger stage than Tuskegee; just as clearly, he believes the wider world would profit from Murray's insights and perspective. Although on jazz, too, Ellison is the published author, he sees Murray as his essential collaborator on the urgent project of giving the music its due as the foremost original art form of American culture. Realizing that he and Murray, in no small part because of their mutual stimulation, had the stuff—and the responsibility—to fill the vacuum in jazz criticism, Ellison tells his friend, "we might as well get started."

His "we" is worth pausing on, for it is remarkable that throughout the correspondence their literary friendship is unmarred by competitiveness—a collaborative, brotherly competition, yes, in the manner of jazzmen jamming at a cutting session, but not any corrosive competitiveness. Perhaps this is partly because each man recognizes that the other plays a different instrument. Ellison's a horn man improvising long, meditative, lyrical solos on trumpet, while Murray swings along on piano in offhand syncopation that he tends to accelerate with a sudden earthy velocity. Yet if readers are not careful, Murray's irreverent, vamping, boogie-woogie style may throw them off the scent of an extremely learned man. On his many vernacular frequencies, Murray is as thoroughly in command of what T. S. Eliot called "the whole of the literature of Europe [America and elsewhere, too] from Homer" as he is of jazz, the blues, and other forms in the African-American oral tradition. In letters and fiction alike, Murray and Ellison share a historical sense of location and dislocation, continuity and discontinuity that they express through the breaks, the changes, the syncopation, the in-choruses and out-choruses of jazz. In their prose and point of view they enact certain vernacular literary possibilities each glimpsed reading *The Waste Land* in the Tuskegee library in the 1930s; aptly, the T. S. Eliot they are in touch with is more the self-described "small boy with a nigger drawl" from St. Louis than the "classicist" and "royalist" who later held forth from London town in a bespoke British accent.

Living on foreign shores—Ellison in Rome, Murray in Casablanca—the two friends may have absented themselves from America awhile, but neither leaves his country behind. As self-styled classical and vernacular literary guardians of the republic, they write *pro domo* and *pro patria* in one and the same gesture. They miss home, and miss each other; they plan a summer trip across several European countries as if they were plotting a military campaign, and here Murray's itinerary is precise yet flexible, his sense of necessary and desired provisions as detailed and subtle as a quartermaster's. Before and after their infrequent meetings, letters whet their appetites for reunions they know likely will be few and far between. (Judging from the letters, they did not see each other more than four or five times during the decade; even so, the continuing, easeful, intimate tone of the letters suggests that the act of corresponding provided regular occasions for their already strong friendship to deepen and develop.) Abroad as well as in the States, the correspondence is a refreshing blend of personal, intellectual, and artistic observation. Murray is shrewd about taking advantage of the PX and hopping planes bound for Athens or other attractive destinations, while Ellison, like a latter-day Romulus or Remus, prowls the streets and back alleys of Rome in search of pickling spices, and afterward distills his frustration into a letter of comic outrage that a great city in a civilized country would lack the ingredients for such vernacular haute cuisine as pigs' feet.

Shortly after making the turn into his forties, while stationed in Casablanca, Murray has a heart attack, which, once detected, is considered serious enough to confine him to the stockade of bed rest with no writing allowed, only reading. In consequence, the two men speak of the need to exercise, watch their diets, trim down, and become fit, as if sensing they may be turning a corner in their lives and, perhaps, from time to time, glimpsing mortality in the mirror as well as somewhere off in the distance.

From abroad, the two friends continue to write as intensely of the American scene as they had done in New York and Alabama, and would do again from New York and Los Angeles in the last two years of their correspondence. In the mid to late fifties their letters register and anticipate many of the volatile changes that would boil over on the American scene during the next decade, especially on the frequencies of race relations, music, and even sexuality. Always, memory is the touchstone for the present and future as well as the past, the Civil War the huge stone under which lies the nation's still to be accomplished rendezvous with its principles, its identity, and its destiny. In their idiom the Negro is "mose"—old Moses who ever seeks the promised land through the fluid, abiding covenant of American democracy. Mose is also an ironic, inside name for the sly and cunning Negro trickster whose subservience is a mask behind which he slips the racial yoke and turns the joke on the white folks. In a riff on Negro preachers, prophetic of Reverent Hickman, who is beginning to dominate his novel-in-progress, Ellison writes Murray, "I'm supposed to know Negroes, being one myself, but these Moses are revealing just a little bit more of their complexity." Ever the disappointed son vis-à-vis his alma mater, Ellison seethes at the contrast between what Martin Luther King, Jr., would soon call "the marvelous new Negro militancy" and what Ellison considers retrograde, reactionary antics at Tuskegee: "here Africans and West Indians are taking over governments and Montgomery Negroes are showing their quality and *they* continue to act like this is 1915."

As his time in Rome is winding down, perhaps forgetting that he has not answered two of Murray's letters, Ellison writes that "[t]his has been one of our longest silences, which means that the world has really been too much with us." He means with him, for he adds that "I've been up to my ass in typescript and have only just climbed out of one level of the mess after another back to my novel." During Ellison's last unsettling months in Rome, Murray seems his friend's polestar, a point of reference he counts on against personal and artistic uncertainties. "You're the only one I really write to," he confesses, before closing the letter with tender solicitude for his friend's health and work, and a touching regard for Murray's wife and daughter as shown by a onetime play on their names and his own: "So, rest, man, and sketch out some more of those episodes. Love to lovable Mokable and Miqueable, from Ralphable."

As the fifties yield to the sixties, the Ellison-Murray correspondence does not cease so much as halt. It does not conclude; there is no sense of an ending. Readers are unprepared when the last letter, like the first, arrives from Murray, and we are left to imagine their conversation of friendship continuing on the telephone and, in a year or two, frequent visits, once the Murrays move to Harlem within a long walk (or short ride) of the Ellisons' Riverside Drive apartment. We are left to imagine what riffs the two exchanged about the accelerating, alternating hubris and nemesis of American culture and politics in the sixties and beyond. Knowing that Ellison and Murray left plenty on the record about the subtle and not so subtle changes in American life during succeeding decades, I cannot stifle a sigh of regret that they did not riff and signify on paper *with each other.*

On the other hand, maybe we should be left guessing. Ellison and Murray are jazzmen, after all, and jazz doesn't tie up all the loose ends. Jazz leaves things up in the air, to be continued, if not on one frequency, then on another. Maybe it's enough that their correspondence in the fifties tells the story of two black intellectuals and writers fully acting out Ellison's proposition ahead of its time. "[I]f Mose takes advantage of his own sense of reality, he doesn't have to step back for anybody." Not only did Ralph Ellison and Albert Murray not "step back" in their books of fiction and essays, in their epistolary conversation with each other they stepped forward and advanced the possibilities suggested by that elusive phrase, American identity. Foremost among these is their shared conviction that what Murray calls the American "social contract" is still evolving and that Hector St. John de Crèvecoeur's eighteenth-century question, "What is an American?," is not fully answered. In a decade of slow awakening, Ellison and Murray brought a vernacular intelligence, defiance, fervor, and, above all, style to American culture. Forty years after the last of these letters, it is clear that, even as they spoke privately to each other, "on the lower frequencies" they were also talking for the rest of us.

JOHN F. CALLAHAN

CONTENTS

EDITORS' NOTE

For authors like F. Scott Fitzgerald, whose spelling is almost flawed enough to constitute an element of style, it is appropriate to incorporate misspellings into the published text of their letters. But this is not the case with Ralph Ellison or Albert Murray. For this reason we have silently corrected the occasional misspellings that occur in letters included in this volume of their selected correspondence. In the case of missing words, we have inserted within square brackets words clearly and unintentionally left out of some of the letters. Finally, we should note that we have included two letters by Fanny Ellison germane to the flow of the correspondence. The first, from New York, is dated June 9, 1952; the second, from Rome, is dated July 31, 1956. Footnotes identify persons, places, and events mentioned in the letters. In the rare instance when anything has been omitted from a letter, the omission is indicated in the text by ellipses within brackets.

JOHN F. CALLAHAN
ALBERT MURRAY

PREFACE

Ralph Ellison and I became close friends and literary colleagues during the academic year of 1947–1948, while I was in New York earning my master of arts degree in English at New York University, and he was working full-time on the manuscript of the novel that was to become *Invisible Man*.

I had been aware of him and of his interest in serious fiction since the fall term of 1935–1936, when I was an eager young freshman at Tuskegee Institute in Alabama on a scholarship from the Mobile County Training School, and he was a junior year upperclassman in the School of Music and a leading trumpet player in the famous Tuskegee School Band. I did not meet him during the one term that we overlapped, but I did know that he was there from Oklahoma City on some kind of special scholarship grant; and of all the upperclassmen, he was the one by whom I was most strongly impressed. I liked his very stylish collegiate wardrobe and was struck by the fact that he seemed as serious about supplementing course requirements with further reading as I was. And I also liked the fact that he seemed to do things very much on his own rather than as a member of a group.

The trumpet was his major instrument, but I also came to know that in fact he was enrolled in the School of Music because he wanted to become a composer of concert hall music. I found out later on that he had chosen to come to Tuskegee because its School of Music was directed by William L. Dawson, the conductor of the renowned Tuskegee Institute Choir who had also recently composed a work that received national acclaim as the first Negro folk symphony when it was premiered by Leopold Stokowski conducting the Philadelphia Symphony Orchestra.

What made Ralph an upperclassman of special interest to me, however, was the fact that he seemed more involved with literary matters than any of the upper-class English majors whom I could observe. When you saw him on his way back and forth across the campus he was more likely to be carrying a clutch of library books on history and literature than his trumpet case or a folder of music scores. I remember him doing copy work on sheets of music at a table by himself in the library every now and then, but even so I was more impressed by the fact that his student self-help scholarship supplement job was not in the School of Music but at the circulation counter in the main reading room of the library. Also, in a matter of weeks I became aware of the fact that he was enrolled in a special advanced course in the English novel that included works by Defoe, Richardson, Fielding, Sterne, Jane Austen, the Brontës, and so on to Thomas Hardy, taught by Mr. Morteza Drexel Sprague, head of the English Department, who was also teaching the special section of freshman English 101, 102, and 103 for which my placement test score qualified me.

The only direct face-to-face verbal exchanges I had with Ellison that year consisted of a few polite words we said to each other at the circulation counter when he was on duty and I was checking books out or returning them. There were freshmen that year who lodged in Ralph's memory, mainly because they were musicians, athletes, or irrepressible hotshots of one sort or another, but I was not one of them.

Ralph did not return to complete his senior year and get his degree in music at Tuskegee, but my memory of his sojourn there was kept vivid by the sight of his name on checkout slips of so many of the library books of fiction, poetry, history, and literary criticism that had become the main part of my own personal extracurricular reading program. Some of the books had been checked out by him more than once between 1933 and 1936, and in many instances he was the only previous borrower.

I didn't actually meet Ralph until we were introduced by a mutual friend and Tuskegee graduate and staff member named Louis A. "Mike" Rabb, who was taking a graduate course at Columbia University when I came to New York on my first visit in 1942. I had graduated in 1939 and had returned as a part-time instructor of freshman remedial English in 1940, after taking graduate courses in education at the University of Michigan following a term as principal of a junior high school in southwest Georgia.

I began teaching regular courses in freshman and sophomore English the following year. At the time I did not know that Ellison had given up music as his main interest, but I was aware of the fact that he had published some articles, sketches, and some short fiction, which, given my awareness of his reading interests, did not surprise me. Nor was I really surprised to find that he no longer thought of music as his primary vocation; he now thought of himself as a writer.

But what he and Mike Rabb and I talked about the afternoon that Mike and I went across from the Harlem Y and up the hill to the CCNY area and the apartment on Hamilton Terrace was not books and writing, but mainly about who was doing what at Tuskegee and what Tuskegeans were doing elsewhere. Even so, what I remember most vividly about being there sipping whatever we were sipping as we went on talking was the bookcase on the wall beyond the writing table where Ellison sat. There, along with copies of André Malraux's *Man's Fate* and *Man's Hope,* I also finally saw copies of Malraux's *The Conquerors* and *The Royal Way,* which I had never seen before.

I had read *Man's Fate, Man's Hope,* and *Days of Wrath* at Tuskegee and at the time I assumed that he had too. I found later that he hadn't read *Man's Fate* until he came to New York and was introduced to Langston Hughes, who was carrying a copy which he suggested that Ralph read and return to a friend. Before I left New York I found copies of *The Conquerors* and *The Royal Way* at Gotham Book Mart on Forty-seventh Street and began reading *The Conquerors* on the train back to Tuskegee.

The next time I saw Ralph in New York he was making wartime Atlantic crossings in the Merchant Marine, and I was a second lieutenant in what was then the U.S. Army Air Corps, stationed at the Tuskegee Army Air Field where the "Tuskegee Airmen" were being trained. I hadn't looked him up; I just happened to run into him on Seventh Avenue near 135th Street. I may have mentioned the musette bag of poetry by Auden, Spender, and C. Day Lewis that I had bought in the "We Moderns" section of Gotham Book Mart, but only because I knew he had read a lot of contemporary poetry at Tuskegee. At the time I had no idea that we would become lifelong friends and literary colleagues. For one thing, I thought that he was as involved with Marxism as Richard Wright was and I had spent much of my first year out of college studying and rejecting Marxism. I also assumed that he regarded himself as a refugee from the South, much as Wright did.

As soon as we began to discuss his current project, however, both of these assumptions changed. It was immediately clear that, like me, he had accepted the challenge of William Faulkner's complex literary image of the South, and that he shared other of my enthusiasms as well.

When I happened to run into Ralph again while I was on another trip to New York during the war, I had a very specific literary matter to talk to him about. He had written a short story about a flying cadet at an airfield obviously based on the one where I was stationed. The story was called "Flying Home," as in Lionel Hampton's popular jazz instrumental, and I had read it in *Cross Section,* a new collection of contemporary writing edited by Edwin Seaver. In this story a student pilot has had to crash-land his plane onto an Alabama plantation after flying into a buzzard. Ellison had made up the incident, but I couldn't wait to tell him that one of our planes actually had flown into an Alabama buzzard not before, but after his story was published. The buzzard that he had concocted at his writing desk in New York had actually come to life! The plane had not crash-landed, because it was a twin-engine medium bomber, rather than a single-engine BT-11 Basic Trainer or AT-6 Advanced Trainer. The impact had caused the vulture to get stuck in the partially split Plexiglas of the pilot/copilot cabin, and when the crew returned to the base the ground level temperature plus that of the plane itself was such that by the time I heard about what had happened and got down to the flight line, the cabin was reeking with barbecued buzzard.

He was delighted by the coincidence of the buzzard in "Flying Home," but he was certainly not amazed, because he then reminded me playfully that "stories endure not only from generation to generation but also from age to age because literary truth amounts to prophecy. Telling is not only a matter of retelling but also of foretelling." So the incident of the buzzard in "Flying Home" was entirely consistent with Ralph's conception of literature. (Incidentally, Ralph was also amused by my account of one of our cadets who could not resist temptation and zonked his AT-6 down to deck level and buzzed an Alabama cotton field at the peak of harvest time, leaving a stalk-brown right-of-way down the middle of all that infinity of post-Confederate whiteness. *Some cotton picking black eagle, man!*)

It was that Seventh Avenue exchange that turned out to be the prologue to what became our lifelong dialogue about life, literary craft, and American identity, a part of which is collected here. As for the most basic and most comprehensive assumptions underlying that dialogue, given the oversubscription to social science surveys and platitudes that now characterizes so many discussions about American culture in our time, perhaps the source of our orientation may not be as obvious as one might have once hoped. Ellison and I regarded ourselves as being the heirs and continuators of the most indigenous mythic prefiguration of the most fundamental existential assumption underlying the human proposition as stated in the Declaration of Independence, which led to the social contract known as the Constitution and as specified by the Emancipation Proclamation and encapsulated in the Gettysburg Address and further particularized in the Thirteenth, Fourteenth, and Fifteenth amendments.

Yes, it would be the likes of him from the Oklahoma Territory and me from the Deep South, the grandchildren of slaves freed by the Civil War, betrayed by Reconstruction and upstaged by steerage immigrants, it would be us who would strive in our stories to provide American literature with representative anecdotes, definitive episodes, and mythic profiles that would add up to a truly comprehensive and universally appealing American epic. Whatever the fruits of that grand ambition, he and I conceded nothing to anybody when it came to defining what is American and what is not and not yet.

The exchange of letters between Ellison and myself reprinted here took place between 1950 and 1960. The letters are arranged in the following chronological sequence: from Tuskegee and New York, 1950 to 1955; from Casablanca, Rome, and New York, 1955 to 1958; from Los Angeles and New York, 1958 to 1960.

All our written correspondence ended when it did because by that time not only had long-distance personal telephone calls become more routine, but so also had long-range air travel, which meant that for an Air Force captain, space-available flights to and from the New York area were fairly easy to come by. Then in 1961 I was transferred from California to Hanscom Air Force Base outside Boston, only four hours north of New York by automobile. I retired in the permanent grade of major in 1962, moved to New York, and began my full-time career as a writer, and so regular local calls ended all written correspondence between us except for Christmas cards.

ALBERT MURRAY

I

TUSKEGEE
AND
NEW YORK
1950-1955

In the autumn of 1946 I was released from active duty as a first lieutenant in the U.S. Army Air Force and placed on reserve status, and I returned to my civilian position as an instructor of freshman and sophomore English at Tuskegee. I spent the academic year of 1947–1948 earning my master of arts degree in English at New York University, returning to Tuskegee in September. My master of arts thesis was a comparative study of symbols of sterility and fertility in T. S. Eliot's poem *The Waste Land* and Ernest Hemingway's novel *The Sun Also Rises*. It was also during this school year that my relationship with Ralph Ellison developed into an ongoing literary dialogue that included sessions during which I listened and responded to his readings of sequences and episodes from the novel he was writing.

I returned to Tuskegee during the summer of 1948, and during the late spring and summer of 1950 I made my first trip to Europe, visiting Lisbon, Naples, Genoa, Florence, and Venice, from which I went to Paris, my ultimate destination, by the Orient Express and took classes in French language and culture at the Sorbonne, the Institute of Phonetics, and Alliance Français. Incidentally, it was also while I was in Paris in 1950 that I met and became a lifelong friend of the painter Romare Bearden, two of whose works I had seen in Ralph's apartment. It was also in Paris at that time that I met and became friends with James Baldwin, with whose civil rights polemics during the 1960s I was to take issue in my first book, *The Omni-Americans* (1970). I also made a motor trip to the Côte d'Azur that summer.

I sailed back across the Atlantic from Cherbourg to Montreal by way of the St. Lawrence River and took a train, and after a brief stopover in New York to make up for the letters I hadn't written to Ralph and to pop in to see Bearden in his studio (which was in the

Apollo Theater building in those days), I came on back to Tuskegee for the fall term.

During the mobilization for the war in Korea that began in 1950 I was recalled to active duty in 1951, and after completing the Academic Instructors course at Air University spent the next four years as associate professor of air science and tactics on the staff of the Air Force ROTC unit on the campus at Tuskegee, where I was promoted to the rank of captain in 1954.

Back in 1947, when I arrived in New York to go to graduate school, Ralph's main preoccupation was the novel he was working on, an episode from which had just been published in *Horizon,* the prestigious British literary journal edited by Cyril Connolly. The novel in progress was under contract to Random House, where Albert Erskine and Frank Taylor, Ralph's editors and sponsors, had taken it when they transferred there from Reynald and Hitchcock. I never asked and never came to know what advance or advances against royalties were involved.

But Ralph did mention supplementing whatever it was by taking odd jobs from time to time. I knew that he had worked in the dining hall before I arrived at Tuskegee and also as a mess man in the Merchant Marine during the war, but his background as a gadgeteer and tinkerer also enabled him to do freelance work as a repair and maintenance man. He was a highly qualified semiprofessional photographer, and his expertise in selecting and assembling recording and playback components became such that his services for installing home high-fidelity systems were also in frequent demand.

Meanwhile, he was writing nonfiction. There was "The Way It Is" in *New Masses,* October 20, 1942; "An American Dilemma: a Review," written for *The Antioch Review* in 1944 but not published; "Richard Wright's Blues," *The Antioch Review,* Summer 1945; "Beating That Boy," *The New Republic,* October 22, 1945; "Harlem Is Nowhere," *Magazine of the Year,* 1948; "The Shadow and the Act," *The Reporter,* December 9, 1949; and "Twentieth Century Fiction and the Black Mask of Humanity," *Confluence,* December 1953. These did not bring in very much cash but they did lead to lecture and panel discussion engagements for which he received moderate fees. Incidentally, I was very much impressed with the informal affiliation with Bennington College he had had during the war years because it had led to his close relationship with Kenneth Burke, the author of *Permanence and Change, Attitudes Towards History, Counterstatement, The Philosophy of Literary Form, A Grammar of Motives,* and other basic books on literary criticism.

When *Invisible Man* was published in 1952, it received a number of enthusiastic reviews, was on *The New York Times* Bestseller List for at least two months, and received the National Book Award for 1953 (no monetary prize at that time). Ralph's main income now came from the increased number of speaking and reading engagements and the larger fees that his newfound fame earned him. In the fall of 1954, Ralph went to Austria to lecture at the Salzburg Seminar in American Studies, and by then was working in earnest on a second novel.

A.M.

BOX 343
TUSKEGEE INSTITUTE,
ALABAMA
2 JAN 50

Dear Ralph,

Thanks very much for the copy of "The Shadow and The Act." I had read it already in the library and had already discussed it with one of my classes, but I hadn't been able to buy a copy of *The Reporter* anywhere. I think it is an excellent piece, by far the best thing on the subject so far, the only other piece worth mentioning being the review of *The Home of the Brave* by somebody in *Commentary* some time ago. (And I mention it only because it called attention to how naively and embarrassingly homosexual—well, you know, come on back to the raft again Huck honey). No doubt you read it. (By the way, did you see that piece by Fiedler on Montana in *PR*[1] for December? I told Mort Sprague[2] that you wrote your reviews with a switchblade knife, or was it a razor? Well, that goddamn Fiedler can at least scratch with a pin).

How is the youknowwhat? Don't let anybody rush you, but every Monday when I get my *Times Book Review* I find myself sort of halfway looking for it. I saw a copy of Steegmuller's[3] book, but haven't read it yet, costs too damn much.

As for myself, I've had a pretty good school year so far. I think the students are a little better. The groups I've had in Drama and in Introduction to Literature are especially encouraging. I've also had a pretty good year with my little writing project. It's a little clearer to me now, but I seem to be only just about halfway through. I couldn't rush it even if I wanted to, but I hope I can get it worked out by May.

I'm going to try to get to Paris in June. I still have about three more years on the GI Bill, and I want to do some French with at least several months of it, maybe nine months. I was thinking that since you are an old seaman, you might be able to help me arrange for transportation. (I'm not taking my family) I don't know anything about visas,

[1] Literary critic Leslie Fiedler, writing in *Partisan Review*.
[2] Morteza Drexel Sprague, head of the English Department at Tuskegee.
[3] Francis Steegmuller, a writer whose office Ellison used for a year while writing *Invisible Man*.

passports and booking passages, and nobody here seems to know. I'm writing the French Cultural Relations Office in NY about possible schools, but I'm planning to go school or no school. How long does it take to get a passport and visa, and where do you get them from?

Naturally I don't wish to bother you if you are still hacking away at that story, but if you get time, do what you can. I don't know just when I'll be in N.Y. again, since I'm going to be economizing for the trip, but I might be able to make it some time in February at that.

Murray

749 ST. NICHOLAS AVE.
NEW YORK 31, N.Y.
JANUARY 24, 1950

Dear Albert,

I suppose by now you've received the information which Fanny had sent you. It was a rather impersonal way of going about it, yet it was one way of insuring that you received the latest and most official directions. Should you run into difficulties please let us know. The trip is much too exciting to allow some fairly mechanical factor like a passport [to] cause you delay.

As for passage, I've been away from close contact with the sea for so long that I'm not up on such things, however I'm told that with the rush for Europe come spring it's best to see about passage well in advance. I would suggest that you try a cargo ship, since many carry passengers and are apt to be cheaper and as fast. It's possible that once you decide, you might take a ship out of New Orleans and save yourself some expenses. We're waiting expecting Virgil[1] to arrive from Japan any day now and he'll have such things at his fingertips. You'll get it as soon as he arrives.

Thanks very much for seeing to it that a few Negroes read my reviews; I get the feeling that most times the stuff is seen only by whites and that, I'm afraid, doesn't mean much in the long run. Although the reactions to the piece by no means displeased me. Some day I'd like to

---

[1] Virgil Branam, a boyhood friend of Ellison's from Oklahoma City and a Merchant Marine messman.

have the time and space to do a real job on the movies and not from any limited racial angle.... The fellows on the *Reporter* are quite alert and on the lookout for competent stuff by Negroes, so you might send them something. They pay a little over ten cents a word and are yet in that formative stage where they are apt to print almost anything of interest. I have several things in mind for them but my you-know-what doesn't allow time for working them out, although two of the essays are in rough draft.

By the way, I took your tip and read Fiedler's piece on Montana and liked it. He's not bad, that Fiedler. And here's a tip for you: Get J. Saunders Redding's new novel *Stranger and Alone* which is to be published on Feb. 17th. I'm reviewing it for the *N.Y. Times*—a very short review unfortunately—but I think you'll find the book interesting. Not as a successful novel, but as a good and important job of sociological statement, and perhaps even more than that; for he has got ahold of some of the psychological motives operating in the Negro-hating mulatto types that collaborate with the white south in making such a travesty of Negro education.... If I'm not careful I'll start my review right here! But see the book. I believe that at last we're going to have a group of writers who are aware that their task is not that of pleading Negro humanity, but of examining and depicting the forms and rituals of that humanity. But see the novel. And if I ever complete my endless you-know-what you'll get a chance to see what different things we make of a common reality. "You-know-what" indeed. Is it a rock around my neck; a dream, a nasty compulsive dream which I no longer write but now am acting out (in an early section the guy is obsessed by gadgets and music, now I'm playing with cameras and have recently completed two high-fidelity amplifiers and installed a sound system for a friend); a ritual of regression which makes me dream of childhood every night (as a child I was a radio bug, you know, and take it from me after getting around with the camera bugs and the high-fi bugs and the model train bugs, you'll have no doubts as to the regressive nature of this gadget minded culture); or is it a kind of death a dying? Certainly after it's all over and done up in binders I will have passed through the goddamnedest experience of my life and shall never be the same. Perhaps that is why it's so difficult to finish. Nevertheless I'm near the end and I'll be glad to get it over with. Perhaps as you say of my reviews there's a switchblade in it—if so, I'll be damned relieved to turn it against someone else for a while. Perhaps you've given me the subtitle: The Invisible Man; a Switchbladed Confession. Who knows, we might both have books during 1950. Let us hope. I've been asked to lecture on the sociological background of southwestern jazz at N.Y.U. in April. The director of course is a combination bopper and exponent of the Herskovits[2] myth-of-the-Negro-past-school of anthropology—*and* under contract to write a book on *jazz*.... Well, I leave bop to Dawson[3] and Herskovits to who the hell wants him, and with my fear of having my poor little brain picked I probably won't say much of anything. So let that be a warning to you; if you have any ideas write them before you talk to these white boys, 'cause they're *all* eager beavers aspiring to win their spurs in *P.R.*,[4] *Accent* or anywhere else that will print a by-line. So write it before you talk it—if you plan to write it, and don't say too much even then.

That's about all, except to express my surprise that you got down to writing. Had you written before you came up last fall you might have had our apartment all to yourselves while we were having Parks's[5] house all to ourselves just a few miles up the river at White Plains. Glad things are going good for you, Mozelle[6] and Mike,[7] give my regards to Bess and Mort and any old ones who would remember me; and we hope to see you in Feb. And you keep writing—all it takes is ——it, grit and motherwit—and a good strong tendency towards lying (in the Negro sense of the term).

Ralph

---

[2] Melville Herskovits, influential folklorist and anthropologist, author of *The Myth of the Negro Past*.

[3] William L. Dawson, conductor and composer with whom Ellison studied at Tuskegee.

[4] *Partisan Review*.

[5] Gordon Parks, eminent photographer who was a friend and sometime collaborator of Ellison's.

[6] Mrs. Albert Murray.

[7] Murray's daughter, Michele, also known as Mique.

MARCH 22, 1950
608 FIFTH AVE.

Dear Murray:
What goes? Are you going abroad or not? I wrote you last month but received no answer. As you can see, I'm back in Steegmuller's office pounding away. Book almost finished—I hope. There'll be rewriting to do but the main thing will be over. Right now it reads like a three-ring circus. All the anti-violence boys will blow their tops should it come their way. Regards to Mozelle from us two.
Sincerely,
Ralph

BOX 343
TUSKEGEE INSTITUTE.
ALABAMA
27 MARCH 50

Dear Ralph,
Yes, I'm still hoping to get to Paris this summer. My leave has already been approved by the school (and, believe it or not, the school is giving me $300 toward expenses). But as yet I haven't been able to obtain passage. I tried the French Line, and they're solid up to 24 July. I've been to New Orleans, but they're all taken there too. I've also had the American Express looking, but all they can offer is a plane, which I will take *only* as a last resort.

By the way, my leave is only for the summer; other people in the English Department had already applied for leave to go to school next year. That means that I have to be here for the fall term. Well that's all right too; I still want to go. Actually I get away as early as May 16 and stay as late as about September the same.

I didn't reply because I thought I was starting fairly early and that I'd be just about set by now, but mostly because I knew that you're tied up. But now that you mention it, if you have any time check a few agencies for me. Naturally I want to go as cheaply as possible, but $500.00 is my range, and I absolutely cannot go any higher than plane fare, which is $666 round trip. Your OK is my OK on anything you or Fanny may be able to find at this late date.

Your short piece in the *Times Book Review* was all right. Mort is doing the book now; I get it next week. I'm sure already, however, that you have represented Redding much better than he represented himself in that talk with Harvey Breit a week or so later. Have you seen *Beetle Creek*? I haven't. *Intruder*[1] was here at last. Boy, that little sonofabitch playing Aleck Sander almost threw the whole thing out of focus here. In the first place he tended to sound like a black Yankee. [...]

Of course you've seen the installments of the new Hemingway novel in *Cosmopolitan*. Did you see *The Cocktail Party* yet? *The Idea of a Theater* is the best thing I've read recently. Haven't seen Burke's new volume yet.

Murray

749 ST. NICHOLAS AVE.
NEW YORK CITY 31
APRIL 16, 1950

Dear Albert,

We're sorry to hear of your difficulty and hope by now you've gotten passage. From our inquiries however, the problem seems to be general. A girl in Fanny's office was successful in getting early passage only after going through the complete list of merchant shipping offices freight shippers and then only because her husband, a former seaman, had connections. The only thing we found that is at all promising is a trip on the Arnold Berstein Line, but the sailing is not until July 5th. Let us know if you're interested. Meantime we're still looking, though it seems that the pilgrims have everything sewed up. Suggest you keep trying such ports as Baltimore, Mobile and New Orleans ... Incidentally, you must be working a very smooth magic to get those boys to shell out that much dough (I mean 'squeeze', such as dough) toward your expenses. I read the account of Founder's Day; isn't it ironic that

---

[1] *Intruder in the Dust*, 1949 movie adaptation of William Faulkner's novel.

Drew[2] should lose his life on his way to take part; even so, if there are photographs or other materials around I'd like to see some of them just to revive my memory of the place.... I see where Dawson's been waving his hands before some white folks. How did it go? The gal on the *Amsterdam News* writes a prose that is strictly from dietetic diarrhea, you can't tell whether she's trying to write criticism or simply suffering from verbal trots.... Recently, at our first dance in years, we ran into a guy named Crouse or Krouse, who is married to a little yellow gal, a rather hard-bitten little thing, from Tuskegee or Greenwood, remember him, them? I think she is a relative of Peck Harper.[3]

No I haven't read *Beetle Creek*, but I plan to. I have read *Idea of a Theater*, which I was unsuccessful in getting Random House to publish, and I think as highly of it as you do. Yes, and the Hemingway; though I still don't know what I think of the three installments I've read. In case you don't recognize him, the writer he keeps needling is Sinclair Lewis, or seems to be. I knew the lost young mistress referred to; she was very petite and smooth and attractive in mink coats and silly hats, and it was through her that we met and had dinner with Lewis. So I guess that's my literary anecdote for today. I've also read Auden's book on romanticism, but prefer something a little more in my own frame of reference, or at least with more precision. Look at it though, if you haven't. The piece on *Moby Dick* is OK.

As for my review of Redding's novel—well. As far as novels go I found it dead before it could get started, so I tried to place it as to archetypal pattern and thus indicate how one might read it without being completely bored. and to be frank, if my own nightmare of a book didn't touch some of that same material, I might have handled him a bit roughly. But hell, it's easy to knife a guy; the creative and difficult thing is to make him aware of the implicit richness of the material as you see it. Then, if you're lucky, you have shared your vision; if not, you still haven't wasted your time for the Negro material will have been thrown into its wider frame of reference and the reader can

---

[2] Dr. Charles Drew, pioneer in the preservation of blood plasma for transfusion; died in a car crash en route to a medical meeting at Tuskegee Institute, April 1, 1950.

[3] A student at Tuskegee.

pick it up and not only understand more of its meaning but can, at the same time, judge it and demand that the Negro writer quit fumbling around and get a good grip on his themes. Some funny things go on on the symbolic level of *Stranger and Alone*. Redding seems to be fighting a battle with color as he tries to designate a scapegoat; and the black, razor-scarred boys were pretty charged up although it is Howden who is the villain. Well, talking with an editor who'd seen an earlier version I learned that Howden was originally a black boy. Black or mulatto it seems that Redding was too much tied up to make him interesting, couldn't identify himself with the character to the extent of making him come alive. Perhaps it is one of those books that are written simply as research for some future writer.

As for Aleck Sander,[4] he is a bit of a bitch all right, and a eunuch, and a denier-of-his-balls. But hell, what use has he of balls when he knows that his roly poly eyes are enough to get him in the movies? And what, by the way, do you think of Baldwin's piece on the protest novel...hell I'm going to close this, it's Monday and after a week of rain and snow the sun is shining and I can use some sun. Only one final thing, I'm lecturing on western jazz at N.Y.U. next week and hope to get a publishable essay out of my notes. Marshall Stearns, who directs the course has received the first Guggenheim for a work on jazz. That's something to think about.

So...give my best to Mozelle and Mike and Mort and all.

Ralph

P.S. I've only one last big scene to go on the book.

[4] A character in the movie version of William Faulkner's *Intruder in the Dust.*

TUSKEGEE INSTITUTE
TUSKEGEE INSTITUTE
ALABAMA

DIVISION OF GENERAL STUDIES   *30 APRIL 1950*
Department of English

Dear Ralph,
I am all set to sail on May 26. I am going to Italy first, Genoa—on the
Conte Biancamano. I should be in N.Y. not later than the 23rd.
See you then.......
Murray

VENICE, ITALY
9 JUNE 1950

Dear Ralph,
Here is an envelope[1] you can use for a bookmark when the Hemingway novel appears. Have been to Lisbon, Naples (short stops), Genoa,
Florence via train and now here. To France via Milan and Switzerland. Seen too much to try to say anything yet. Wonderful, but am impatient (somewhat) to get the hell on into Paris and settle down. Write
you from there.
Murray

NOV. 1950

Dear Ralph,
I've been able to get back to work, and as of now the book marches
very, very well. At last it seems that I'm really going to be able to finish it. My incident has at last come to the surface—my containing incident, my "action pretext"—and I now feel that I have the whole
thing worked out in my head., all there is to do now is to get it all down
in the kind of sentences and paragraphs I like. Feel very very fine
about it, but I also know that I am a little over enthusiastic; however, it
really does seem only a short matter of months now....

---

[1] From the Gritti Palace Hotel.

School is not bad this year, classes that is; Tuskegee is about the same, only a little more so, as the saying is. The teaching load and schedule is as convenient as ever. Monday, Wednesday, Friday have Composition and Theory of Literature at 11:00 and 1:00. Tuesday, Thursday, Saturday have English Lit. Survey at 10:00 and Comp at 11:00. Repeat, not bad. And *I* can think fairly clearly here even though almost nobody else can or wants to or has any interest at all in what I'm doing, nobody else here I mean. But you know what they are interested in as well as I do—you know it as well, and you understand it better. You've probably heard by now that Dr. Pat is going to be traveling in Europe and Africa November thru February. Don't ask me what for. Pat certainment doesn't know, and I've heard that he really doesn't want to go, that it's really Catherine. Anyway, no good will come of it. Europe is not going to be able to do anything for Pat, and Pat is not going to be able to do anything for Africa—but he's going to think he can, and there's where the Africans are going to be the ones to get shitty end of the stick. No goddamn good can come of it, man; I'm telling you.

Mozelle and Mique are visiting friends in St. Louis. They'll be gone for about ten days. So I have the whole house to concentrate in. Mozelle is still teaching; she just decided to use up some sick leave. Mique is very happy about the whole thing because the trip is what she is having instead of a birthday party. Boy, Mique is SEVEN!

By this time you have seen the Faulkner story in the October issue of *Harper's*. The whole issue is worth having. I think. So far, I have not been able to do much reading this fall, but who wants to be reading when at last he has something to write? However, I'm going through the books I brought back from Paris—and, by the way, I think that my French is continuing to improve. I'm still working at it every day.

Ralph, boy, Mort Sprague has a new baby girl. Surprised everybody. I had no idea of it at all when I left this spring. Mort of course, admits that it absolutely slipped up on him. So you see, goddamn it, the Ellisons are subject to be coming off any old chicken butt day now.

Hello and love to Fanny, than whom not even Mozelle is more wonderful and thanks again for that weekend. Write as soon as you can get around to it, and tell me about the present status of that bundle of blues and shocks you're blowing. Tell them like Hemingway, that you're doing three-cushion stuff. Good crack. Strictly my kick.

Murray

749 ST. NICHOLAS AVE.
NEW YORK 31, N.Y.
MAY 14, 1951

Dear Albert,

You are hereby warned that I have dropped the shuck. About the middle of April, in fact; and strange to say I've been depressed ever since—starting with a high fever that developed during the evening we were clearing up the final typing. I suppose crazy things will continue to happen until that crowning craziness, publication. That hasn't been set and I'd like very much to see you in town so that you could read the ms. When are you coming up? With Duke's new band attracting attention and my recovery from my six hundred page obsession you certainly have excuse enough.... Otherwise things are normal. Fanny is well and glad it's finished, I'm back at 608 Fifth trying to get started on my next novel (I probably have enough stuff left from the other if I can find the form)

Our best
Ralph

TUSKEGEE INSTITUTE
TUSKEGEE INSTITUTE
ALABAMA

DIVISION OF GENERAL STUDIES   29 MAY 51
Department of English

Dear Ralph,

I got your card and the wonderful news. Kicks, man. Maybe we'll have some noise by autumn. But waiting for the reactions must be pretty rough at that. Well, you can bet on some stupid ones, but let's hope that the good ones are really good. When a guy doesn't like you, you can always tell him to go to hell, but when a guy does like you, you want him to like in the right way.

I wish I could get up there for a little while right about now, but I won't be able to make it any time soon. I haven't written you in so long that you've forgotten about me and the Air Force. I'm going back on active duty on June 8th. Well, that would be a very good reason to come up too, but I really have this thing of mine going again right now and I can't put it down. It's been going very well all of the spring, and now I have it almost finished. At the rate I'm going now I have a good chance to get all but the last chapter done before I go. And since there's very little rewriting and cutting to do only the worse possible luck can keep me from finishing the whole damn thing by September.

I'm assigned to Keesler Air Force Base, Biloxi, Mississippi, and my specialty is plans and training; but the ROTC people are opening up two new Air Force units (Tennessee State and A&T in Greensboro) and they want me too, so I don't know how long I'm going to be at Keesler, which is not too far from home in any case. The period of this tour is twenty-one months. The pay as of now is $430 per month. I must say I AM looking forward to that!

Another reason I can't get up to NY before I go is that I'm trying to get things arranged so we can get a house started soon. I have the GI Bill and a little cash and now that I am certain of that much per month, I'm going to build that dream house we've been taking notes on for so long. The architect (my friend Bill Mann, who called you on the phone that time) is turning my plans into blueprints and specifications now and I'm almost set to get a wonderful piece of land way out on Bibb Street (beyond Miss Delaney's) and so I have a good chance to have it all up by some time this winter.

So the Air Force deal doesn't seem so bad to me after all. Naturally I'd rather be going back to Europe on a Fulbright or something. But I think these twenty-one months can be turned to a lot of good. I've got to have that house, boy, for my wife, my child and my books; and the Air Force is going to be my way of getting it. We will have been married ten years come May 31st, and Mozelle is the kind of girl that wants a home.

Well, as soon as I get settled in this new job and get the novel to the typist and back I'll be ringing your bell to raise some hell. But I sure would like to have a session with you before too much longer.

And so old Duke's back in there blowing. Have you caught him yet? Bill Mann heard him on the radio not long ago. Said the stuff was still there.

Did you keep the same title for the book? Is the handwriting still on the belly? I sure hope it is as good as I think it is. But I'm afraid that you must face the fact that it will NEVER get the promotion that the MacArthur show got. But after all, MacArthur got going with that fade away act, and your hero is already invisible. So maybe you got a chance. And then there are bound to be thousands and thousands who will buy copies because they'll think it IS a book about MacArthur, by Ralph Ingersoll. Think of them reading page after page looking for MacArthur. And lo, the veterans are fleeing him.; that's why they're at the Golden Day. We've got it made, boy. Now if we can just work Truman in there, somewhere, like say a true man confession on the dust jacket.

I hope to cash in on this too. The title of my book is *Point of Departure* (that means Tokyo). I'm changing my name to Mac Murray and since I'll be an author then that'll make me Arthur MacMurray. There's a graveyard scene figuring in the climax, which means Old Soldiers Never Die. And when I say north and south I mean North and South Korea, of course. Tell Fanny I've just got to get this thing finished before MacArthur finishes fading (fadding). Maybe we'll all have enough money for a year in Europe when our twenty-one months are up.

NEW YORK
JUNE 6, 1951

Dear Murray,

I hope you get this before you start your hitch. Your news was a surprise, to say the least. I was expecting to look up and see the three of you any old day. It makes me kinda sorry that I didn't carry through during Nov. (?) when I called you and was all set to take a quick run down there. As luck would have it, it was during the big blizzard and you couldn't be reached—and I fell back into my old groove and decided that I'd better remain here and work. Besides, I would have had to borrow the dough. Come to think about it, that was probably my last chance to see you in your natural habitat; after *Invisible* I'm just apt to be persona non grata—though I hope not. Anyway, I was having a little difficulty about that time and thought that such a trip might help, but I got over it and went on to turn in the book during April, having finished most of it at Hyman's[1] place at Westport. I went there just about the time Shirley[2] was doing the page proofs of *Hangsaman* and it was just the spur I needed. I had been worrying my ass off over transitions; really giving them more importance than was necessary, working out complicated schemes for giving them extension and so on. Then I read her page proofs and saw how simply she was managing *her* transitions and how they really didn't bother me despite their "and-so-and-then-and-therefore"—and then, man, I was on. What I needed to realize was that my uncertainty came from trying to give pattern to a more or less raw experience through the manipulations of imagination, and that the same imagination which was giving the experience new form, was also (and in the same motion) throwing it into chaos within my own mind. I had chosen to recreate the world, but, like a self-doubting god, was uncertain that I could make the pieces fit smoothly together. Well, it's done now and I want to get on to the next.

Erskine and I are reading it aloud, not cutting (I cut out 200 pages myself and got it down to 606) but editing, preparing it for the printer, who should have it in July or August. I'm afraid that there'll be no publication until spring. For while most of the reader reactions were enthusiastic, there were some stupid ones and Erskine wants plenty of time to get advance copies in the hands of intelligent reviewers—whatever that means. I guess it's necessary, since the rough stuff: the writing on the belly, Rinehart (Rine-the-runner, Rine-the-rounder, Rine-the-gambler, Rine-the-lover, Rine-the-reverend, old rine and heart), yes, and Ras the exhorter who becomes Ras the *destroyer,* a West Indian stud who must have been created when I was drunk or slipped into the novel by someone else—it's all here. I've worked out a plan

---

[1] Stanley Edgar Hyman, folklorist and critic, whom Ellison called "an old friend and intellectual sparring partner."

[2] Shirley Jackson, fiction writer and wife of Stanley Edgar Hyman.

whereby I trade four-letter words for scenes. Hell, the reader can imagine the four-letter words but not the scenes. And as for MacArthur and his corny—but effective—rhetoric, I'll put any three of my boys in the ring with him any time. Either Barbee, Ras, or Invisible could teach that bastard something about signifying. He'd fade like a snort in a windstorm.

Who knows, perhaps we'll have books published in the same year. I'm anxious to see what you've done and I've already told Erskine that you expect to have it typed by September. Come to think of it our writing novels must surely be an upset to somebody's calculations. Tuskegee certainly wasn't intended for *that*. But more important, I believe that we'll offer some demonstration of the rich and untouched possibilities offered by Negro life for imaginative treatment. I'm sick to my guts of reading stuff like the piece by Richard Gibson in *Kenyon Review*. He's complaining that Negro writers are expected to write like Wright, Himes, Hughes,[3] which he thinks is unfair because, by God, *he's* read Gide! Yes, and Proust and a bunch of them advance guard European men of letters—so why can't these prejudiced white editors see it in his face when he goes in with empty hands and asks them for a big advance on a book he's thought not too clearly about? No, they start right out asking him about Wright-Himes-Hughes, with him sitting right there all cultured before them, fine sensibilities and all. The capon, the gutless wonder! If he thinks he's the black Gide why doesn't he write and prove it? Then the white folks would read it and shake their heads and say "Why, by God, this here is really the pure Andre Richard Gibson Gide! Yes, sir, here's a carbon copy!" Then all the rest of us would fade away before the triumph of pure, abstract homosexual art over life. Right now, poor boy, he demands too much; not only must the white folks accept him, recognize him, as a writer, they must recognize him as a particular type of writer—And that, I believe, is demanding too much of the imagination. Especially if it must be backed up with an advance.... No, I think you're doing it the right way. You've written a book out of your own vision of life, and when it is read the reader will see *and feel* that you have indeed read

[3] Richard Wright, Chester Himes, Langston Hughes.

Gide and Malraux, Mann and whoever the hell else had something to say to you—including a few old Mobile hustlers and whore ladies, no doubt. You've got to get it done by September—hell, I says this is only the point of departure, you can highball and ball the jack and apple jack in the next one, when you tell them about that philosophical, prizefighting, foot racing, chippy chasing, Air Force character you're going to meet up with in the next twenty-one months, name of Little Buddy.

Kidding aside I'm glad you've worked the hitch in with your larger plan in that you and Mozelle are getting that dream house. You've done so much since my days down there that I feel like a rounder. I never had much of a sense of competition (or at least I have a different kind) but with middle age staring me in the face I'm feeling the need to justify myself, or least Fanny's working and my thinning hair. So I'm trying to get going on my next book before this one is finished, then if it's a dud I'll be too busy to worry about it. I could use a little money, though, I really could. Anyway, just to put that many words down and then cut out two hundred pages must stand for *something*. I'll get you an advance copy if possible. Erskine's having a time deciding what kind of novel it is, and I can't help him. For me it's just a big fat ole Negro lie, meant to be told during cotton picking time over a water bucket full of corn, with a dipper passing back and forth at a good fast clip so that no one, not even the narrator himself, will realize how utterly preposterous the lie actually is. I just hope someone points out that aspect of it. As you see I'm more obsessed with this thing now than I was all those five years.

Let us know where you're stationed should you transfer from Keesler and we'll be glad to see you, as always, the first time you can hitch a flight up here. We might go to Chicago during August but we're not certain. Meanwhile get the book finished. I want to learn more about Little Buddy and ole Reynard, the more than life-size man-with-the-plan. Give our love to Mozelle and Mike.

Ralph

OFFICERS' MESS
MAXWELL AIR FORCE BASE
ALABAMA

SUMMER, 1951

Dear Ralph,
Finishing Air University Friday (24th). Coming up to NY week of 26th. Hope you haven't gone to Chicago yet or that you're back. Will try to reach you as soon as I arrive. Hope to get there not later than Wednesday, sooner if possible.
Writing (rewriting) behind schedule because of Air University, but doing very well I hope. Temporary delay right now because of eye infection, but hope to be able to work again by weekend.
See you soon.
Murray

TUSKEGEE INSTITUTE
TUSKEGEE INSTITUTE
ALABAMA

DIVISION OF GENERAL STUDIES   *30 DEC 51*
Department of English

Dear Ralph,
I finished it on the 26th and it is all typed up and I hope ready. Mort Sprague is reading it now (he had not seen a sentence of it before), and there are two or three other reactions I'd like to get, and then I'll be mailing it to you and Fanny. It runs 225 pp., and I feel pretty good about it right now, but by no means certain that I have it made, and I do mean MADE. I *feel* pretty good about it, but I can't really *read it.*
I'm absolutely certain that I have a number of very good things in there, but there's a lot of tricky stuff too. But if my pet chapters come off it'll all jump.
As you know, from the point of view of composition it is (in texture) a jam session on the theme of old Jack the Bear, and I'm supposed to be in there blowing a little of everything that I can think of,

blowing it as I feel it and think I know it, not as I was taught and not as anybody else thinks I should. Boy, I really think I got me some soloists in there nearbout as good as old Cootie and Rex and Johnny and Ben Webster and Harry Carney; but you also got to have a pianist-arranger like old Duke to make them cats really blow, and naturally THAT'S got me worried.

Well, anyway it's all typed up now, and you and Fanny and Erskine and 'em can read it for yourselves. You said maybe we both would have books coming out the same year; I'm leaving it up to you to decide. Maybe I really broke the bed down, and then again maybe I ain't done nothing but hit it a lick and promise. Maybe I ain't no certified cocksman yet, but that goddamn chick is pregnant, doc; you examine her. Maybe it'll be a nine-pounder and maybe we'll have to put it in an oxygen tent, and maybe it'll be a fucking miscarriage; you examine it.

Xmas fine. My friend Bill Mann went (flew) to Mexico and left his car with me, so we have been getting around to a lot of visits that Mozelle and Mique felt they owed people. Am now working out lesson plans for this quarter's work in Geopolitics. This quarter: Asia, beginning with Turkey and the Middle East and going all the way across to Japan and Korea. Next quarter: the great powers, U.S.A., U.S.S.R., Great Britain.

Saw Duke and his big road show in Birmingham in October. New band OK. Show pretty good, but not enough Duke, never is.

Do you have a date for Invisible yet?

Erskine told me he was going to Europe in October. Did he get off? When is Francis Steegmuller going again?

By the way, I've been meaning to ask you if you ever saw that Faulkner story, "Notes on a Horse Thief". It was published by the Levee Press, Greenville Mississippi, 1950, 71 pp. 975 copies, signed by the author. I have copy 780.

Murray

749 ST. NICHOLAS AVE.
NEW YORK 31, N.Y.
JAN. 8TH, 1952

Dear Murray,

Yours was really good news. I was beginning to think that you decided to sit on the egg six months or so longer, but now to learn that you've not only finished but are about to ship it up to us was just about the best Christmas greeting I've had in a long time. We were half way expecting you during the holidays—especially after old 'bass clef' Deren called to invite us to a party and suggested that we bring you along if you 'happened' to be in town. We went there looking for you in person but found you only in spirit. The chick was draped out in something like a sarong, her hair blazing, her feet bare with anklets of little bells that tinkled as she got into that Haitian groove. She really had the feeling for that stuff too, man—mostly in the shoulders though 'cause as she explained them Hate-ties don't fool around with bumps and grinds lessen it's death dance.

But old Maya was shaking and tinkling with the feeling, and when we could capture her for moments in all that mob of people, talking with a great deal of insight. But it wasn't until around four a.m. when I happened to go back to the bedroom to get one for the road, that she broke down. She said, in the quietest, most confidential tone of the wild evening, "Ralph, what is a bass clef chick?" And I toppled, man, from the ankles, hit the flo' and rolled! He's here, I cried. He's arrived! Who, she said. What do you mean? Murray, I said. And when I stopped laughing and looked up, man, there she stood without her anthropology on! Then I had to assure her that I was laughing at you not at her. Then as I grabbed for our coats I tried to explain what a bass clef chick meant to me—which took me into gut and bucket, blues and jive, meta and physic. So then she wanted to know what was meant by a chick calling somebody's name! And I said, He's here, he's truly been here! But what about calling his name, she said. And I said, Look, when the bass clef is grooving with overtones, earthing and skying, jooking and jiving, moaning and crying, doing-and-dying, penetrating and being penetrated and she hits him where he lives and he jumps bear or rabbit, bull or hound and begins to riff then, lady, his name has been called. She's still digging after it man. We left her digging, and I told Fanny who didn't hear most of it that it was a damn shame what you had done to anthropology.

Seriously though, she's a nice person and I'm glad that we finally met. But you, man; I've been hearing about you from all over. You have taken that low-down southern cullud jive of yours and spread it all over western civilization. I was talking with Bellow and he told me about you in Paris. He was both amazed and amused over your ease of operation. And I said, "Who, him? Hell, man, the world is his briar patch." If he didn't understand me he will when your book comes out. Hurry and get it up to us. I'll tell you whatever I can. And if Random is hesitant, I have a good friend at Knopf's who is anxious to see it.

Yes, maybe we'll have books published during the same year. I completed the page proofs in December and expect bound copies sometime in Feb. Publication date is set for the day after Easter. And the current issue of *Partisan Review* carries the prologue. Things are rolling, alright and I guess I'm now a slightly mammy-made novelist. There is quite a bit of excitement, with more calls for galleys than can be supplied, but who's puking and who's laughing I do not know. Keep your fingers crossed. I managed to keep in everything but that sour cream in the vagina that Ras the Exhorter talks about. It was too ripe for 'em, man. They called me and said, "Mr. E., that sour cream just naturally has to go." Maybe they know about "duck butter." So I guess I sold out. I compromised; all the stuff that really counts is still there, and I didn't dodge before they drew back to strike. In fact, I was so busy chunking myself I didn't have time. One thing both of us can be sure of is that whether our books are miscarriages or what not, this kind of labor of love is never lost, not completely lost, because just the effort to do what has never been done before, to define in terms of the novel that which has never been defined before is never completely lost. Hell, besides I'm trying to organize my next book. I've been a tired, exhausted son of a bitch since I've finished and I want to feel alive again. It's an awful life, for years now I felt guilty because I was working on a novel for so long a time, and now I feel guilty that I'm no longer doing so. Fanny's after me to do some stuff on Negro culture and perhaps I shall.

We had a quiet Christmas. Erskine did not get to Europe but his wife did and they have been separated since her return. Steegmuller is back in his office, I think to stay a while. I'm putting a hi-fi sound system in their apartment, for which a friend of mine has designed and is building a handsome room-divider bookcase. They're fine.

My copy of *Notes on a Horse Thief* is no. 114. Your copy of *Invisible Man* will be numbered one of the first I can get my hands on. Give our love to Mozelle and Mique. And, MacNeil, be careful with the Mann's automobile!

Ralph

(*JAN. OR FEB.*) 52

Dear Ralph,

I'm sending p. 31 herewith[1] but was absolutely certain that it was there all the time. The page markings are all screwed up but I thought that the spring binding would hold it all in order. Maybe you found it by now.

Saw the prologue to Invisible in *PR*. It reads very, very well indeed. I guess printing does make a significant difference after you've seen it in manuscript for so long. Interesting to speculate what Rahv et al. will find happening when old Ras and Barbee and them really get going. They really should get a kick of some kind out of that stuff about the Organization or Brotherhood or whatever it is.

Right now I'm conducting an experiment to see how the local Psych. boys will react to Kardiner's *The Mark of Oppression*. I've checked out several library copies and am passing them around, and next week the big wets over at the vets are going to review and discuss it at their monthly pow wow, to which I have been invited. Personally I find it just about the worst thing on the Negro since, well, since they were justifying white supremacy with the Bible. No time to get into what I think of it now, but I must say that I find myself in complete agreement with Lloyd Brown's reaction to it in (of all places) *Masses and Mainstream*, Oct 51, with a few objections of my own. Will let you know what the vet specialist said. Expect mostly verbal masturbation.

---

[1] I.e., of the manuscript of Murray's unpublished novel.

So you finally got down to see old Maya. She has a lot of good stuff but she doesn't know a goddamn thing about American scobes.[2] When it comes to us she's just another fay chick, and all the anthro and ritual doesn't help her very much. I say goddamn a motherfucking *Haitian* ritual. My kick is the *local* nitty gritty.

Joseph Campbell is the guy I really want you to meet. He knows myth and ritual like nobody else around, and he can also use it to get a hell of a boot from, say, a guy like Slim Gaillard.[3] He doesn't know a lot about spades as such, but he's got the stuff you learn with.

Murray

FEB. 4, '52

Dear Albert:

It has taken me a hell of a lot more time to get down to writing you about the novel than it took me to read it four times. So without further delay let me say that we both think that you've written yourself a book. I found it beautifully evocative and poetic (indeed, I'm not sure if it's a novel or narrative poem), especially those sections concerned with the past: Lil' Buddy, Luzeana, rabbithood, the womb, the nest—in the chinaberry tree. We found his discovery of his mistaken identity and encounter with L. Charley on the freight especially moving, poignant. For here I think your writing is saturated with the experiences, the rhythms, the texture, the 'signifying' in the broad colored sense of the term, the moods, the preoccupations (think you could get ole Deljean to sic my dog on her cat?) the search for manhood via adventure, and, of course, the search for the current self through the translation of the past into the meaningful focus of fiction.

All of this is rendered in terms of inwardness, yet because it is bathed in emotion and presented in terms of details: Dog fennel, water, smells, hollers (what the hell does 'tell the dya' mean?), speech rhythms, walking and dancing rhythms—all the complex interaction between sensibility and environment, it comes out whole. A balance is

[2] scobes = slang for Negro.
[3] Jazz musician.

reached and dreamer and dream are made manifest, wheel within wheel to use an inadequate and mechanical metaphor. To put it in another way, while lying in bed he turns himself inside out—and we see the whirling world that made him, moving again in that wonderful process called boyhood. And of course there's that other dimension, the hero meditating on the hero theme at the same time as he seeks the hero's mission. And it is here that I ran into trouble.

For while I disagree with hardly any of his formulations of the nature of fiction nor with his theories of jazz, etc., I think the reader is deprived of his, the reader's, adventure because here you turn from presenting process to presenting statements (Listen, I am probably too much involved in my own techniques of illusion to be a balanced critic, so take this with the knowledge that I have just emerged from a long period of madness). Nevertheless I would like more Emdee, actually he's not as real as Lil' Buddy, though he's right there in the environment—or Jaygee, because with them Jack could arrive at his theories through conflict just as Stephen arrived at his through talks, discussion, arguments with Cranly, Lynch, the dean, etc. His ideas are not the usual ones (sic.) and I think much *unrevealed* revelation lies in the story of how he attained this kind of transcendence. Perhaps my desire to have what you choose not to present is proof of the success of what you've given us., still I feel the same about Eunice.

How 'bout that chick? Why does he go after Sugarbabe when she is his woman; what does Sugarbabe symbolize apart from bass clef, maturity, mama, or Daddy Bear's own darling that Eunice her dialectical opposite doesn't? And the reverse: For what value does Eunice stand? Does she stand for unconscious fear of loss of manhood, Eunice = eunuch? If so, why? Man, you've got to watch that stuff! You're riffing over your own head. Certainly she is reality too. In short, I feel that Emdee, Eunice, Edison (look at how the E's fall in line, gate) and Jaygee form a sort of missing middle (you'll probably say a missing book which you had no intention of writing, so hush my big fat mouth) from the *process,* the unfoldingness of the novel. The hero is interesting and indeed is heroic, (for he is a cultural hero in the milieu of the college just as L. Cholly is in the folk world of Gasoline Point), exactly because he mixes both of these sets of elements within his personality. Thus it seems to me that while he is saying yes, yes, yes to the complexity of the world, he is saying no, no to more than cracker-dom and such asses as the doctor in the hospital. In order to think and feel as correctly as he does about so many things that mister has had to wade through a heapa hockey, illusion or whatever you want to call it. I know, 'cause I done a bit of wading myself. In fact, Jack speaks for me too and I'm damn glad you've taken on the difficult task of telling that part of the story.

Because, as you know, we've taken on in our first books a task of defining reality which none of the other boys had the equipment to handle—except Wright, and he could never bring himself to conceive a character as complicated as himself. I guess he was too profoundly dissatisfied with his life, his past life, to look too long in the mirror; and no doubt he longed for something, some way of life so drastically different that it would have few points of contact with what he knew or the people he knew it with. But you, hell, you'd eat chittlings at the Waldorf! Not because you wanted to brag or be different, because you know they're as good a food for the gut and poetry as any other, and I would too. More power to you. That's about all of this except for the following: If the publisher should want more wordage I suggest that you simply expand on what is already there. For instance, tell them how here as in the blues, sex means far more than poontang, but the good life, manhood, courage, cunning, the wholeness of being colored, the beauty of it (am I making suggestions or simply showing you that I see what is already there?) as well as anguish, and the deep capacity of Sugarbabe to stand for, to symbolize it all. The only other thing that I would watch and I had plenty to watch in this thing that I finished, are those [folk] rhythms from which you derived part of your style. I know how powerful they can be, indeed they can move a man to write, make him will to endure the agony of learning to think and see and feel under their spell—even before he learns what he must say if he is to achieve his own identity. Well, you have an identity and what you're saying no one but you could say. So watch the trailing umbilicus of rhythm. And I say this knowing full well that you might have consciously had Jack think in these terms by way of ironic comment on his literary approach to life. Intention does count, doesn't it? Here finally is the only criticism that I make brazenly and without humility. (I) I don't think the stuff on page 92 *works* after you leave Pound. (II) I think it's a dam gone piece writing. Those Moses down there don't know what they're living with but you'll show it to them, articulate it for them.

I turned the ms. over to Erskine today (p. 31 was there all the time, but the pages slipped out of the binder and I was so damned irritated to have my reading interrupted that I wired you on impulse) and he said that he'd get to it as soon as he got a couple of other things out of the way. I'll keep you posted. Of course if they're interested he'll write; and if they're doubtful (though I can't see why they should be) I'll take it to Harry Ford over at Knopf; he's anxious to see it. You think that knuckleheaded Hamilton[1] is off somewhere writing a big book? Man, you had me looking at photographs of that period in an effort to make Fanny see it as concretely as you made me see it, and there in the center of all the KIYI's[2] was old Gerald. I tried to find the portrait of Sprague, your son Mort, since you've writ him large, but I don't have one. Do you know by the way that I used to work back there in the stacks? High up? There's a sculpture of Booker[3] sitting on the floor, and other relics, and as the day turned to dusk in the late spring the outside light turned a deep indigo blue. The same old nest, the same old briar patch. I only wish that I had known consciously that I was preparing myself to become something called a writer, rather than the aborted composer that I am. The bastards defeated me there, but I think they might have let well enough alone. Nimble is the word, they taught me to be many things in order to be myself. So I thank them although I don't forgive them and one of these days I intend to get hold of that kind of false artist, false teacher, for which Dawson stands. Just thinking about it all makes me mad all over again.

[1] Gerald Hamilton, a close friend of Murray's at Tuskegee whom Ellison considered a character.

[2] KIYI, a social club.

[3] A statue of Booker T. Washington, on which Ellison based the statue of the founder in *Invisible Man*.

I finally saw Ada Peters.[4] I spent an afternoon trying to give her something with which to make more than a provincial estimate of Wright. She was full of the old "he married a white woman" crap. I really don't see why she didn't talk to you and Sprague. At least she'd have a background with which to approach his work. Anyway I talked and I hope she does a good job.

Incidentally she mentioned *The Mark of Oppression,* let me know how the meeting comes out.

As for the novel, I'm still sweating it out. Good things are being said and the publisher's hopes are high, but I'm playing it cool with my stomach pitching a bitch and my dream life most embarrassing. I keep dreaming about Tuskegee and high school, all the scenes of test and judgment. I'll be glad when it's over. The prologue has caused some comments, but I don't think Rahv[5] has decided what he thinks about the book as a whole. He does know that it isn't Kafka as others mistakenly believe. I tell them, I told Langston Hughes in fact, that it's the blues, but nobody seems to understand what I mean. But the thing is arousing interest. I've been asked to participate in a *P.R.* symposium on the artist and American culture, and *Commentary* has asked for some essays. You should submit something to them, they pay well and I think they feel that there's something not quite right about Baldwin and Broyard.[6] They're getting me a book on jazz to review, so maybe I'll have a chance to get some of this stuff from my N.Y.U. lectures down on paper.

Why don't you, by the way, do a short story about that bad cracker cop who got so puffed up with pride and recklessness that he kicked the keys off the piano?[7] The son of a bitch, couldn't he see that was sacrilege? I'd have blown him down my damn self! Our love to Mozelle and Mique,

Ralph Taft Edison Ellison

---

[4] Ada Peters, English instructor at Tuskegee.
[5] Philip Rahv, editor of *Partisan Review.*
[6] Anatole Broyard, late author and book reviewer and friend of Ellison's.
[7] See Murray's *Train Whistle Guitar.*

Dear Ralph,

If old "Jack the—" was able to get by you without getting anymore scratches than that, I guess he ought to make it pretty good out there. I sure the hell don't know who else would be better prepared to trap him than you are. It well might be that old J the B has already had his best review. That is, unless old Invisible puts enough of them hep. (By the way, *Invisible Man* equals IM equals I'M equals I AM: and Taft Edison = Taft Jordan plus Harry Edison equal a double-barreled trumpet player, plus Thomas Edison minus Wm. H. Taft equals light bringer equals shining trumpet).

That's what I call extreme bop, and I just play it for my own amusement and for the amusement of close friends, and there's a lot of it in Jack the—and I don't expect and don't want any reaction public at all. But there are some other bop riffs that I did hope would operate. Miss Eunice was rendered in bop and is supposed to operate *crucially*. I felt that that was the only way to render her this time (since she's going to be used again!) EUNICE means HAPPY VICTORY, man, and I can't say a hell of a lot about that yet. In my mind it also suggests union, oneness, equilibrium. Notice that the full name is Eunice Purifoy. I was hep to eunuch implications too, but in the sense of unreadiness, unfitness. Remember, this guy must fear abortions in the sense that he is unready, he *is* a eunuch and I described her to look as much like that Egyptian princess that Mzle looks like as I could—but in another sense he is NOT a eunuch at all but a prince in disguise preparing to—well, he's running around with Falstaff and them. At first I was going to call her GRACE (plus Purifoy) but I thought that would be too obvious, what with everybody reading Kierkegaard these days, I played around with the name Charlene too, but I was already echoing L. Cholly in Blair (and I didn't feel the need to pull the Thomas Mann trick of Privislav Hippe-Clavdia Chauchat in the *Magic Mountain*). So Eunice seemed to be just the thing etymologically, and also with certain tan or mulatto overtones (which I play around with in the next (!) one). Thus, for me she represents a more complicated order or level of abstraction. Well, anyway, she was bopped in or sketched in deliberately (because I was holding back and also because I thought I could make bop work in that way.) Edison, Emdee, etc. were deliberately rendered too. I was trying very consciously to avoid what Joyce had done so goddamn well in the dialectics of *A Portrait of*, and I wanted to see if I could make them with "three cushion shots."

Sugar Babe Goodlough is Earth Mother and sustaining element whereas it is old Jack the hero who is going to have to sustain Eunice, etc., etc. say she is sleeping and he ain't prepared to kiss her awake yet.

I wondered if that stuff after Pound would work, so I'm not surprised that it doesn't. (Extreme bop must admit) Man, but it sure is good to know that this thing can still be thought of as a book after four readings. Mort's reaction was very enthusiastic. The first thing he said was that it struck him as being both a novel and a narrative poem; and he said that the "story" kept him reading. (I was hoping that it would be poetry, which is why I wrote it in pencil and kept reading it aloud.... Remember that time we were talking about visual dialogue and sound, 1947 ca. Me at N.Y.U....) But not as such, not just as such, because I was hoping even harder that it would be a novel.

Well, I think it is the poetic intention which accounts for the closeness of the texture and for the 'statements'. Was fully aware that Aunt Gertie had told Uncle Ernie that remarks are not literature, but thought I was getting away with some little cantos and unwritten diary notes there. And then also there was old Hans Castorp and all of that stocktaking in *The Magic Mountain* which Pappa Thomas the Mann was getting off at just about the time that Aunt Gertie said what she said to whom she said when she said it in Paris. Well, even there in the *Magic M* were the magnificent dialectics of Settembrini and Herr Naphta, but I was following Castorp when he was alone and then there was also Uncle Ernie's Robt. Jordan. Man, but I was trying to do so much, and was trying to do it with a jazz band and not a symphony orchestra. Solos, man.

You must think I'm crazy by now, but I'd just as soon put a scene by scene soundtrack of jazz records in an appendix as not. (Did you play Duke's "Jack the Bear" for Fanny when I slid that in there about Jimmy Blanton?). There's "Cotton Tail," "Mainstem" and a hell of a lot of stuff in there not only in there like the rivers running thru Annalivia Plurabelle, but also there like the soundtrack in a goddamn movie: whining (grinding) Boy, Bessie, Leadbelly, all kinds of stuff, man (I hope, but not too strongly). But so much for old Jack the Bear for this time, but tell Erskine or Ford when I say Jack the Bear I mean all possible Jacks (and Metaphysical knaves, and bears to include Mr. Faulkner's.) I wonder if Erskine could see any connection between Duke's Jack (Victor 26536-A) and mine.

Have a number of short stories on the drawing board, including the one you suggest and also a scenario or ballet or something taken from Frankie and Johnny. They will have to wait. BECAUSE I'm going to have to go on to novel #2 (it seems). I think it's that cross country jazz thing and I keep wanting to call it "Black and Tan Fantasy" for some reason or other. I don't know, here's where we wade through crap in a piss storm. I think it's going to have a band leader piano player with a scar on the side of his face name of Dude or something. Eunice will be there to purify and be purified and old stuff old Johnny NoName will be in there being called Gilbert Morris, since you can't sign in anywhere as Jack the Cub. I hope to put Taft Edison's ass to work too. But that's going to be rough going, since that son of a bitch is an umpteen kilowatt operator. Man, old Invisible ain't so invisible to me but, I sure got to watch out for that distorting mirror, got to keep telling myself that it ain't glass—it's a DIAMOND! Anyway I'm trying to get going on the notes and outlines. Maybe I'll have to do a bit of touching up on old Jack but Black and T F or whatever it's going to be is what I hope to sweat with right now.

Not much to report on the review of *Mark of Oppression* except that the guy who reviewed it cut it to pieces! In cold "and er and er" scientific language. Guy named Johnson, Ph.D., clinical psychologist, and as of last week also a Saturday morning Disk Jockey (Auburn—Opelika station) and currently getting a record shop started out at Green Forks. There was one fool at the meeting (Johnson's boss) who was in great awe of the book because it was by *specialists* and finally made the amazing statement that Lloyd Brown and Kardiner come to the same conclusions. Of course he had read neither the book nor the review, but he is a Ph.D. and a clinical psychologist (now that is the way I'm used to having Ph.D's act, like Red Davis,[1] who uses terminology to masturbate with. The fact is that Kardiner's book *does* fit guys like that!—and the interesting thing about it all is that I already knew they insist that it fits everybody else) Johnson simply pointed out that the subject matter of the study was too damn much for science and then went on to show that the conclusion of the book couldn't possibly [be] arrived at by the scientific method. As simple as that sounds I found that very important. Some fool is always defending science against the layman (good religious term) whereas all the layman wants to be sure of is that science is truly scientific—by its own standards!

Hope old J the B will give us an excuse to get up there some time this spring. Thanx for reading it four times. I found your remarks very encouraging although encouragement ain't exactly what I require. The stuff is either there or it ain't, and there's always more where that came from (I hope). So maybe they will buy it and maybe they won't, but if they don't I hope I can make them regret it some day,

Albert

Box 343
TUSKEGEE INSTITUTE
ALABAMA
6 JUNE 52

Dear Ralph,

It seems that I won't be able to get up that way before the 19th or 20th. Will you still be in town? I have an assembly program to do here on the 18th.

Invisible seems to be doing all right in every way. Imagine having a book that good on the bestseller list! I saw the notices in *Time, NY Times* (Two)[2] *Herald Trib* (1), *Sat Rev., Nation, NR, PR, Bk. Of the M. News,* and the *New Yorker.* Also saw *Jet*'s expected stupidity and J. Saunders Redding's expected chickenshittery. (Was somewhat shocked to find out that J. Saunders was *that* ignorant.) For my money Delmore's[3] piece in *PR* was the best. *Time* did a lot of good on the

---

[1] Alonzo "Red" Davis, professor of psychology at Tuskegee.
[2] A review in the daily *New York Times* and in the Sunday *New York Times Book Review.*
[3] Delmore Schwartz.

stands, which is about what you would want from them anyway. Was surprised at Mayberry. Felt that Irving Howe was the wrong man. Scandalized at West's gross misreading in the *New Yorker.* All in all tho I must say the reception was better than I feared it would be. You're doing all right, man. And your stomach [can] settle down again now. How's number Two coming? (Item: *Jet:* Although Ellison's, etc. etc. his second novel won't be ready for five years. What the hell are those people talking about?)

See where old Champ Hemingway is going to have a non-titled bout come late summer, and I'm sure that the wiseguys have the odds stacked the other way—and I hope to hell he breaks them all.

By the way, people are reading the hell out of *Invisible* around here. The library has a waiting list of about 90 at all times and there are quite a number of private copies being passed around. The *Time* notice certainly is responsible for all that. Everybody very very impressed; you may become Tuskegee's Frank Yerby., no? I don't think you're really going to become persona non grata after all, although there are some who claim to remember when it all happened, and MOTON kicked you out. Some fool asked Pat if he wanted him to write a newspaper rebuttal, but Pat told him that it was an outstanding book. DAWSON told me he found it an outstanding work of art, that he plans to write and tell you how well he thinks you carried out your designs. (Pat, I understand, has already written; his secy. asked for your address. I told her to send it in care of Random House. I'll never forgive myself for Ada Peters, who may have come meekly to you, but will be her arrogant and thoroughly dishonest self when she gets back down here.)

If you're not going to be in town when I get there, let me know. If you're going to be in Connecticut or some nearby place, maybe I can still see you. What about Europe, are you going to be able to make it any time soon? Somehow or other I keep expecting a letter saying you're about to check out for six months or a year or something.

Mzle/Mchle OK
Will have 40 pp. or new ms. Seeyouall
Murray

MEMO   *FANNY McCONNELL*
                                                              6-9-52

Dear Murray,
I was about to send you a note which I was to have enclosed when I mailed you
Jack The Bear last week, saying that a letter from Ralph would follow. Now,
however, I've spoken to him on the phone and in answer to your letter which he
received this morning he says:

> *Yes, we'll be here this summer when you come.*
> *Bring a copy of your MSS. along with you.*
> *That he was just about to write, but will "save" it until you come.*
> *And as ever so many thanks for your two letters—*
> *especially the long one about* Invisible Man,
> *(which is an important item in the scrapbook).*

Over the past ten days we've gotten two very interesting letters—from Patterson
and Moton—very nice letters they were but perhaps overly civilized.
  I hope that Mozelle and Mike come with you this summer. We'd like to see all
of you.
  We caught a glimpse of Deren Friday evening strolling along a Village street
with five men. I use the word "men" euphemistically.
  Best to you all,
  Fanny

                                          TUSKEGEE INSTITUTE,
                                                  ALABAMA
                                              20 FEB 53

Dear Ralph,
I got that copy of your acceptance statement, but you forgot to enclose
PAGE FOUR. What I have is excellent of course, but what about letting me have that punch line, goddamit.

Proteus is the right kick, boy; and it is my kick too. Both the writer and the hero have got to learn to riff on it. You got to be nimble or nothing, I keep trying to tell them (& myself too)....

How are things with No.2? Get with it, Jasper; they aint seen nothing yet—aint heard nothing yet. Remember, you're the goddamned trumpet player, and you already got em clapping their hands and patting their feet.

Looks like I still got about ten or fifteen pages to go on this Me & Lil Buddy thing. The Air Force has been taking up a hell of a lot of my time for the past few months, but we are going to have our annual (federal) inspection in the middle of March this year, so that the heat should be off after then, and I should be able to get it done and get back to the novel, which I am now calling Johnny on the Spot.

It seems that I'm finally about to get our house plans in shape. So maybe I'll actually be able to start construction some time this year. And, by the way, I'm ready to start buying that sound system now. I saw some stuff advertised by Hallicrafter that I think I might like, but if you have the time I would rather you select it for me (piece by piece, of course). I'd like to start getting it now and have it out of the way, because no telling when I'll be able to spare the cash after I get all tangled up with the house itself, what with all the travelling I'm still planning to do.

Man, this '53 Ford Victoria (light blue bottom, sungate ivory top) is strictly my kind of tooling. They can HAVE that Lincoln. I don't know what's for the summer yet, but I WILL be zinging up that way before too much longer.

Duke is scheduled for the Propeller Club here March 13. If the local disc jockey can get him down to the studio, I am booked to interview him. By the way, have you heard that new thing by Tiny Bradshaw (of all people!) called "Soft"? (King-4577). It ain't great, but it sure does MOVE.

Haven't been doing a hell of a lot of reading recently, but I have read *Rome and a Villa* (don't know what I think of it); Baker's Hemingway (OK, but I like my lectures better); Howe's Faulkner (much better than I had expected); and I've just finished Aldous Huxley's *Devils of Loudun* which I found very stimulating. You know, I spend so much time digging around in the primitive religions that I forget how exciting the Christian church is, and yet I have been knowing all that stuff ever since I've been big enough to know anything. Man, what don't I know about that shit, all the way from my Presiding Elder (in that thing that I was playing around with about Sycamore Junction) to your Rinehart and all the other Papas and Daddys.... It also occurs to me that perhaps I have been missing a whole level of statement in that possession stuff in the Marcellins. (Hey, did you say Ghost Writer or Ghost Rider?)

Couldn't you pull your *Bear* program, too much radio church! What did old Faulkner say to you at that party, by the way? Boy, I got a hell of a charge out of seeing you standing there in that picture with DeVoto and MacLeish.[1] Both of those guys take me back to the days of me and old Hamilton and the Library. The early MacLeish (Poems 1924–1933) was really my introduction to contemporary poetry, and I still have some copies of the Devoto-edited *SRL* which I got from Hereford and Payne.... And the very last book that I saw you reading when I was up there in June was *The World of Fiction* by Devoto that you bought in Brentanos that day you went shopping with me!

That must be some interesting stuff you're getting into down at Princeton.[2] How is Bellow doing down there? Have you had any pow-wows with Wilson?

A.M.

WINSTON SALEM, NC
MARCH 18, 1953

Dear Al,

They've got the old rabbit back in the patch, wearing a black robe and trying to outdo ole Barbee! All I needed was to have you in the audience to give me a few amens while I riffed. I'll write you from the apple.

Rhine

---

[1] Bernard De Voto, historian and literary critic (1897–1955), and the poet and playwright Archibald MacLeish (1892–1982).

[2] Note scribbled on copy of Book Award acceptance. Remarks mention R.E. attending Edmund Wilson's "Patriotic Love" lectures at Princeton.

730 *RIVERSIDE DR.*
NEW YORK 31, N.Y.
APRIL 9, 1953

Dear Murray:

Man, I hope you received my postal from Greensboro, as I was as close to the cotton patch as I had been in sixteen years, and I wanted you to know just in case those crackers jumped salty. As it was they treated me fine: plenty of newspaper space, photos, two interviews Winston-Salem and one in Greensboro; a TV show, during which I was interviewed by Robie McCauley (who, incidentally, invited me to lecture to one of his classes at Women's College—unfortunately I couldn't do)—in short, those people are acting civilized. Seriously, it was a most rewarding trip, especially meeting some to the very intelligent little girls at Bennett, where a young white instructor from Boston has done quite a job of introducing them to modern lit. There were also a few old heads who seemed to look ahead; indeed there were several who went through *Invisible* like trained critics. They reminded me of ole Eubanks, who discusses the book in terms of levels! Man, I'm not lying, I swear. Eubanks[1] says to me, "Ellison, you know you're a hell of a nigguh? This goddamn stuff is History, man. It's *history!* You read this shit one time and you get to thinking about it and you go back, and damn if you don't find something else. You got to dig that stuff man, 'cause it's loaded!" There was a little guy in Winston-Salem, a much more literate man, who kept me up all night talking about things which I aroused in him. He told me that I had completely bewildered Saunders Redding until he (John Hauser) and my cousin had straightened Redding out. He was so aroused that he swears that he (Hauser) is going to write a five foot bookshelf full of novels from things which I left for others to take off from. Man, that little Negro (he looks like a younger version of Brockway) is *extremely* gone! He's a kind of village atheist, only he's far more intelligent and forceful, who gets a bang out of shocking the *ignorant* educated Negroes, with whom he refuses to

---

[1] Tuskegee graduate, manager of food service at the Harlem YMCA, and a friend of Ellison's and Murray's.

identify himself—although his job as manager of a housing project should make him a member of the club. It's always good to be the kindred soul.

In Greensboro I was twice a guest at the home of Eva Hamlin Miller. Little bouncy butt has two boys, is married to a successful dentist known as 'Slick', and owns what is really the show place of the Negro side of town. On one visit I was the guest of the Greensboro Men's Club, which is quite exclusive, I'm told. All I can say is that the Negroes were served some fine food which we gave no quarter, and good whiskey with which to wash it down. Beyond that it might have been an evening bullshitting with the boys on the block in front of Sage Hall. Up here, the big Negroes start out their affairs as pretentious as hell and have to knock out about a fifth of booze a piece before they settle down to enjoying themselves, but these Greensboro studs started performing the moment they hit the door. I like that. Boy, but their local versions of some of the fancier men's fashions knocked me out; the cat who started that fancy vest business should be jailed, because there are one or two studs in Greensboro who have taken it and committed a crime against the western aesthetic!

But let me tell you what happen to me. On the 15th of March I made the keynote speech opening Bennett's Homemaking Institute. Well, I had arrived at Winston-Salem on Saturday, where I spent the day and night with my cousin and his family, who drove over to Bennett about noon. First there was lunch with the student body and then Dr. Jones walked me over to his office, where a reporter and photographer from one of the local papers waited to interview and photograph me, after which I sat and talked with Jones a while. It was then that things started taking off. When it became time for vespers he hands me a black robe, which he tells me I am to wear. Man, I started to cut out right there, but as *he* was getting into his black robe I got into mine, then we went stroking out [along] the tree-lined walk [to] the chapel building, nodding to teachers and townspeople and young females all a-blooming and a-smiling in the spring sunlight. Well, in the vestry of the chapel Jones produces a printed card from his sleeve and says to me quite confidentially, "Don't let this bother you, but you speak right here."

I looked. It was the order of the Methodist service and he was pointing to where it said SERMON.

Man, I really started to protest. But Doc looked at me as though to say 'come on, m.f., this ain't the time to start no shit,' the next thing I know I'm walking with him, a preacher and a young chick, back behind the choir stall where the machinery that drives the organ bellows was pounding away and snatching me back to years ago when I had played in such a passageway when I was a child. From then on it was a nightmare. We divided, the preacher and the chick going to one side, Jones and me to the other then to march ceremoniously upon the platform to come to rest, each group of us behind a pulpit! Behind me the organ, before me the Gothic space and upturned faces. The organ is strictly brooding and upper register, and then in the distance, unseen and to the rear and above the congregation, sweet girlish voices began intoning the beginning of the Methodist ritual and the slow ho-ly, ho-ly, ho-ly ritual march beginning in the now opened doors on both sides of the chapel, sweet and ethereal down the length of the room and up to take their places behind us on the platform.

Well, gate, my past hit me like a ton of bricks. I know all the hymns, and the whole order of service and in spite of everything the emotions started striking past my defenses, not a religious emotion, but that of *remembering* religious feeling—which, perhaps, is little different. Anyway, there I was in a black robe, sharing a hymnal with the doctor (LL.D) with my throat throbbing and my speech notes rendered worthless because of the atmosphere. Someone had been so naïve as to select 'achieving peace through creative experiences' as the theme of the institute, and I knew that I wasn't going to tell them that creative experience brought peace, but only a fighting chance with the chaos of living. I looked down there at those chicks, man and felt that I was a repentant Rinehart. I was full of love for them because they were young and black and hopeful and, like all the young, prepared to be swindled by another fourflusher who had no idea of what it meant to be young, idealistic and willing to learn. I could hardly talk, but I tried to level with them; tried to direct them towards reality and away from illusion. Once I heard my voice and, Jack, it was as sad and gloomy a voice as I've ever heard; and I knew then why even the most sincere preacher must depend upon rhetoric, raw communication between the shaman and the group to which he's spiritually committed is just too overpowering. Without the art the emotion would split him apart.

That's about it. Evidently I was effective. During the days that followed the kids kept coming up to speak about it and to ask questions. And all I had done really, was to tell them to dig the world each for himself. I took part in two of the workshops, one on creative writing and one on poetry. You should have heard me reading *The Wasteland* to those chicks! It's easy to make a fool of yourself around that many young gals.

Man, I must have a million cousins in N.C. I met one of my father's sisters and a cousin who knew my mother and father before they were married. What was more I got a chance to learn how many of what I thought were my own special characteristics are really family traits. My aunt, whom I've never seen before, started kidding me in my own damn idiom! Man, I come from a line of mad studs. I learned that my granddad stood up in the street in South Carolina and talked a mob of mad crackers out of lynching one of his friends. All I can say is that the old man must have talked the unknown tongue. Anyway, he got away with it because he lived to look at me when I visited him when I was four.

It's good news that you're winding up on ole Lil' Buddy, let me see it as soon as you're done. As for no.2 I've been busy laying the structural framework. Thus far it looks like a much more complex book than *IM* and there are several things to be gotten into focus. Incidentally, I'm doing a piece on the background of Negro writing for *P.R.*, in which I plan to touch on Wright and Baldwin, both [of] whom have novels. Take a look at their works, I don't think either is successful, but both are interesting examples of what happens when you go elsewhere looking for what you already had at home. Wright goes to France for existentialism when Mose, or any blues, could tell him things that would make that cock-eyed Sartre's head swim. As for Baldwin, he doesn't know the difference between getting religion and going homo. Here he is trying to write about storefront religion with a style that one good riff from a Negro preacher's sermon would smash like a bomb.

Boy, I heard about that Victoria. You be careful and don't confuse it with one of those sabre jets. Incidentally I talked with Dr. Pat on the first of March, he told me to let him know if I plan to be down that way this spring and I intended to; now, with the news of his resignation, I suppose that's out. Nevertheless I plan to drive out to Oklahoma this spring and I might take the southern route, in which case watch out. I shall be at Fisk from the 21st to the 25th, at Antioch on the 30th (of April) and at Princeton on the 5th of May; after that I plan to scout the southwest. I've got to get real mad again, *and* talk with the old folks a bit. I've got *one* Okla. book in me I do believe. (Hey, I said both of them, ghostwriter and ghostrider, both of them sanctified and gone!) Speaking of Tuskegee, Chauncey Eskridge was through here the other day and he's one cat who really knocked himself out over knowing a guy who's written a book. He tells me that the new chaplain at Tuskegee tells him that the people there are making a game of trying to guess who I was talking about. You should set up a class in adult education down there, man, 'cause some of those cats sound too simple for pity. And please keep them out of the city.

How did the interview with Duke go? I was at his opening at the Band Box. We've become friends with his sister, Ruth, after I was on her radio program a couple of times and have seen Duke at parties. The first time he went for Fanny like a glad dog making for a meat wagon, so all I did was head for his old lady and he stopped that crap. He's a damn nice guy nevertheless.

The Faulkner meeting was very brief. I had gone to Random House on the morning of the Book Award Ceremony to be photographed with DeVoto and MacLeish, when Saxe Commins told me to come place my coat in his office and meet Bill Faulkner. So I went in and there, amid several bags, (suitcases, man suitcases!) was the great man. You've heard the crap about his beat up clothes? Well, don't believe it. He's as neat as a pin. A fine cashmere sports jacket, tattersall vest, suede shoes and fine slacks, the correct tie and shirt collar rolling down! And I mean *down* down. Saxe says, "Bill, I want you to meet Ralph Ellison. He's one of our writers who's won the National Book Award."

"Glad to meet you, Mr. Ellison," Faulkner says.

"Well, Mr. Faulkner, this really completes the day for me," I said.

"Yes," he said, "I guess this really is a day for you."

"Ralph's book is *Invisible Man*," Saxe said.

"Yes, I know," Faulkner said. "Albert sent me a copy almost a year ago."

"You know," I said, "you have children all around now. You won't be proud of all of them, just the same they're around."

"Yes," Faulkner said, "I was surprised to learn how many people like the stuff."

"You shouldn't be at all surprised," I said. But on this lame note I was snatched away by some publicity person to stand beneath the photogs' lights. Later I saw Faulkner at the party but then it was all small talk over bourbon. He was quite friendly and shy and his voice is soft, southern and courteous. Last week I saw him at the men's faculty club at Columbia at a reception for a visiting Japanese intellectual. He was even more uncomfortable than me as we stood around with cups of tea listening to the Japanese be polite through an interpreter. I think Faulkner, whose hands perspired all through the show, cut out even before me. It was raining like a bastard outside, but he was dressed down. You thinks he's been hanging around with Mose?

MacLeish and DeVoto are both easygoing and friendly men, nothing stuffed shirt about them. You haven't seen the photos, I've a bunch of them here when you come up. Mrs. DeVoto sent me a translation from a Yugoslavian paper in which it was stated that both MacLeish and De-Voto were Negroes. She said, "Move over"; I said, "There's room for many a thousand mo'." Life is strange, isn't it? I had no idea that when I bought DeVoto's book that I'd ever meet him. I met and was photographed with Justice Douglas, also, but *Ebony* killed the pictures. He's more like a rancher than a judge and I liked him. A spade photographer had us holding hands for about twenty minutes, it seemed, but he took it as a joke. I told him if I never received justice again this was one time I had held its hand. Then he startled me by asking me if I had graduated from the University of Oklahoma—me with my bald head![2] Man, I'm

---

[2] When Ellison went to college in 1933, the University of Oklahoma was still seg-regated.

sounding off. I'll be writing you about that sound system next time. You take it slow and give our regards to Mozelle and Mique.

As ever,
Ralph

What's up with Mort? I was talking with Frank Taylor and Jim Agee about his attending Hamilton College and they, who both are graduates were surprised. Give him and Mike my best.

Speaking of M.D. reminds me that I used the Tuskegee library to point up to the kids at Bennett the kind of freedom that lies available in the south but which is too often ignored. I told them what a wonderful collection of books I found there through a few people's thinking and working not as Negroes but as librarians and scholars and who were building something of value to any human being with the intelligence and curiosity to use it. Naturally I was signifying, man; but I get a kick out of seeing Negroes from liberal arts schools puzzle over how a writer could come out of Tuskegee. I wish you could come up to Fisk, Bontemps hinted in the *SRL* that I had created another stereotype and I'm going to talk on minority provincialism as a problem for the creative writer. One thing I intend to do is point out where the so-called New Negro boys crapped up the picture. I don't know why those guys want to mess with a contentious Mose like me anyway; I done told them I ain't no gentleman, black or white, and I definitely ain't colored when it comes to writing.

Tushhoggedly yourn,
Ellison

SPRING '53

Dear Ralph,

You should have come on down into the deep south early so that you could have been here for the Founder's day weekend this time. Horse, the trustees were supposed to name Pat's successor, and the shit just missed the fan by inches. One S.J. Phillips of the Booker T Fourbits & the Booker T Birthplace & Booker T Sales Agency & George Washington Carver Birthplace notoriety, upon hearing of Pat's resignation, had gone out and tom-stumped the South and was here with his whitefolks all lined up against the yankees and damned near scared the drawers off of everybody. Here's a sonofabitch who's been literally swindling off thousands of dollars from people who thought they were making contributions to Tuskegee and Tuskegee Sponsored projects—who is perhaps Pat's only truly *deadly* enemy, and whose hatred for this place is second only to his ambition to turn it into a three-ring circus,—here's this anachronistic fourflusher (perhaps the greatest smoke defrauder of our day—who else has ever gotten the US Government to make a MILLION HALF-dollars and let him SELL them for WHOLE dollars and more?) whom any kind of investigation would land in the pen before a gnat could lick his ass, this motherfucker who is so loaded that if he let out a mild poot he'd blow himself to pieces—here's THIS stud whom any fool would think that the trustees could only be interested in jailing or hanging or both; here he is with his good southern whitefolks completely sold and gone on the idea that HE is not only the greatest living exponent but also the ONLY living heir and continuator of the true gospel of Booker T Washington (most of Booker T's offspring work for him—for whiskey money)—and here he is in the natural flesh all up and down the block and in the barbershop telling people to "shake hands with your next president." Man, you missed it.

I don't really know what happened in the board meeting, but they *didn't* name the new president, and wont before June 1st. But the point is that that jasper's name was actually presented and actually received some votes and is, so far as we know, STILL to be reckoned with. I don't say imagine that: I'm TELLING you! There was many a cat around here with the Bledsoe Blues last week, cousin, and I'm here to clue you: that goddamned Phillips is STILL in there fucking with that fan, and that shit aint near-bout as funny as it ought to be.

It was good to hear from you, boy, and you sounded even better than ever. Seems like you had yourself a natural ball in N.C. Sounds like you were in there foxtrotting your old tail off.

Am looking forward to that *PR* piece. Incidentally, I have already read *The Outsider* and I seem to have had exactly the same reaction that you had. Look man, you can lose your hat ass and gas mask farting around with them damned French cats if you don't know what you are doing. I know how you feel about Wright and all that, but I just

caint help saying that that oscar looks more and more like an intellectual parasite to me everyday, a sort of white man's NEWNIGGER, if
you know what I mean. So now he's hep to Camus' *The Stranger;* that
was the very first thing I said to myself. Ain't nothing happening in
this one, Ralph. I personally would rather read some of Himes's *If He
Hollers,* something that is out & out crap as James M. Cain is crap, with
no real literary pretensions at all. I haven't seen Baldwin's book yet,
but what I saw of the manuscript in Paris didn't show me much, and I
caint figure out why they printed that excerpt in *New World Writing.* As
for that style, Baldwin has already admitted to me that he really
doesn't know anything about the actual grain and texture of Negro
expression. But what the hell, man, you been going around signifying
for years about castration.

The Duke visit was strictly my party. He was only here for one day,
but they turned him over to me for that day, and we hit it off fine. Boy,
and on the radio I'm playing all this stuff like Bojangles & Jack the
Bear & Happy Go Lucky Local, etc., and talking about tradition &
style & form & reality, and mop! and there's old Duke in there riffing
right with me and then going on to define his music in terms of ONO-
MATOPOEIA!!! The band was in very good form out at the Club that
night too, playing anything that *I* wanted to hear. By the way, I saw Cat
Anderson about that tape you were talking about, and it's all set; you
can make a copy of it whenever you like. Here is his address: 186 Lex-
ington Avenue, Brooklyn; Phone: ULSTER 72731. He said he was
going to write his wife and tell her to expect you.

A. M.

OKLAHOMA CITY, OKLA.
JULY 16, 1953

Dear Folks,
I've been here about three weeks and this being twenty years in the
past is getting me down. Miss you all heap much. Write from heap big
city where take big root with chief squaw. Night too lonely in homa
Red Man, how!
Ellison

730 *RIVERSIDE DRIVE*
NEW YORK 31, N.Y.
JULY 24, 1953

Dear Albert:

I've finally returned from my jaunt into the past, somewhat tired but up to neck in experience. I don't know what the hell will come of it, but there's no denying that I've had it. I stayed in Oklahoma City a week and a day, and despite Phillips having contaminated the plane, the flight from Montgomery was without incident. I must have hung around the Dallas airport for over an hour before my plane came, then within another hour I was at home once more.

It's very amusing how things worked out, for once in the city proper I had no more than started removing my bags from the limousine than I looked up to see my boy-hood buddy coming along smoking a cigar. It was as though he'd been sent as a welcoming committee, man. We must have talked for two hours before we realized that it was after two o'clock in the morning and that we'd both better be getting along, although at that hour the streets seemed remarkably full of Negro bell-hops, taxi drivers and Indians. That's my home town! My friend said he'd been talking about me constantly for over a week but that he had just returned from a trip, and thus didn't qualify as a welcoming committee, though he was damn glad to see me. Nevertheless, he was good medicine; it was as warm a return home as ever I've had (excepting, of course, my returns to Fanny, who this time greeted me with chilled champagne and glowing eyes).

Indeed, that's one town in which I just drip with *charisma!* Not only were most people glad to see me and buddies now from way back, having bitten the nipples on the same breasts and bottles together, and shared the same adventures and loves and hates (though some such professors were at least as old as my dad) they all wanted to tell me what kind of guy I was and the good things they predicted for me. And there were newspaper stories and receptions given by the city libraries, with some of the Negro clubs (including the Tuskegee bunch) participating. And there were all the old teachers who many a rough day ago had wished me not only dead, but thronged with worms, now taking credit for having made me what I am today—whatever the hell that is! But that's life, I suppose, and that's the way it's supposed to be. So I forgive them their lies if they forgive me mine and say, "I'm your own dear baldheaded, tense-bellied, world-weary boy; thy very own!" Yes, and let them watch me like hawks and harpies, waiting to see if I'd grown a tail or spoke Shakespearean jive out of my anus, or walked on my elbows. Then, "Gee, you haven't changed at all. You still have your baby face!"

And bears! Man, that's the top town in the nation for the study of bearology. They've got all kinds, little, big, medium, monstrous and lil' biddy bears. And many of them my friends from way back, though others have become bears since I left home—which, God knows is long enough to do even Goldilocks in. But many are young bears with ideas and who have come up in the last few years. But boy, they're all authentic... "Now don't tell me this is *Raf*...come on over here boy, and hug me (this from some fool I wouldn't have hugged even twenty years ago). You living in New York now I hear. They tell me you New York fellows is rough on women." Or "Boy, your wife sure don't know what she's doing, letting you come running down here by yourself. I'm liable to decide to keep you down here myself." (This from my lady King-Konga!) And from another while dancing, "Mr. Ellison, have you forgotten your western boy ways?" Or, "Raf, I bet you down here just giving these old nowhere-Okla. City women a fit. I remember you, you that quiet, straight-faced kind. I got the dope on you. You better come and see me before I get in touch with the *Black Dispatch*." And upon being introduced to another, who thinks I've forgotten her, "What's my name? I know you've forgotten me!" And then, when I've identified her, remembering what a bitch she used to be: "that's it, but don't say my name like that, honey, you make me nervous! Ha, ha how'd you ever remember me? Done made a fine young man, too—how's that you said my name?" Bears will be bears.

And of course all the Negroes were busy waiting to see what would develop between me and my love of twenty-three years ago, wishing for some scandal, or perhaps hoping for some affirmation that true love never dies. Anyway, I met her husband at least a dozen [times] and he never once mentioned her name. Which of course was stupid, since she *did* come [out] of her own regard for times past (she and my mother were good friends) to see me; just as I would have gone to see her had he been a bit less of a fool. Just the same, I'm not ashamed of my taste in women, even for those adolescent days—though how she let herself be sucked into marrying that joker is beyond me. No, don't tell me the answer.... let sleeping lovers lie, and lie, and lie.

I found that my memory of the city and the people [was] extremely vivid, although both have changed. Some years ago a Mose who drove for the governor caused a lot of excitement by pitching him a ball in the blue room of the capitol building, a formal boogie, man! Well, today Mose is living within spitting distance of the capital and the white folks are accepting our presence with a certain amount of grace. The city has expanded tremendously and there are several new additions financed by Negroes, and for the first time in the history of the city large numbers of Negroes are living in houses which were never the whites' to abandon. All in all, it's a prosperous town, too, and what with the continuous decentralization of our industry, should continue to grow. The people are still aggressive, though some of the old teachers are discovering that they really want segregation and are trying to discourage their students from attending the University of Oklahoma. They aren't getting anywhere, however, and I'm told that over three hundred Negroes are attending classes there. The old order changeth and a lot of asses are out in the cold wind of reality. But for the provincialism, I'd return there to live. I made it fine until evening, then I missed Fanny, the city, music, books or just conversation. Time would adjust that, I know, but then there's so little time.... boy, but the barbecue is still fine and the air is still clean and you can drive along in a car and tell what who is having for dinner; and it's still a dancing town, and a good jazz town, and a drinking town; and the dancing still has grace. And it's still a town where the eyes have space in which to travel, and those freights still making up in the yard sound as good to me as ever they did when I lay on a pallet in the moon-drenched kitchen door and listened and dreamed of the time when I would leave and see the world.

All in all, it was good to return, though so many, many of the old ones whom I'd hoped to see have died. And I couldn't see the old fellow who led the migration to what is the present Negro section because only a few days after I was there his wife, (the mother of the jerk who married my old girl) was killed with her sister in a car accident. I've been asked to lecture at Langston during the coming year so perhaps I'll see him then.

Perhaps one of the nicest things to happen to me came when the Randolph-Slaughter-Rohne clan (these are the "family" from which I was estranged when I learned that one of the wives had accused her husband of being my father, and to which up to that time I had felt as close, if not closer, as to my blood relatives) were called together for a Sunday morning breakfast. There were some twenty of us, including several lively children, and we ate tons of chicken and drank gallons of coffee and just played havoc with the hot biscuits and looked over old photographs (gad, but I was a big-headed brat!) and relived old times until well into the afternoon. The sad thing about it, of course, was that so many were missing: my mother and father (who I learned used to say that he was raising me for a poet! Poor man.) and their mother and father and grandfather and great grandmother, those to whom it would have meant more than it did to any of us, unless myself. So we broke bread together and there was forgiveness, even for her who caused me all that damn trouble. Which is what growing up is for and homecoming too. So, I came and there was much for me to be forgiven, though not so much from the clan and I received it. I suppose now that I'll spend the next twenty years trying to understand what happened and how, and what was real and what imaginary. But that's my role and I accept it.

Just the same I didn't forget how wonderful you and Mokie and Miquie were to me and I never will. This time I look forward eagerly to return, so don't let Foster forget that he's committed. Tell him, by the way, that Fanny does indeed remember his wife, and pleasantly. Fanny says that she's a fine gal. She also gave me the good news about your story, and Arabel[1] wants very much to see the novel version, which I hope you'll consent to, even though you might have reasons for not hav-

---

[1] Arabel Porter, editor of *New World Writing*, published by The New American Library of World Literature.

ing it published. Certainly it can only help, for Arabel is quite taken with Luzana.[2] I better close this now because I'm working on a paper on the novel to be read at the Harvard conference on the contemporary novel on the fourth of August. There'll be Simenon, Frohock, Hyman, Katherine Anne Porter, Frank O'Connor, Pierre Emmanuel, William Sloane, and Carvel Collins participating. I'm to speak thirty minutes about the American novel, which are apt to [be] thirty of the damnedest minutes I ever spent. This doggone integration thing maybe is going too fast. Anyway I'll write you how it goes, meanwhile take it easy and give my regards to Mike Rabb, Mort and Mann and the others, especially Mitch and Viv (that lovely woman) and tell Mort I'll write him soon and just to confound you I'm enclosing what came out of the typewriter when I sat down to test the keys upon my return. Guess the trip made me a little soft in the head. Just the same here it is.

  Sincerely,

Ralph

P.S. I just talked to Laly and she says hi.

Deep Second

Now when the plane-stirred winds drew down the enraptured
       dawn
I fell upon the slow-awakened past of joy
Eagerly, eagerly, going forth to dawn-dance
Diving blithely as a boy
Plunging arrogantly twenty years through ordered space,
And when to my older eyes the town appeared reduced and
       dowdy as worn-out doll

Tossed into a corner of the newer city
There was only this to do; accept,
Accept the smack, smack! of Time upon my flanks and plunge me
       boldly
Into that inner past to fit
The puzzle of now and then together;
The girl and woman, man and boy;

[2] Luzana = guitar player (see page 57 footnote).

Blue kites against the bluer sky and silver planes
Swimming beneath the surface of the air as once we swam
Fish-like beneath Arbuckle Mountain streams.
And learn that streets loom larger in the mind than ever
Upon the arches of the hills:
That kisses linger in the memory as indelibly as pain
Or harsh words thrown through adolescent anger.
Fined too, the dream which went before the passion,
(That child father to the childish man) of him who dedicated me
And set me aside to puzzle always the past and wander blind
          within the present,
Groping where others glide, stumbling where others stroll in
          pleasure.
And now returning after all the years to crawl the paths most
          others
Had forgotten. My second coming into deep second, that frontier
          valley
Between two frontier hills, that world bounded by Walnut and
          Byers.
And then in the enraptured dawn at last possessing
That which all the others would now have lost:
The path still vivid, the old walks layered beneath present ways;
The inner houses behind the present walls revealed;
The earlier birdsong sounding behind the now-dawn's awakening
          thrill.
And all the past was shaken up, and all the old speech singing
In the wind, and their once clear skins and once bright eyes
Looking through to see me in my passions venture.
Recaptured, held, their promise still promise and all their days
          dawn
In my awakened eyes. And me a red cock flaming on the hill,
Dying of the fire of past and present, and yet exalting
That in me and only me they live forever.
I who can give no life but of the word would give them all—
Their past unsullied and their present gleaming with
          child-smiles:
Their fathers rich with humanity and their mothers beautiful

And lovely: And their thoughts true and their actions wise:
And from that past we knew,
Would make for their children a dew-fresh world.
Oh, I would with them make of us all heroes and fliers,
Even now, though where once our blue kites dipped and sailed
I now plunge past in silvery planes—
Even in this Now, where derricks rise and engines throb upon our
        playing fields
And young girls laugh and glide within the room wherein my
        father died
And where my mother learned the grave transcendence of
        her pain—
Would make their heroes and world-makers and world-lovers,
And teach them the secret of that limping walk, that look
        of eye,
That tilt of chin, the world-passion behind that old back-alley
        song
Which sings through my speech more imperious than trumpets
        or blue train sounds—
Yes, would heal the sick of heart and raise the dead of spirit
And tell them a story
Of their promise
And their glory.
Would sing them a song
All cluttered with my love and regret
And my forgiveness
And tell them how the flurrying of their living shaped
Time past and present into a dream
And how they live in me
And I in them

There it is, some of it sounds familiar, but for the life of me I can't be sure. Anyway, Deep Second is a block, or rather three blocks on East Second Street, wherein I spent much of my childhood and youth, and where I spent much of my time, talking and looking at the passersby upon my return. I was born not far from there, had my first job there, and my father died there in the old University of Okla. hospital building, which is now a Y.W.C.A. This ain't much but it's probably the first time anyone was mad enough to try to get Deep Two into a poem.

R.E.

FACULTY CLUB
HARVARD UNIVERSITY
CAMBRIDGE, MASSACHUSETTS

DANA-PALMER HOUSE   *AUGUST 6, 1953*

Dear Albert,

Up here you have to be pretty nimble, but there are a few fair squares, even here. We've had a fine, though rather hectic, time. Talk about the novel is running out of our ears. Much of it too abstract and aloof. Which of course, left me a role to play.

To hear Anthony West, Frank O'Connor, Hyman, Simenon and all the rest boot the question of the 'extended lie' around before about a grand of people is fun, if little else, yet I suspect that novel criticism will benefit. At least we all agreed that a more sensible terminology was necessary. This, by the way, might [be] an interesting place for you to teach. You'd be among peers, not dolts.

Incidentally, we're told that Henry James once lived in this house, which probably is true—I haven't been able to sleep in it.

Ralph

BOX 343
TUSKEGEE INSTITUTE,
ALABAMA
16 AUGUST 53

Dear Ralph,

Just got back from the workshop at Ohio State yesterday. Your letter from Harvard was here when I arrived. Had received the other one before going out but was too tied up to reply, and didn't find time to write you from there. The Okla trip seems to have been definitely worth making (That was some letter, Dub). The Harvard get-together or whatever it was must have been an interesting professional experience too.

Did you finish that story [for] *New World Writing*? The one of mine that they took was precisely the one that I would have picked for them, some how or other. Miss Porter wanted to know if she should turn the rest of the ms over to an agent, and I told her OK by me if you think I should have one. What do you think?

As for the ms of the novel, I don't quite know what to do. I had already started reworking it before I left for Ohio, which means that I'm all tangled up in it now, tearing it down and rebuilding it very differently. I'll send a copy of the old version up to her, but I like what I'm trying to do now much better. It doesn't have the same kind of thickness, but if I can bring it off it will say a hell of a lot, and I'll still have the old structure left for one of my jazz projects, wherein I'm hoping to be able to riff my old ass off.

We leave for Cuba sometime this week. I had to get permission from the Pentagon in order to go. Regulations. I had forgotten, or rather I had thought that Cuba was in the same category as Mexico (since you dont have to have a passport to visit there) but it aint like that. Military personnel have to request special permission (which only the Pentagon can give) four weeks in advance of the desired date of departure. It's all OK now, however, and I'll be getting away as soon as I regroup from the workshop offensive. Thanks for the copy of Bellow's book. Will get into it as soon as I get back. Reading about Cuba now.

Have allocated part of the check for Luzana towards that hi-fi set. (They gave me $205, and I'm putting $125 away as a start on hi-fi and with the rest I'm getting myself a small filing cabinet and a leather notebook). Bill Curtis suggests that about $300 should fix me fine but says that you have the latest poop. I'll see what Bob Moton can do as soon as I hear from you.

Everybody doing pretty good here, too many doing too damned good, however Foster very happy to know you, Vera very happy to remember Fanny, and both expect you back as said.

Murray

p/s 17 Aug 53:

Galley proofs just came for the L. Cholly K.[1]

---

[1] "The Luzana Cholly Kick," excerpt from Murray's novel in progress, published in *New World Writing,* 4th Mentor selection, 1953.

730 RIVERSIDE DRIVE
NEW YORK 31, N.Y.
SEPTEMBER 22, 1953

Dear Albert,

I had planned to wait until you returned from Cuba before answering your letter, but only today, While looking steadily and quite guiltily at the calendar, did I realize that you were not only back at Tuskegee but perhaps very much at work. We take it that you'll give us the high points of the trip when you get a chance.

As for us we've been very busy as usual. We spent part of Fanny's vacation up at Provincetown on Cape Cod, fishing unsuccessfully for striped bass; and besides trying to prepare a piece on the Negro and twentieth century fiction for *Confluence.* I've been converting my notes from the Harvard conference on the novel into an essay. (I see from *your* letter that I didn't go into details about that jaunt, thinking perhaps that the *Times* would carry a full report. Instead they gave the assignment to Frank O'Connor, with whom I clashed for hamming things up with his I-me-my Irish bullshit). You'll notice that he doesn't mention me at all in his piece, but after I told him—over the air, though I didn't realize it at the time—that jokes were all very well, but that I hadn't realized that we'd been asked to Harvard as entertainers, otherwise I'd have prepared to tell a few jokes of my own, since I know a few good ones, he cut out some of the clowning and we were able to discuss a few ideas. Before that he was busy throwing his brogue and rep[utation] around, telling everyone how much better a writer than Joyce he was, sneering at every achievement of modern fiction, and when cornered, falling back upon theological arguments that were very much beside the point. Well, he *does* have an Abbey Theatre background and I guess that finding himself upon a stage before an audience of two thousand or more he couldn't resist going into his act. All he did for me was to get my Indian blood boiling and I went for him. I'm still hearing about how everyone was glad that I did. Besides if he is the champeen writer and intellectual of the century (incidentally I told him that a few of us knew who had done the real pioneer job of clearing the forest and sawing the wood from which his own work was able to take its meaning) then let the bastid act like one. Clowns? Hell, I've been teeing off on clowns all my life, and besides I don't think he's all that hell anyway. You should have been there, man, just to place a few good sized hickeys on his ass. Anthony West revealed himself to be pretty much a creation of the library. When I spoke of the national framework of experience which effects the form of the novel, he confused it with nationalism as political philosophy. For a moment I thought I was arguing with Ralph Powe or Saunders Walker. Just the same it was a worthwhile experience and I did well enough to have them threaten to have me back next year.

You asked if I finished the story for *New World Writing*. I did to my satisfaction, but after sending me an enthusiastic letter and a contract, Arabel turned up with reservations at the last minute promising to let me know the cuts and additions they desired, but I succeeded in getting the ms back only yesterday. Now they want the story for April but I don't know. I have the feeling that their desire for more exposition is motivated by their knowledge that the story was once part of the novel. At best the story is simply an amusement, but having taken so much of my trip to write it I don't feel like bothering further. I'm glad that they took your story and I'm glad to see you getting into print. This is a very necessary part of writing, until the work is printed it's still tied to your own subjectivity. Put it into print and the spell is broken and self-criticism is born. As for the problem of an agent I think that since you are so far from the city you might consider one. Don't, however, sign a contract with one; they work for themselves primarily and though they can place your work and perhaps get more money for it, they would hardly fall out with a publisher over one writer where they have other of his authors on their list.

Find who Arabel would suggest and let me check. Send her the old version of the novel, it won't hurt.

As for the hi-fi, three hundred is promising. There will be an audio fair next month and I'll look around to see the latest developments and send you a suggestive list. It's better to get the latest and I'll get you set up as cheaply as possible without sacrificing quality. Which reminds me that I promised Mokie a kitchen mixer. Tell her that I haven't forgotten and I'll get to her before long. That's it for now. I'm pooped and bound for bed. Give my best to all who deserve it and keep up the good work.

Ralph

TULSA, OKLA.
OCT. 16, 1953

Dear Murray,
I find myself back here in Okla. much sooner than I expected. I lost my cousin. Read ole Luz just before I left home and found him fine in print. Wished section in which narrator discovers identity had been left in though. Regards to all.

R.E.

730 RIVERSIDE DRIVE
NEW YORK 31, N.Y.
OCT. 23, 1953

Dear Murray:
I've been back home a week today and I'm still a little tired. I dropped you a postal card from Okla. City, where I had gone to attend the funeral of that cousin who among my relatives was my best friend, and whom I visited this summer. She'd had an operation, appeared for a week to be recovering, then she was no more. So I went back.

I went back a long way back, for she's buried not far from my father. I made my first trip to that burying ground when I was three, so I returned thirty-six years [later] to the place where much of my temperament was formed. Perhaps it is a law of civilization, of human life, that you must plant a man to make a man and the father's tomb becomes the second womb of the son. Anyway, that was thirty-six years ago. Then the place seemed far from town, now the city has grown up around it, has absorbed it as life always absorbs death, and as I have absorbed that planting of my father. Now it has taken on a gentle serenity of waving willows and bending sycamores that was not so years ago, when the sheer terror of death looked out of the raw red clay mounds, the crude granite stones, the wild countryside. Now there is grass and trees and flowers and the usual polished stones the familiar names—mostly of whites and Negro pioneer families, for now the Negroes have their own cemetery and only those who paid their first toll to death years ago still come here.

So we laid her down, this cousin of mine who was my father's favorite, and then went home. She was quite an interesting woman and I'll have to tell you about her some time.

I remained in Oklahoma from Monday to Friday, then flew out of there. I felt roo[t]less and frustrated, I was living in that earlier time, living in that old house where my cousin had lived when we were young, hearing the old rain in the night, the old thunder, the old lightning, and in the morning the hens sang soft beneath my window. The weather was warm, the Indian summer sad. And when I tried to live in the here and now there were the reminders of the joy of two months ago cut through with juke boxes yelling "She a Hand" and t.v. is the thing this year. Then everywhere I went I saw shotguns being oiled and guys preparing for the hunting season. Several whom I know took off for South Dakota for the pheasant season, and it was all I could do to remind myself that I couldn't go along. So I'm back at work, but somewhere out on the outer fringe of my consciousness I hear the bass music of shotguns singing. Look out pheasant, look out quail, here comes a bear in soldier's clothes, firestick and all!

I'm lecturing at Antioch College the week of the thirtieth of November, so maybe I'll actually get another taste of hunting. At least I'll get down to Cincinnati to my mother's grave. Perhaps this has been my life's pattern: Death, hunger, hunting and death. If so, then I'll be true to the pattern. Anyway, forgive me these thoughts. Enclosed you will find some memories of the summer. I'd have enlarged them but have no darkroom at the moment. Later perhaps. I'm also sending shots I made of Sonny and his family whose names I can't remember—and they were so nice that Sunday morning. Please see that they get them with my regards. That's all for now, write when you can.

Sincerely,
Ralph

P.S. Tell Larry Robinson that Janet and Big Ben[1] send him their regards. Janet is in Okla. City, Ben in Tulsa, where, during the interval created by our arriving an hour ahead of schedule, tailwind hurled, I called him. Damn! But those big bad Negroes of yesterday sound so mild when you meet them nowadays. Tell Larry that the gal is still gay and still possesses that unusually beautiful coloring. I don't believe I've ever seen anything like it.

R.E.

BOX 343
TUSKEGEE INSTITUTE
ALABAMA
25 OCTOBER 1953

Dear Ralph,

Things are finally settling down around here now, and I'm beginning to know what my 53–54 routine is. This was the damnedest school opening, ever. They didn't get through redoing our offices until the last minute. That plus the new AFROTC curriculum plus the usual registration confusion plus two new officers to break in just about had us snowed under for a while, but I guess everything is under way now, anyway have more time for the things that really matter to me.

Naturally I got a hell of a kick seeing old Luze in print, and the reaction here has been surprisingly good. Examples: There's a Luzana in every community; He's an epic hero; The title sounds like the name of a Dance step; etc, etc. Only one jackass so far, who said he read it and understood it but didn't care for the style and that white folks wouldn't have any idea at all of what it was all about. He said he was giving me the reaction of a common reader, whereupon I told him that what he was really giving me was the reaction of a pseudo-critic, because the so-called common reader doesn't go around making it his business to analyze paragraphs in terms of whether or not somebody else was going to understand them. I said, Man, read for your goddam self, I'll take care of the white folks: they done already give damn near $300 for writing like that, and they say there's more coming.

---

[1] Tuskegee schoolmates.

I'm beginning to get back into that Blair–Sugarbabe–Will Spradly–Jack stuff again now. I've done the first chapter, and I think I have a pretty good outline for most of the rest of it. Maybe it'll work this way and maybe it won't; the important thing is that I'm just as interested in redoing it as I was doing it the other way.

By the way, the stuff that you thought had been cut from The L Cholly K is in *Johnny Emanon*, the no name jive, that is. They didn't cut old Luze although they originally said they wanted to make a few changes in the galleys, but I see I missed a wrong word or so in a couple of instances.

How is your current project coming? I dont know what you're doing, but that Okla stuff is coming through in your letters like it aint going to wait too damned much longer. Cuba was a good little trip. We were down there for a week. Can't write you a report on it now, but boy, them Havana scobes are the goddamnedest operators I've seen yet. Man, every other mose in Havana has himself a hustle. It's the damnedest thing you ever saw. Imagine all of the slickest slicks in Harlem operating in Times Square and up and down 5th Ave and Broadway and in and out of the Waldorf, the Astor, The Stork and Toots Shors. Batista may be running Cuba, but them goddamn spades are running the tourists, boy, as only jaspers can. The mose to mose feeling is very strong however, so I was *in* from the second day on. Damn near got involved in a big mess. We couldn't get into the Tropicana because we had Mique with us (since naturally Mokie wasn't going to leave her at the hotel), but the guy at the door made the mistake of saying something about reservations, which the (mose) taxi driver said was a crock of shit. Well, no sooner than we get back into town than they have the manager on the phone begging for mercy, scared as hell that they are going to ruin him. He begged them to bring us back and they wouldn't do that, and he begged them to let him talk to us and they wouldn't do that either. He explained that it was the child and that they knew good and well that Negroes came there every night and were there right now, but that didn't do any good either. Man, I had to beg them cats to keep that stuff out of the papers, hell I'd had to check in with the Air Force Attaché to get there in the first place. I had to go to the newspaper itself and explain that shit,

Ralph Ellison & Albert Murray

64 · Ralph Ellison & Albert Murray

man. Boot cops and all were ready to start jumping! For a little while there I thought I was going to have to un-ass the area but fast.

So had to miss hearing some of the best drummers, but I did hear some good ones, and I met some of those that I didn't hear, and I got myself a real Cuban Bongo, which one of them stretched for me.

Went out to San Francisco de Paula and saw where old Hemingway lives. He was in Africa of course, but I met the Negro boy who has been working for him for the past seven or eight years, and there is an old man living in a shack right outside Hemingway's gate who must be at least part of the old man in the book.

ITEM: One day I was cruising around in a taxi with a bunch of them Havana studs (who make passes at every chick they meet as a matter of course) and we came up behind two very interesting posteriors, but when we caught up with them they turned out to be two BEARS of the How-do-you-do-ma'am variety. Man, the guy driving stepped on the gas so fast you'd've thought something struck him. Then he turned to me and said, "Mau-Mau!" I thought I'd die. Boy, them chicks looked just like they were going somewhere to cut somebody's throat.

Well, the big thing down here right now is Foster's[2] Inauguration, which comes this weekend. Mort is the chairman of the planning committee, so he has been busier than I have.

By the way, I see that your name is on the schedule of events for this school year. Have they arranged anything definite with *you* yet?

Murray

p/s Old Mike Rabb is the new secretary to the Board of Trustees! Can you hear him?

730 RIVERSIDE DRIVE
NEW YORK 31, N.Y.
NOV. 20, 1953

Dear Albert:
I finally heard from the school about coming down. These are the suggested dates: Jan. 17, 31, March 7, 14. Which of these seems the most

[2] Luther Foster, incoming president of Tuskegee.

interesting? (I've been asked to Bethune-Cookman for the nineteenth of March and I believe I could knock off Dillard around the same period. The important thing is to be at Tuskegee when things are most interesting. Incidentally, my note comes from Julius Flood.[1] Would you please find out if the entertainment committee understands that I do this kind of thing as a part of my living, especially since it takes time from my writing. Perhaps Flood understands this, but I'd like to make sure before I answer his letter.

There isn't much to report from here. I was part of a symposium on the art of narration at Bard College two weeks ago, along with John Berryman and Georges Simenon. Driving up Fanny and I were caught in a blizzard and I spent the following week in bed with the flu.

Still getting good reports on Luzana, and I had lunch with Arabel Porter the other day and her reports were likewise good. Just tell those dog-ass pseudo-critics that you are writing for Negroes with enough integrity to accept themselves and when you do that white folks are bound to like it just like they like jazz which originally was mose signifying at other moses. Naturally, like any real work of art jazz made a helluvalota white folks want to be mose, simply because jazz is art and art is the essence of the human. Besides only dog-ass folks run away from that essence, so the hell with 'em. That's it for now. Try and let me have this information as soon as possible as I'd like to answer Flood.

Sincerely,
Ralph

Box 343
Tuskegee Institute,
Alabama
27 Nov 53

Dear Ralph,

I've seen Flood, and he understands about the money part, and Mort has been looking into the other and will write you soon if he hasn't done so already. As to the date, I don't know right now which would be

---

[1] Julius Flood, director of the Tuskegee entertainment course.

the best. I'd say perhaps the best thing to do would be to fit it into your other southern schedule.

Murray

Dear Murray:

Thanks for putting the needle to Flood. I suspect that he resented it but it produced action. I'm damned if I understand just what's going on down there, or why they want me. They sent me no idea of the format of their program, nor of theme; while I'm at no loss for things to talk about, it would be nice to try to integrate my remarks with whatever program they have. Perhaps that's what they're leery of. Anyway, don't bother them with it. Mort [Sprague] was the guy who suggested that he would work something out, but as you say he tends to leave the field to shit artists like my boy Mike [Rabb]. He'd better make his weight felt or next trip he'll have Red Davis or Mike for president. And mind you, I'm fond of Mike and can't stand Davis, but what the hell has that to do with educating men and women? Mort's either going to have to make his values felt or quit. He was fine for us, but that was damn near twenty years ago and it's *now* that his qualities should be most effective. It's all right to hate ignorance in important places and brown-nosing and whatever that shit is that Walker and Davis put down, but hell, if his values aren't worth teaching to Foster—and even getting his head whipped a bit to get them across—then he's playing himself cheap. Not to mention those kids to whom he owes a responsibility by birth, by sensibility, by intelligence and by position. The whole thing depresses me. A man shouldn't let himself be boxed in and then pout about it. Well, more about this later.

Unfortunately Fanny, after quitting her job, took another recently and won't be able to come on the trip. She prefers to take the time off for the Salzburg trip. Thus I'll come down sometime around the eighteenth or nineteenth. Eubanks has been invited down for the following week. So I'm trying to get him to drive down when I go, but if he doesn't I'll be flying since my dates are too far apart to drive them in time without killing myself. I have a problem as it is, for after Tuskegee it looks as though I'll have an eighteen day interval before I go to Dillard on the eleventh of March, to Southern on the fourteenth, to Bethune-Cookman on the nineteenth and to Howard on the twenty-second. I'd prefer to come home during the eighteen day period, but with the cost of flying what it is I plan to try to write somewhere between Tuskegee and New Orleans. Man, I'm getting out of this racket, the pay is bad, the colleges try to make it worse, and the result in terms of reaching the kids is dubious. I'm getting to look like a fat, baldheaded old fart fast enough; and little more of this and I'll start sounding like one.

I had the pleasure of seeing Bellow get the book award this year[1] which is encouraging for all of us. There ain't much originality, man, and they're waiting for you. Jack up old Jack, we need him. As for me, I'm in my old agony again trying to write a novel. I've got some ideas that excite me and a few scenes and characters, but the rest is coming like my first pair of long pants—slow as hell. Never mind, I'll get it out, it just takes time to do *anything* worthwhile. Incidentally, I just had a talk with Bellow and he's getting some of the same shit I received last year: the envy, the snobbery, the general display of lousiness, which some of the bright boys tried to pass on to me. He's shamed them both by winning something they want and by writing about them as they really are, without love, without generosity, sans talent, sans life. I thought they were simply reacting to my being a mose, but hell, they can't stand for anyone, not even one who's been around themselves (until he gets up and produces something that breaks their perception of style and form), to come along and try to leave his own agony on the heart of world. He tells me that years ago Greenberg advised him that there was nothing more to be said in terms of fiction and that he, Bellow, should follow him and make a career out of criticism! Well, they ain't taking it gracefully. There is just as much sneering over Bellow's award as there was over mine, if not more. So I've learned a little more why Hemingway and everyone on back to

---

[1] Saul Bellow won the 1953 National Book Award for fiction for *The Adventures of Augie March*. The award was presented in 1954.

Goethe, and probably back to Homer, have said to hell with critics. Today they see their world going to hell, all their standards fall flat and still they're afraid of anything that lets in the big wide contradictory sight see sound of the world. Stick to mose. Man. He's got more life in his toenails than these zombies have in their whole bodies. As though you didn't know it.

Had quite a bit of fun hunting during the season and discovered that I could still hit them once in a while. I got ducks (none of which were good because they had eaten fish) quail, grouse and squirrels. I hunted most of the time with Noble Simms' uncle and another old guy, who were fun enough in the beginning, but grew rather boring. They told no lies and had none of that old time humor, so next season I'm finding me some young studs and some kind of dogs. Those old cats had me walking my ass off, stirring up the birds—and then missing most of them. Indeed I've still to see one of them kill anything, and we hunted all season. He's the guy who took me out to have some fun at my expense only to have me imagine that I was back in Dayton in 1937 and started hitting every living ass. Poor man thought I'd tricked him although I never pretended that I was a stranger to a shotgun. Hunting is still a good way to live, man; and I'm glad that the instinct is still alive within me. It's much healthier than this backbiting and verbal murder, character assassination and bitchery that seems to be the current mode among the intellectuals. Tell Mokie that we're glad she found the machine useful—as I knew she would. One gadget you ought to avoid though, man, unless you want to work you balls off, and that's one of those floor polishers. I made that mistake and I'm about to end up with housemaid's knees from smearing on the goddamn wax! It's fun enough though, even if it does lead me to violate my taboo against work.

. . . I've run into some new bearisms which I'll report to you when I see you. Ran into a bear who was operating under F.D.R. with the stuff she had learned to work on Mose—and got away with it! Mau! Mau! Come up here if you can, if not I'll be down there in a couple of weeks and whatever happens don't go sour; you'll just have to do what the others aren't capable of doing, that's all. The world is changing so fast that most of these studs are going to crumble up before the very complexity of the freedom they thought they wanted and didn't, so forget them. It's the boys who'll call you papa, or at least will think of you as such even though they never give utterance to the thought, who'll inherit the earth. Be of good cheer.

Ralph

730 RIVERSIDE DRIVE
NEW YORK 31, N.Y.
FEBRUARY 8, 1954

Dear Murray:

Here is a copy of my letter to Flood, telling him to get off the pot or get into it. I rather like that guy but he isn't making sense at all. Perhaps I'm oversensitive about trains. Too many cinders in my gall bladder.

Anyway show this to Mort though I meant it for you since I feel you should know what I've said to Flood.

Hope to see you and Mokie and Mique—which, if I don't is liable to make me mad enough to sue old Julius for breach of contract.

Rough it, man.

Ellison

730 RIVERSIDE DRIVE
NEW YORK 31, N.Y.
FEBRUARY 8, 1954

Dear Mr. Flood:

In reply to your inquiry of Feb. 2nd, the fee arrangement set forth in my recent letter was meant to include round trip plane fare to Atlanta and return to New York—plus a fee of $175.00 for one formal lecture and any attendant talks the committee feels necessary and reasonable. I shall, of course, be personally responsible for my transportation from Atlanta to Tuskegee and return.

As to your personal suggestion that I travel by train, I must say thanks, while per force rejecting it. Trains consume precious time from my writing, are uncomfortable, and are still frequently dangerous for a black man. Thus whenever possible I take to the air—regardless of who pays the fare. When it is impossible to fly, I drive; when it is impossible to drive (buses sicken me), I remain at home. Naturally this is not a criticism of those who prefer the railroad.

There is, however, a less personal factor which makes the train impractical: When the entertainment course committee rejected the first date agreed upon, the resultant rearrangement of my schedule has made it necessary that I remain here for business until the very last minute. I accepted your last minute change of date without comment because last summer when I was approached by Dr. Foster I had made Tuskegee the focal point of my lecture schedule. Indeed, since it was suggested that I might spend two or three weeks at the school, I rejected lectures at Sarah Lawrence and at Vassar so as to be free for what I considered my most important engagement—thus leaving a gap of from sixteen to eighteen days between my stint at Tuskegee and my next lecture.

I don't like to burden you with these matters but they *do* nevertheless have a bearing on the question at hand. For while I am primarily a writer, it is my lecturing which makes it possible for me to give most of my time to creation. And while I approach my lectures with the feeling of responsibility, I consider them chiefly as a means to continue writing; thus they must at least repay me for the time which they take from my typewriter. I wish, indeed, that it were possible to give my services with no consideration for such realities as I was able to do last summer while on vacation.

This, incidentally, is the reason I asked Lieut. Murray to speak to you and it explains why you have "nothing in (your) files" regarding the matter of fees—though not at all why you have no previous knowledge of these matters. It was to avoid such misunderstanding precisely that I had Murray approach you.

I'm sorry to contribute to confusion of what appears from this distance to be simply a failure of liaison arising, no doubt, from the circumstances that it was not *you* who initiated these discussions with me, but Dr. Foster and at a time when things at Tuskegee were still in flux due to the change of administrations.

To return for a moment to the matter of trains, may I point out that if you are concerned with cutting expenses the saving would be nonexistent? The Crescent Limited with roomette (there being no berths on this train, according to the information clerk at Penna. Station), plus a modest $8.00 for meals and tips would come to $128.00; while the plane fare to Atlanta and return would come to only $111.67. Tips and taxi and/or airport limousine fare would past raise it some $5.00 more but the saving would still be on the side of the airlines. Thus the trains are not only impractical for me, they are of no economy to you.

I am naturally very much in favor of helping the Entertainment Course stretch its budget. As a former student I realize how important the course is to the intellectual horizon of the student body. Thus if I don't find it necessary to return to New York upon the completion of my talks at Tuskegee I would be perfectly agreeable to refund to the committee that part of the return plane fare that remains after flight fare from Atlanta to New Orleans ($21.35 plus 15%) has been deducted. The College Fund will get me for far more than that anyway, though I'm not complaining. Actually I prefer to remain South, so that unless a new lecture in this area comes up during that eighteen day period the chances are that I shall.

In closing may I assure you that I would be most disappointed to miss this trip to Tuskegee, but if the fee makes the engagement untenable, please assure the committee that it may feel perfectly free to cancel without embarrassment. I ask only that you kindly inform me by return mail.

Cordially,
Ralph Ellison

Box 343
Tuskegee Institute,
Alabama
[1954]

Dear Ralph,

Flood says it's all set for 21 Feb, so we're looking for you anytime around that time. Will Fanny be able to come?

These cats don't really know what the hell they are supposed to be doing, but they're about to get something worked out, I guess. The man said have it, but they really ain't got no natural place for it, and I know damned well why, but they'll be ready when you get here.

There's one young fellow in sociology, however, who without knowing you were scheduled to come has made Invisible required reading and has put in an order for 150 copies (NAL). I told him that I would see to it that you met some of his classes. He's not really so hot but he's trying.

This new administration, by the way, ain't showed me much but negative so far. As yet this guy seems to have no real idea of how much and what kind of help he needs. Man, here's a dude that's done inherited something that he thinks he ought to be proud of, and everybody knows it's a pile of shit but him. This jerk needs help bad, boy. And so far the only one who seems to be giving it to him is Red Davis! (a shock which is surprisingly low at the moment). Did I tell you that old Mike Rabb's stuff paid off and that he is the new Secretary to the Board of Trustees? Mort of course rates high with this square, but you know Mort; he doesn't want to get in there and politic, and when things take a turn toward the stupid his first reaction is to back the hell out. So there he is on the bench pouting, while out here on the field is Fumbling Foster losing from five to ten yards on every play. That cat is too light, Ralph, he needs some black eyed peas and cornbread.

The only really enjoyable thing that's happened so far this term was the two-day stopover that Sugar Ray made here (while he and Count et al were touring together). They didn't play here, just stopped to rest up a bit. We hit it off fine and spent most of the time together. Listening to the Gavilan fight with him was something that old papa Hem might well envy. Man, when somebody asked old Sugar if he were going to let them talk him into going back into the ring again he said if you ever heard tell of him in there again you could bet he had a switchblade knife with him.

It's not really set yet, but I might have a flight up to NY around the 1st of Feb to get some poop on the UN. Let you know if.

This ROTC stuff still hasn't let up much yet, but I'm still trying to plug away at this rewrite job on Jack the Bear, or whatever it is. And by the way what happened to those articles you mentioned some time ago?

Murray

Dear Albert:

This is a most difficult letter to write not only because of the news itself, but because it reveals the terrifying possibilities which often flow from what appear at the time of making them to be simple decisions. I tried to get Eubanks to come to Tuskegee with me over a period of months[. H]e was committed to come and address the food show and be honored, but some complex of motives caused him to decide not to and you know about his sending me the speech too late for me to deliver it and the jokes we made about it. Yesterday I received word that Eubanks was killed by a psychopathic dishwasher over a wage dispute. He was both shot and knifed. Over and over my throat flexes with that old tragic cry "if only...if only...if only...." and it's true, had he come to Tuskegee he'd still be there to relive the experiences of the visit.

I suppose the word has already reached Tuskegee. Martha Ann Sumpter phoned it to Fanny. If not, please pass it along. He was one of the good ones, and a rare one. I'll never have a friend with *his* combination of traits again, nor will you, nor will anyone who knew him. Should anyone wish to write his mother, her name is Mrs. Lillie Eubanks, Akin, S.C. Her phone number is Barnwell 3917.

I'll write you later about my trip here. Please give my regards to all.
Ralph

Dear Albert:

After all the wandering I'm at home for a while. Last Thursday and Friday I was down in Baltimore, where I talked at Coppin State Teachers College and, the next morning, before a class in Negro Literature at Morgan. I suppose now I'll be free until June, when I'll return to Tuskegee if the boys haven't changed their minds. As much as

I hated to leave I think I did the right thing in going to New Orleans, although I didn't see the parade because I couldn't ride in either the airport limousine or the white taxis and thus spent hours steaming. I called some white folks some unheard of mfers that day! Nevertheless, despite my anger over the jimcrow (they must have invented the hitching post nigger, for they have millions [of] life-sized figures of Negroes fishing), despite having to spend four nights in hotels that were hardly more than whore houses, and despite the food, which put me in bed—I got some solid work done on my novel. They gave me an office to work in and I got down to business. They, meaning Dillard; which I found a most interesting school. They have the best lit. students and the most alert lit. faculty down that way, two white fellows and a Negro gal setting the pace. Southern is a bustling place, but I was there too briefly to get a real idea of what was going on. Except one night at a party at the dean's home the Negroes started needling me and I started asking questions and soon had everybody yelling at me, defending their right to be second rate! Naturally it was a mose doctor and a mose physicist who yelled the loudest. One Negro even drew his Caddy on me! For a while there it was outrageous, then one of the women went upstairs and brought down her child and I turned to the father and asked if the child represented his attempt to produce a second class baby and he finally admitted that in some things at least Negroes had a responsibility to measure up to or to lead the field. It ended well enough, though, with one of the wives giving me a kiss as I, unrequested, left.

I keep running into people who were at Harvard last August. Three are teaching at Bethune-Cookman operating on a high level—although I believe this was the most uneven school of the tour. They do have the best college food I've eaten anywhere, the department being headed by a Tuskegee grad. But it was Howard that was the most disappointing. Those people ask the most provincial questions put to me anywhere. They spent most of the time trying to push me into an autobiographical corner and when I wouldn't budge things would get quiet and I'd have to give them another lecture. Brown, Frazier, Davis, Lovel and others were there but none of them would say a mumbling word—not even when I attacked some of their assumptions concerning Mose and America and culture.

Later at a party Sterling Brown was very friendly and came along to see what kind of strange creature I was, but it was sad. But it had to be an old friend who made me mad. After most of the guests had gone (fortunately) Walt Williams started telling me that I was really developing, but I mustn't pontificate too much(!) and that I should speak more like Matthew Arnold! I told him that it might be more entertaining to some audiences if I learned to sing, but that my interest lay in the quality and validity of my ideas. If he found them wanting I'd be glad to be corrected. No, I showed that I had thought a lot about these matters but I should remember that there are other ideas. What ideas and what were their value, I asked. You should speak more like Arnold, he said. That goddamn Howard is a graveyard, man. Holmes seems to do nothing but speculate on the sex lives of others, several of the bright boys are suffering from liquor impotence; we were told (Fanny met me there) that this was the first time that Sterling Brown had been seen in the home of one of his old friends in six years; another once-good-man who's taken the cure. Depressing. John Hope Franklin seems to be the only real scholar and Margaret Butcher the most alert English teacher as well as the most socially conscious. The rest seem naked before the blast of reality. Can you imagine me standing up before a group of so-called leading Negro so-called scholars and saying that they had failed to define "Negro" except in blood terms, and not have one open his mouth? Maybe it's because they're afraid. The government has cut their funds again and there's talk of doing away with the school if integration comes and there they sit, the mask of illusion slipping down. And yet, when those boys see a guy like John Franklin functioning as an historian, writing papers, attending scholarly meetings, etc.—they think he's crazy. Then one day he'll be appointed the head of the department in some big college and they'll think it's simply a fluke.

There were some funny things on the trip: the Globetrotters running out onto the Municipal Auditorium in New Orleans dressed in stars and stripes and the crackers applauding to raise hell. Goose

Tatum ran out and tried to drag a white policeman in to arrest one of the opposing players and the cop must have brushed his coat sleeve compulsively for thirty minutes where Goose's big tarbaby hand had gripped him. It was a minstrel show and magic, man, and the white folks were simply fascinated. I found also that the coach at Dillard was a Pierro,[1] with whom I grew up. His wife also brought out the chittlings—though Mokie could teach her a few things. The amusing thing about Dillard lay in the fact that its chief backer is a Jew and he has put these Negroes in a stage set of a campus with white buildings of semi-plantation architecture! They left off the verandahs perhaps because they just couldn't stand to have these young moses sitting around drinking mint juleps while the white folks rolled past and stared.

Before I forget it, will you please send me the name of the fellow who heads the English department? I have to write him about the lectures in June and I've misplaced my notes. I absolutely refuse to enter into correspondence with Sandy!

How are things going? Things here are well enough. The *New World Writing* advance copies are out and I had some sent to you to distribute to a few faculty members. I was allowed only a few. Incidentally, I tried to pay Sonny for driving me to the plane but he refused it. I didn't mean it as pay and would still like to do something for him. If you have ideas let me know. Meanwhile, our love to Mique and Mokie and let us hear from you soon.

Ralph

> BOX 343
> TUSKEGEE INSTITUTE,
> ALABAMA
> 25 APR 54

Dear Ralph,
Your letter was waiting when I got back from the U of N.C. Was up there at another one of these AFROTC conferences. The advance copies

---

[1] An Oklahoma family name.

were here when I got back too. Delivered them all very promptly and every body tickled to death. Thanks for mine too.

Your tour very very good reading, too bad you don't have time to write it up as such. More important to keep at the novel however. Glad to hear that you were finally able to get it going again. I don't know WHEN I'm going to be able to get down to business again. This is the godamnedest term yet.

I'm booked to be at Mitchell[1] for about five weeks this summer, beginning around June 10th. Mokie is planning to go to Columbia, and Mique is to go to camp somewhere, maybe out to that Perry-Mansfield place in Colorado (if Fanny knows of someplace up that way where kids can take Dance while in camp I wish she would let me know about it—so far, the Perry-Mansfield is the only one we know of which specializes in the arts).

Looks like I'm going to be up there when you are down here, but of course, I'll still be up there when you get back too.

Dr. Robert Reid is the Head of the Department of General Studies. He is the guy I guess you want to get in touch with. Damned right. Don't write to Walker, you'll never get ANYTHING settled.

Was finally promoted to CAPTAIN on the 11th of March.

Will write again when there is more time.

> *Box 343*
> *Tuskegee Institute*
> *Alabama*
> *5 Aug 54*

Dear Ralph,

Had a good trip down. Everything running smoothly all the way. Being both papa & mama for Miss Mique these days and doing all right. Hot as I don't know what down here these days. Caint remember when it was this hot here. More like Miami during the war. They say it hasn't been this hot here since 18-something-or-other.

---

[1] Air Force base, Hempstead, Long Island, New York.

Nothing to report on the Foster regime except that the ass dragging continues apace. Mort is getting ready to go back to school this Fall, working very hard catching up on his reading.

Guys very excited about my hi-fi stuff. Excited about it *all*, but especially the amplifier.

Having checked into the situation here I've decided that the best thing to do on that speaker is to get a kit. That way I can be sure that everything is cut right, and at the same time I can have the experience of putting it together. Am going to have to use a wall cabinet. Corner won't work in that room.

Don't have to attend that workshop at Chapel Hill, so will not get back to NY before y'all take off. Mokie is coming back on the train.

Things are moving slowly at the office, so maybe I'm going to have a chance to get some real work done. Will take some leave when Mokie gets back. Hope to take her and Mique to the beach somewhere.

Reading Melville again (Man, that stuff on "bears" in Ch 9, *Confidence Man* is gone!)

Murray

730 RIVERSIDE DRIVE
NEW YORK 31, N.Y.
AUGUST 9, 1954

Dear Albert:

I was pretty annoyed with you and Mokie—but especially with you—because we had no word of how your trip went. Of course when *I'm* driving somewhere I'm the same way; I set out and arrive in good order and think nothing of it until the week or so it takes me to get my breath—then I write. I called Mokie, but she was busy and we were unable to reach her until Sunday, when she came up and spent the afternoon and part of the evening helping Fanny sew. It looked like a sweat shop when they got through, but Fanny's going to have some damn good looking clothes. Mokie, by the way, says that she has an idea who's being poppa and momma down there. Me too, and I suspect that Miss Mique has you well in hand. Give her our love. I'm disgusted with this lutherism[1] you sent, it's the most inept piece of transparent crap I've seen yet. I had some hopes for the man but this, if it expresses his thinking, is as lame as the outpourings of any mushmouth who has convinced himself that his uncletomism is wisdom. All this and Walker too.... I think Mort is doing the correct thing. I plan to write him, meanwhile I'm sure you'll give him the dope on our bull sessions. I've been working away at constructing other organizing forms for this novel, which has led me to more reading in Faulkner criticism. I found the *English Institute Essays,* 1952, published by the Columbia University Press of interest. Most of the book is given over to Faulkner's *The Sound and the Fury,* but there are also three essays on rhetoric, one concerning Joyce, that are of interest.... That Bear stuff in *The Confidence Man* is indeed gone. I guess I told you that the bank image in *Invisible* was suggested by the figure of Black Guinea. That son of a bitch with his mouth full of pennies! I've also just read the galleys of Wright's book on the Gold Coast, *Black Power,* and though I'm somewhat annoyed with his self importance I think the book is important and I'm trying to work out a comment. Take a look at it, perhaps I could send you the galleys if I don't have to return them.

I'm glad the system worked out OK, and I think the kit idea the best solution. If I can be of help let me know, Sarser might well give you some kind of discount—only let me know before next week.

Things are getting frantic here over the trip. I've found a young writer who wants to stay here while we are away. His name is Alvin Cooper and he has been working on a novel for several years. I don't know what it's like but it sounds sociological. Anyway, it looks as though he'll occupy the fort while we are away. As usual I've waited until the last minute before allowing the trip to become real for me, so that now I'm shopping and putting things in order and find myself short of dough even before I leave. If you still want to lend me something until I return, I can use any amount up to three hundred dollars, preferably the whole sum. This would be just the right amount of medicine to chase away that nagging anxiety of insecurity of getting

---

[1] Luther Foster, president of Tuskegee.

busted in a foreign land. If you can send it and should you need it suddenly don't worry, as I can always get an advance from my publish-
ers—who would like to have me spending some of *their* money so as
to be in a position to needle me about the work in progress.

I hope you'll get work done on your book and that you'll start turning out essays on jazz which can later be part of a book. You have the
stuff and I think it'll do you good to have part of your identity an-
chored outside Tuskegee. Thus far you've stayed there and transcended its limitations. You've evolved the stuff, so now put it on the
line. You're the only one I know who makes sense of all the ramifica-
tions and since it looks like no one is going to do anything with this
material we might as well get started. I still think that that conversation [sic] we had with Maya one of the damnedest I've ever partici-
pated in! Tiger, rabbit, bear and priest (Campbell), strictly a jam
session in metaphors and the jungle queen getting her butt kicked
with each snap of her tail.... Incidentally, I found that record, "Blue
Monday," I asked you about. It's by Smiley Lewis and it's in the classic
mold, a mose singing triumphantly about hard work:

> Blue Monday, oh how I hate blue Monday. Got to work like a
>   slave all day
>
> Then comes Tuesday, oh lawd Tuesday I'm so tired I got no time
>   to play
> Then comes Wednesday, I'm beat to my socks
> My gal calls and I have to tell her I'm out
> Cause Thursday is a hard working day
> And Friday I get my pay.
> Saturday morning, oh Saturday morning!
> All my tiredness has gone away
> Got my money, got my honey
> And I'm out on the stem to play
> Sunday morning my head is bad
> Boy it's worth it for the times I've had
> But I got to get my res'
> Cause Monday is a mess

Boy, if I could sing that stuff the way Smiley Lewis does I'd run all these fancy singers out of the country. Call that primitivism if you want to. If you hear anything else by him let me know.

Back to jazz, I've heard enthusiastic reports on Basie from two other sources. I'm sorry we didn't get down to hear him together. I plan to make it before we leave. Take it easy, man. It's raining here and I've got to go out in it. Monday is, after all, a mess.

Ralph

Box 343
Tuskegee Institute
Alabama
11 Aug 54

Dear Ralph,

Know what you mean about that letter writing business, but never seem to be able to just sit right down and be civilized enough to write just a plain functional expected letter. Always trying to wait and write out of readjustment, I reckon. Never send post cards, for instance. Got to get operating better than that. Will.

No, I really am Jack the mamapoppa in this house these days, cooking my cottonpicking ass clean off, cleaning, and supervising. Miss Mique had two girl friends in the other day, and invited them to stay for dinner! during which (ham, potato salad, brown-&-serve rolls etc) one of them asked Mique, "Whose cooking do you like best, your mama's or your daddy's?" To which Mique replied, "Both." Later she told me, "You entertained them very well, we had fun."

On that speaker cabinet kit, if you have time you can have Sarser send it on down as soon as possible. I'll send the money as soon as he lets me know how much, or C.O.D. if that's OK.

[E]nclosed is the $300.00 you mentioned. I don't think that I'll be needing it before you get back and get set. And if you get over there and still find that you're running short, don't let this 3 keep you from letting us know. Too much to do over there to be pinching pennies too sharply.

Determined to get some stuff down this year. And as for me and Tuskegee, boy the less I'm identified with this sonofabitch the better. I will never give these bastards an inch. Boy, these mfkers are all through and won't know it. I have one thing to say to them from now until the time I unass the area but def: "You niggers ain't shit, you niggers ain't shit, you niggers ain't shit, you niggers ain't even shit!"

Looking for Mokie this weekend. Seems she might be bringing Gwen's Pete home for Vivian.

Have done 139 pages of *The Fable,* and am starting over. Not participating enough. Figured I should be in deeper before getting to that horse thief stuff. Don't know what I think yet.

Murray

AUGUST 19, 1954

Dear Albert:

Man, we're almost off, struggling with baggage and general anxiety. I forgot to tell you last night that I was sending along the key to my new file, (it's in the front closet) in which all of my papers are located. Should anything happen to us see what you can do with the junk. You and Stanley Hyman can play—or fight—at being literary executors. A hell of a thing to wish on anyone, but since we have about the same rifling that's what goes with it. Of course I'll try like hell to save you that problem. Take it easy, write your book, give my love to Mique and Mokie, and warm regards to the Mitch's and the Morts. This here is one monkey who's yelling at the buzzard to straighten up and fly right before he even hits the airport!

Ralph

R. Ellison
Salzburg Seminar in American Studies
Schloss Leopoldskron
Salzburg, Austria

10 DEC 54

Man, I had forgotten about sending this key until Mokie asked me yesterday if I had done so. Here it is.

How are things these days? Me, I'm still pluggin, doing some more purging too. Always some shit to be gotten rid of. So many things I seem to be seeing through for the first time. The "literary" apprenticeship as such endeth, beginneth the journeyman American. What I have learned I've learned, but a lot of the stuff that I've tended to ignore as crap I find I need too....

Boy, my hi-fi is jumping. I'm using a Karlson "Ultra Fidelity" enclosure and am tickled to death with it. I ordered it unfinished and finished it myself, painted it black and covered that goddamn swallowtail with red & black grill cloth.

Am now trying to get an overseas assignment to Europe, North Africa or the Middle East at the end of this ROTC deal next summer. Would like to have the free trip and that much more money for the next two or three years. Also should like to be able to take Moque and Mique. Possible.

Things are generally quiet here. Foster is in India don't ask me what for. No signs of improvement. Boy you should have seen these cats when one WVS (Shadrack) Tubman was here, Man, you would have thought they were getting ready to inaugurate the son of a bitch. I believe Foster would dry-run a prayer meeting (wasting valuable time for bear meetings, which he'll never be able to recognize for what they are).

Hi to Fanny.

Murray

> *Box 343*
> *Tuskegee Institute,*
> *Alabama*
> *11 Jan 55*

Dear Ralph,

Flying this weekend, the weather permitting. Should arrive Friday afternoon sometime. Returning Sunday. Cross-country, me, Hurd & Carter. See you.

Albert

> *730 Riverside Drive*
> *New York 31, N.Y.*
> *April 12, 1955*

Dear Murray:

Here are a few riffs from old Cliofus, who seems on the way to out lie Sallywhite. This chok-drinking Charlie character appeared just as I was typing up this copy to send you, I don't know where the hell Cliofus got him but here he is anyway. As you see, the stuff is still crude— which means it's still building. Anyway, here it is.[1]

Things are all upset here, the damn prize[2] is something of a problem, for here we are still paying off our debts from the last trip and now we've got to prepare for another. The apartment has to be sublet (if the landlord approves). I have to do something about the car, and we've got to get money for Fanny's passage. Here we go again. I could take an advance, but this isn't good because we'll have to have something to live on when we return. I'm sure we'll work it out, but just the same it's a pain. I'd have had yours down to you but I discovered that $3000.00 of income which I thought I'd paid last year actually was received during this tax period—which literally knocked the crap out of our payment schedule. Nevertheless, I'll take care of you before Sept. 22—our sailing date.

What's happening with you Murrays? I've talked with Doris recently and she mentioned something about Europe but was very vague. Tell me something. How're Mique and Moque?? Has spring shown? Man, I'd like to hit the road even though I'm sure I'd get disgusted with what they're not doing down there. But I always liked the place in the spring and I'm sure it would be as good for my soul as anything. Tell Nance incidentally, that I hope he got his fellowship even though I've neglected to write.... I helped record the Ellington–Symphony of the Air concert a few weeks ago and wished you were here to catch it. Don Gillis took up half the program but nothing happened until Duke started waving his shoulder, then the symphony started sounding like his band, strings and all. Even Don Shirley with his fabricated personality and cocktail lounge, white boy approach couldn't ruin it. We've caught a couple dances at the Savoy recently with Cootie Williams and Buddy Tate and I'm glad to report that the joint still jumps and the gutbucket is as full of rich life as ever. Let them

---

[1] Ellison's enclosure is what he called an eleven-page "Copy of [a] Working Draft" from his novel-in-progress. The excerpt is not included here but will be among the drafts to be compiled in the scholarly edition of Ellison's unfinished second novel.

[2] Prix de Rome.

look for white hopes of jazz as much as they will, the true stream still runs deep and blue. Tell Mitch[3] that when he comes to town, if ever, we'll have to go jumping. And tell him to hold down the Twenty-Nine[4] because I'll be back there the first chance I get. This is about it but before I drop it I should say that I hope you're not allowing those asses to turn you away from writing. The only mistake you ever made was, perhaps, to assume that they could ever really tolerate you among them. Man, you're a walking condemnation of everything they stand for; and though I'm sure you've done very important things for some of the students simply by being there, too much of your psychic and moral energy has to go into simply keeping the stink of some of the administration out of your nostrils. Now, with Mort away, it must be a real crapper. Well, the only way to stick them and stick them hard is by going ahead and publishing a book. A novel or a book of criticism, anything that expresses your sense of life—this is more important than the dough which you're going to have anyway, and you pointed out there's no contradiction between you having dough and writing. If you have something short, send it up to Arabel, she's dying for material and worrying the life out of me. But whatever and whenever— write and publish! End of sermon.

By the way, there's a Hemingway piece in the current *True*, which I haven't read. I'm catching up on the gal he recommended as worthy of the Nobel Prize, Isak Dinesen, whose *Seven Gothic Tales* I read down there during the thirties. I'm in the midst of *Out of Africa* and it's really very good. I understand that there are several others and I'm out to find them. I've also been having once a week sessions with Bellow, listening to him read from his work-in-progress and reading to him from mine. For about thirty minutes we cuss out all the sons-abitches who say the novel's dead, then we read and discuss. Wish the hell you were taking part. If you fly up bring along some of the stuff and give it a try. It's the only genuine literary life I know these days; the rest is all cocktails and bull shit and the cocktails aren't always

---

[3] Dr. Rudolph Mitchell, obstetrician and pediatrician, Murray's neighbor at Tuskegee.
[4] Roadhouse on Route 29, Macon County, Alabama.

good. When I find myself at one nowadays I feel like asking with Choc-drinking Charlie,[5] "Where the hell's the *hat* that goes with these castrated pants?"

Take it easy, man. And write me. I'm in a violent agitated frame of mind and need a friendly voice. Give our love to Mokie and Mique.

Ralph

BOX 343
TUSKEGEE INSTITUTE,
ALABAMA
17 APR 55

Dear Ralph,

Looks like you got yourself some boy in that Cliofus[6] (also Cleophus, and I also used to know a guy named Cephus, called See First, See First Adams! lives in Plateau right now)[.] Cliofus is a good Southern sounding name (House-nigger classicism) and of course it is also derived from the Muse of History (like old daddy Eubanks said, Man this shit is HISTORY!) Boy, you got yourself a cat that *blows* history. Riffs is right. Jam session history. Strike a chord and that cat will blow everybody down but the rhythm. (Man, when that motherfucker gets good and warmed up all you can do, the best you can do is pat your feet and clap your hands and let him blow—you know how them cats get all down on their knees, turning their horns all sideways, YOU KNOW HOW THEM CATS GET TO BLOWING VIOLIN NOTES, BRASS NOTES, OBOE NOTES, DON'T CARE WHAT KIND OF NOTES (growls farts horseneighs trainwhistles airplanes womangrunts) any-and-everything once they get started like that. Strike another chord, change the key, or even break the rhythm and that son of a bitch is not only laying with you he's in there working in a lot of EXTRA shit of his own. Man once you get that clown cutting, all you got to do is sit there at the piano like old

---

[5] A minor character in Ellison's novel-in-progress.

[6] Storytelling character in the "Working Draft" Ellison had enclosed with his letter of April 12, 1955.

Duke and chord them goddamn FRAMES around his ass. Work out, man. Work with him.

Saw the Hemingway piece. Have also been checking on Isak Dinesen, have *Out of Africa* right on the head of the bed. I have always associated you with *Seven Gothic Tales*, [y]our name is probably still on the card of the library copy. Library also has *Winters Tale.* Would like to round them up myself. Random did sell them all didn't they? Are there more than three? I know that the first two are now in Modern Library. If you come across *Winter's Tales* get one for me. Picked up a couple of interesting things on a Marboro[7] sale, C. Vann Woodward's *Reunion and Reaction,* and Owen's *Slave Mutiny.* By the way, Dawson has a piece in *Etude* (Mar or Apr).

Have been tied up for the past several weeks getting ready for Annual Federal Inspection. Over now. Bill Campbell just took over as the new PAS (Professor of Air Science) been to Korea, Japan & Okinawa since seeing you here in '53. Carter and I move out sometime this summer. Don't know when yet, or where to.

Look, man, I'm NOT going to accept that money until AFTER you get back from Europe, so goddamn.

Harry Ford sent me that copy of *Masters and Slaves.* Do I write him at Knopf's or will you send me his home address, or has he gone to Europe yet? I forgot when they said they were going.

Kenneth Clark and I were talking about real estate. If anything turns up that looks pretty good, I'm definitely interested. That would be a good project to have while I'm overseas. In fact I've just initiated plans to build a small resalable house here, so I'll have somewhere to leave my books, and also because it's a good investment. Mann and I are planning to build three and sell two to help pay for the third.

Yes, Spring is very much here now. But a lot of plants were ruined in that cold snap a few weeks ago. The wisterias had just reached full bloom and so had the Judas trees and the dogwoods. All of a sudden Mop! Two days of freezing temperature and a week later the countryside looked almost like autumn. [D]amndest thing to happen that late

---

[7] Chain of bargain bookstores.

since way back in the 19th century. Peach crop of Georgia absolutely blasted. The weather is right again now though, and the stuff is in the air like it always was, and the rubbers on the grass alas, a lass rubbing ass on the grass....

Old Mike Rabb was up there with the choir, business mgr thereof, but he was so busy that he hardly got out of the goddamned hotel. Very tickled at himself. Great trip. Almost half of the choir had to be recruited from the ranks of the alumni.

Club 29 out on Highway 29 is as was except more so. Got Little Ester out there this week. Going for frequent live shows out there these days.

I guess you've heard by now that Major Abbott died last Friday, which reminds me that we didn't mention the fact that Neely died last Fall.

Old Mort is back. Finishing up his paper, should get his Ph.D. sometime this summer. Moque and Mique are fine. Moque has been on a sewing spree, so she and Mique have sharp new outfits. Boy, and Mique reached the age of monthly sanitation the other day. Hell of a feeling. This father business is just about to enter another phase. I think we've established the proper perspectives. Now the job is to maintain equilibrium. So far so good, but now comes the crucial test of parenthood.

You and Bellow keep that stuff moving. I'm doing what I can right now, which ain't much, but I'm coming and I'll be there when I get there.

Love to Fanny, and how's that hairdo?

Murray

p/s In as much as they've turned Miss Shirley Ann Grau[8] into the new hope or something, I've been forced to read beyond that camera panning paragraph that reminds me of a gimmick I got from Edna Millay. Man, that chick is a goddamn drag. She has no real identification with that stuff, and has made no real effort to handle it honestly. Hell, the white jazz musicians are way ahead of that bitch (with her black monkey images and her "might can"s). Writes like she gets that stuff from the servants. She better talk to Jack Teagarden or somebody. Hell,

---

[8] Southern author of *The Black Prince and Other Stories.*

even Eddie Condon or Benny Goodman could do her a lot of good. If that goddamn crap is really better than my Briarpatch stuff, I better start all over again. That Goddamn Albert Erskine said last summer that he liked it and that I should publish some more of them like in *New World Writing,* but that there was absolutely no market for volumes of short stories these days. Maybe I ain't got it yet, but that chick ain't got it yet either—but look at the critical reactions she's getting.

II

ROME, CASABLANCA, AND NEW YORK

1955-1958

From the late summer of 1955 until April of 1958, I was assigned to the Southern Air Material Area (SAMA) of the U.S. Air Force Europe, located at Nouasseur Air Force Base on the outskirts of Casablanca in what at that time was known as French Morocco. I received notification of my new assignment in May 1955, and on July 14, Bastille Day, the news media carried headline stories of anti-French terrorist bombings in Casablanca by the native Moroccan anti-French independence movement of Arabs and Berbers.

On the other hand, there was already Ralph's news that the American Academy of Arts and Letters had awarded him the Prix de Rome, financing a year's residency at the American Academy in Rome, which meant that we would be able not only to see each other during the next year (or maybe the next two years, since the term of residency was renewable) but also to do some traveling in Europe together, because my automobile would be shipped to my new duty station just as my household furniture would be, and I was already planning to drive up to Europe on leaves of absence. And for military personnel and family members, there were also "space available" leave-time morale flights to Europe and one Mediterranean round-trip cruise all the way to Istanbul by way of stops in Italy, Libya, and Greece.

When I arrived in Casablanca on August 20 with my wife Mozelle and our twelve-year old daughter Michele, the revolt against French control was literally exploding. There were anti-French terrorist attacks and atrocities across North Africa from Tunisia and Algeria all the way to the Atlas Mountains area of Morocco. But at that time there was no Arab hostility toward the U.S. military presence in North Africa and the Middle East. So although we were in an active zone of violent anticolonialism, we were not considered to be in any great danger so long as we avoided all of the clearly defined restricted areas and transportation facilities. In fact, we lived in a small villa within the city limits of Casablanca for a year before moving into newly completed on-base housing.

So it was during our tour of duty in Morocco that France abrogated the 1912 Treaty of Fez, ending its protectorate status which was administered by a resident general, and recalled the erstwhile sultan of Morocco from exile in Madagascar to become King Muhammad V. But for the most part the nature of U.S. neutrality was such that the political situation was all nearly as much a matter of newspaper and magazine stories to me in Casablanca as it was to Ralph in Rome. In any case there are not many references to it in our letters. But I am surprised to find no record of my mentioning the shrill, primordially female sound of ululation of those veiled Arab women as a procession of the ex-sultan rearriving as king surrounded by his elite blue-black Senegalese guardsmen passed along the streets of Casablanca en route back to his palace in Rabat. Even now I remember it as if there were birds singing in the overhanging trees, an image I also associated with hearing organ and choir music in Gothic cathedrals.

In Rome, Ralph was challenged to come to pragmatic American terms with what he was supposed to have learned about ancient and Renaissance times back when he was a schoolboy in Oklahoma. "At table," he wrote to me in Morocco, "I hear the classicists talking the stuff, who did what when and why and where, and I feel lost in a world that I've got to get with or die of frustration."

But it was also in Rome that he invented the crucial episode of the assassination in the Senate Chamber for the novel that he hoped would follow *Invisible Man* within the next year or so. Having accepted several invitations to write essays or literature, toward the end of his time at the American Academy, Ralph found himself torn between fiction and his critical prose. Nonfiction from this period includes "Society, Morality and the Novel," written for *The Living Novel,* 1957, a book of critical essays edited by Granville Hicks; and "Living with Music," *High Fidelity,* December 1955. In response to a copy of a lecture on Negro writing by Stanley Hyman he also began what became the essay "Change the Joke and Slip the Yoke," which was published as an exchange with Hyman in *Partisan Review* in the spring of 1958. During his two years at the Academy in Rome, Ralph also served as American representative at literary conferences in London, Mexico City, and Tokyo.

As the letters between us indicate, Ralph and I carefully followed the jazz and literary scenes from Casablanca and Rome. But we paid particular attention to the growing Civil Rights movement in America, and the efforts in Congress to advance or frustrate integration. In response, Ralph wrote most of "Tell It Like It Is, Baby" (1965), whose title is from a letter sent him by his old Oklahoma friend Virgil Branam.

A.M.

HQ SAMA(E)
APO # 30
NEW YORK, NY
23 AUG 55

Dear Ralph,

The trip over was more or less routine, Mozelle and Mique took the whole thing in wonderful stride. We arrived on schedule on the 20th, and since that time have been billeted in a swanky hotel in the resort area. I've been assigned to the Education and Training Division at Command Headquarters. That's a very high level operation it seems. Haven't actually started work yet, still getting processed in.

The main thing is to find a house (villa) or an apartment so we can get the hell out of that hotel and get settled. This is not really going to be a very difficult problem, but I'm in a hurry. My main difficulty right now is not having the car. It seems that it might be six or eight weeks before it gets over, the back log is so great.

All I know about the situation here is what I read in the papers (*Stars & Stripes*). There are troops and there are road checks, and there are many restrictions for the time being, but we haven't actually been near anything rough yet. Things are going OK so far. The address is as given on the envelope.

Murray

AMERICAN ACADEMY IN ROME
VIA ANGELO MASINA V
ROME 28, ITALY

OCT. 22, 1955

Dear Albert:

I started this letter a few days before we left, but didn't have time to finish it so I'll pick up where I left off before going into the trip, etc. So as I was saying: I went into a store on Madison Avenue the other day and saw a slightly built, balding mose in there stepping around like he had springs in his legs and a bunch of frantic jumping beans in his butt (pronounced ass), and who was using his voice in a precise, clipped way that sounded as though he had worked on its original down home sound with great attention for a long, long time—a true work of art. I dug this stud and was amazed. I was sitting across the store waiting to be served when he got up and came across to the desk to pay for his purchase and leave his address—when the salesman made the mistake of asking him if he wasn't *the* Joe (pardon me, Jo) Jones.

Well man, that definite article triggered him! His eyes flashed, his jaw unlimbered and in a second I thought ole Jo was going to break into a dance. His voice opened up like a drill going through thin metal and before you could say Jackie Robinson he had recalled every time he had been in this store, the style of shoes he bought and why he'd bought them and was going into a tap dancing description of his drumming school, politics, poon-tang in Pogo Pogo and atomic fission—when I remembered what you had told me of his opinion of Alton Davenport and uttered the name. Man, his voice skidded like a jet banking up there where the air ain't air and he started stuttering. "Did you say Davenport?" he said. "And Birmingham, Tuskegee, and points south," I said. And he was off again. In fact, he damn near exploded and the fallout must have swamped the fat-ass Alton way the hell down Birmingham way. I thought I'd better get him out of there to cool him off, so we moved out on the street with him still blowing. I finally managed to tell him that I knew you and he calmed down. He gave me his address to pass along to you so here it is: Jo Jones, 123 W. 44th Street, NYC Room 903. Judson 2-2300. What a character! I'm afraid that he's not only a great drummer, he is—in the colored sense—also a fool. When we separated I followed him at a distance just to see him bouncing and looking as he headed over to 5ᵗʰ Ave., and it was like watching a couple of hopped-up Japanese playing ping pong on a hot floor. Man, they tell a lot of wild stories about boppers but this stud is truly apt to take off like a jet anytime he takes the notion. He probably has to play his bass drum with a twenty pound weight on his trap foot. In fact as I moved behind him I expected any minute to see him re-react to the outrage of Davenport's teaching music and run a hundred yard dash straight up the façade of a building. Drop him a few calming words, man; he needs them.

As you can see, we are here. It took us eleven days on the Constitution, what with one day stops in Algeciras (Spain), Cannes, and Genoa. The food was lousy and the trip was a bore and [we] were damn glad to get off at Naples, where we drove by car to Rome. We're about settled now, here on the Janiculine Hill, in a huge villa where all the Rome Fellows and some Fulbrighters live and work. We have a bedroom and a living room and I have a study located in a one room cottage built against the old Aurelian Wall, which surrounds part of the estate. My windows face the garden which supplies our vegetables and flowers and I'm fairly remote from interruption and most workaday sounds. The only writing I've done however has consisted of an article on music and some letters. For at the end of our first week [we] were carried on a tour of northern Italy. We went by car and saw the art of Orvieto, Perrugia, Urbino, Pisa, Assisi, Todi, Rimini, Ravenna, Florence, Sansepolcro, Sienna and many places in between. We were gone nine days and if we never see anymore we've certainly seen some of the greatest. My eyes are still whirling and we simply must go back to some of the places to isolate and study those works which most moved us. If I had about one choice it would be Florence and the Ufizzi Gallerie. I'm aching for a car now, just to get around at will. The Renaissance has sent my imagination on a jag ever since I was shooting snipes in Oklahoma, but here its around you everywhere you turn, the same sky, earth, water, roads, houses, art. And not only that, it's all mingled with the Romans, the Greeks, the Greco-Christians. At a table I hear the Classicists talking the stuff, who did what, when and why and where, and I feel lost in a world that I've got to get with or die of frustration. We've got one of the keys, though, for here is where the myth and ritual business operates in a context not of primitive culture but beneath the foundations of the West. Some of the classical people here are snobbish about this mess but it belongs to anyone who can dig it—and I don't mean picking around in ruins, as important as that is. I've just read a novel titled *Hadrian's Memoirs*[1] which is interesting in its reconstruction of the times, warfare, politics, philosophy, religion and the homosexual love life of the Emperor. It's really more of a scholarly synthesis than a novel [...] but it's worth reading. As soon as I can discover who knows what around here I plan to get a reading list so that I can orient myself in relation to the classical background.

Man, I wish I could get over there with a tape recorder and copy some of your records. I bought that French set and it took up a good number of the reels I had so that I need a hell of a lot more jazz tapes to keep me on my proper ration. A man has, after all, to keep his feet on his home ground. As it is I have the Academy ringing with Duke and Count and Jimmy Rushing. I could just use a hell of a lot more. Books are a problem too; I'm only the fifth fellow in literature and they haven't built up much of a library. I guess I have to load up on my Penguins as soon as I can get down into the city. That Fanny is more like you, she's down there every day seeing all the sights. I've been only three times, and then on business. I'll catch up though. She's also speaking some Italian while I've had only one lesson ...

No important news from home. We have friends living in the apartment and since I couldn't sell the car I stored it. Which bothers me now, for I have been told that I could stay here two years if I wish, and perhaps three. Right now I'd trade it for a Volkswagen and a gallon of gas! Have a letter from Foster requesting ideas of what program of Tuskegee should be, I haven't yet written that self-liquidation is the trick.

How are things going with you, Moke and Mique? All three of you stay the hell out of the way of those bloody French. In fact, I suggest that you fly Old Glory everywhere you go. And by no means go

---

[1] *Memoirs of Hadrian,* by Marguerite Yourcenar.

around in anything white, 'cause it's better to be shot for a mose than an A-rab any damn day (as you can see I'm still learning how to operate this Italian typewriter). By the way, write me the price of those Moroccan scatter rugs; we have tile floors and we could use a couple in our living room. If they are cheap enough I'd be willing to pay the duty to have them here. Those I remember are white with brown, black, yellow etc. designs. Got to feather this nest, man. Now if I could just find me some chitterlings ... Allen Tate's wife, Caroline Gordon, is here and as soon as I know her better I'm going to ask her. Cause sure as hell she's going to come up one day wishing for some turnip greens cooked with a ham bone and I have a notion that all the southerners in Rome have a joint which they keep secret. I met Snowden, the Negro cultural attache at a party and he was operating semi-officially so I didn't bother him at the time. Incidentally, I'm still cutting my own hair; he has less than I have so I didn't ask him about an initiated barber. Nevertheless, I suspect old Snowden can speak the idiom and I'll bet my money that he's an operator. If not I'll find me somebody down around Bricktop's place. Some seamen from the Constitution promised to introduce us to that part of Rome when they came in next trip, so by the time you get over we'll have situation well in hand. Till then if there's anything I can do for you here or through friends in New York, just let me know. Kiss the girls for me and tell 'em love us loves yall.

As ever,
Ralph

HQ SAMA(E)
APO #30
NEW YORK, NEW YORK
2 NOVEMBER 1955

Dear Ralph,
Good to hear from you, man. Good to hear you in there riffing like that. But then you're bound to be riffing if you're cutting dots for that goddamned Jonathan Jones. He's every bit as crazy as that goddamned Sonny-assed Greer, the main difference being that he drinks only cokes and claims to be a narcotics agent. You got to hit em and git,

blowing over that Birmingham-KC tempo, Jim. Remember what he told that fay drummer that time. This poor square cat was clunking and plunking up there on 52nd and one night he looked out there's old Jo sitting there not even looking. Whereupon this cat falls to and commences to fair-thee-well all but cook supper on them skins as only a grayboy feels he's got to do. Sweated himself into a double krupa trying to make old Jo take notice, then at the end of the set he came over and asked if he dug him. "You're distorting me, man," old Jo lectured him right then and there, his teeth set into that razor-edged footlights not-smile, his eyes crowfooted, his nose narrow, his voice nasal, "This way, man, this way. Lighten up, lighten up and loosen up. Watch your elbows, man. Watch your shoulders. What you mad about? It's music, man, music, music. From here man, here, here, here. It's heart and soul, pardner. Man, you're distorting the hell out of me." Man, that cat didn't use nothing but brushes the rest of the night.

Glad to know that you've not only arrived and gotten fairly settled but also have already begun moving around. There is one hell of a lot of stuff stacked up in that Italy, boy. I certainly know what you mean when you say it does that to your imagination. You know I've always been in there with you on the Renaissance. Man, I had to get the hell on out of Florence but fast [back in 1950] otherwise it might have taken me months. Went on to Venice and Lido to lighten up a bit. Rome was out of the question after all of that, what with Paris still to be done.

Ready for them Romans now though, and them Greeks too, and also them Egyptians. By the way, speaking of reading, I did "Hadrian's Memoirs" last spring. Found it completely absorbing. Also picked up some of Robert Graves' Roman stuff.

But speaking of books, man, I've bought SEVENTY since I've been here. *Regular* editions, condition good to excellent. GI library salvage sale. TEN CENTS EACH!! Stuff like this: Ten volumes of that Rivers of America series, Six volumes of the American Folkways series (*Deep Delta Country, Palmetto Country, High Border Country,* etc), Van Tilburg Clark's *City of Trembling Leaves, Track of the Cat;* Mencken's *Supplement One;* Buckmaster's *Let My People Go;* Perry Miller's *Jonathan Edwards; Robber Barons; The Big Con; The Great Rehearsal; Reveille in Washington;* Douglas Moore's *From Madrigal to Modern Music; Gods, Graves and Schol-*

ars; Michener's *Voice of Asia, Return to Paradise;* Capa's *Slightly out of Focus;* Vincent Sheean; etc, etc.... Good thing old Uncle Sugar is hauling this stuff around for me for free.

We've now taken a small villa and have just about gotten settled into the new routine. Mique of course never missed a beat, school nor otherwise. And Moque you know just lays in there strumming like old Freddie Green does in that Basie rhythm section. Me, I'm zeroed in and zunking. We were in a hotel for five weeks, but now we're out in one of the quartiers.

Know what you mean about your car. When ours came the whole place changed shape. We've been doing Casa systematically for practical operations, and now we're beginning to get out into the other towns and the country. We've been to Rabat and Port Lyauty. Next: Fez, Meknes, Tangier. Then MARRAKESH, the mountains, and the Sahara. And that's just Morocco!

Fanny mentioned news service. Not too bad here: *Stars & Stripes* everyday in PX. Two British papers, and all the Paris papers toute suite, which I can manage well enough to keep up, and which I'm using as a part of my language routine anyway. PX stocks just about all mags, all of Moque's.

About those rugs (and Berber blankets), this is the country, but we haven't been buying yet because we're still learning about them. Plan to get them not in Casa but at the getting places: Rabat for your own modern designs, Fez for the very finest Moroccan designs, Marrakesh for solid rugs and blankets. Fine copper and fine leather in those places too. Of course they have the real thing right here in Casa, but it goes a little higher here. They got just about everything to eat here too. There are North African Collard greens, and no later than last Sunday morning Moque and I saw hog maws and chitterlin's in the Marche Centrale. Man, these Frenchmen know a good thing when they find it.

No problem on haircuts here. Moroccans come in all textures. No problem there either. You just haven't checked the jazz boys yet. That was the first question I asked old Don Byas in Paris. Them Africans ain't no help at all in an operation like that, same-same your hipsters. Nix.

My music isn't here yet, but we have our own radio on the base, and the French stations play some jazz every day. Radio Tangier is better than the base.

Political situation firming up fine right now. There will still be some more terrorism for a while yet, but it looks like the Arabs have done it to them. The French are afraid that they're going to lose their hats, asses, and gas masks, but actually they probably won't. The Arabs will still need somebody for a while, and the French could salvage something as the British usually do. Well, they *might*.

Murray

p/s What size rugs did you have in mind?

7 Nov 55

This thing came back to me for more postage. So now I'm including Faulkner's latest, just in case you haven't seen it yet.

AMERICAN ACADEMY IN ROME
VIA ANGELO MASINA V,
ROME 28, ITALY

Jan. 30, 1956

Dear Albert:

I've been intending to write for quite some time now but first there was the holiday hurly burly then two weeks ago Fanny had an appendix attack, which though it did not require an operation, was very painful and has left her weak and has had us quite anxious. But the round of illnesses didn't stop there; I am just recovering from bronchial pneumonia after eight days in bed and gallons of antibiotics. (Right now as far as I'm concerned they can give Rome back to the Etruscans. This whole joint is like a hospital most of the time. Americans don't seem to get the same energy from the food here and I'm told that it takes just about a year to adjust to the dampness of the climate and the germs that fill the air from the constant pissing on the streets, monuments, churches, cars, and anything else these studs can lean on and direct a stream against. The dogs here run around in a perpetual state of confusion because their messages are always being scrambled by the human beings.) The best of Rome remains its past, I'm afraid, and I've given up any faint notions I might have had that the salvation of the world lay in Europe, just as I've learned that a lot of the crimes against taste which the Americans are charged with are just so much hoeky. Hell yes, Hollywood is lousy but it just isn't powerful enough to be responsible for all the degeneration of Italian taste. Some of the stuff they show in the art galleries wouldn't be allowed to take up wall space in the States, and if you think television in the States is bad, man, you should see it here. Some outfit did a show called "Americans in Rome" in which I took part along with some of the others at the AAIR, and while at the station we had to observe an hour of their regular TV fare. Man, it was worse than a gang of fays trying to imitate a gang of moses—like a vacuum full of crap! Well, the Italians are in spite of all this, a kind, warmhearted people and we like them and are making slow but definite progress with their language. I'm taking two lessons a week and getting down into Rome proper several times a week. Haven't been able to find any Negroes though, except the Snowdens, who are too much on the defensive. They're Boston and Washington, DC and you know what that means. The fays here resent him and insist that he *must* be a Tom, otherwise he wouldn't have been given the job. Actually he seems no more incompetent or competent than the US cultural attaches I've seen in other countries. Anyway, he seems under great strain and gives the impression of a man who wishes to hell that he had eyes growing in the back of his head. Madame Luce[1] is roundly disliked by some of the American colony, a great deal of which is pederast and ultra snobbish, not that one has to [be to] dislike La Luce. It makes for a very amusing though quite unsavory atmosphere because Americans away from home are the most insecure people in the world and become even more the victims of their status striving. So that here snobbism has become a prime value and they can't seem to see that the leaders in this farce are really the most ridiculous and insecure of the whole lot. When we see you I'll spell this out as it's truly instructive.

---

[1] Ambassador Clare Boothe Luce, playwright, wife of Henry Luce, publisher of *Time* and *Life* magazines.

Thanks for the Faulkner, I'm sure I would have missed it otherwise. The library here is a farce except for classicists, architects, etc. No literature and magazines. That haul of books you've been buying makes me anxious. I've only picked up three beat old copies of Mencken's *Prejudices* and the biography of a civil war figure at the flea market. Ordered a study of the Ulysses Theme from England, which looks promising; have been reading Stendhal's journals and rereading the *Idiot* in a new translation and *The Sound and the Fury.* Sypher's book on Renaissance style, etc. This is the damnedest place, full of scholars but thus far no one knows much of literature or of the life out of which literature comes. I've also reread the *Royal Way* and now find it quite thin. It makes me sad but I'm sure that under other circumstances I'll feel differently about it. Maybe I've reached the age when some of the things we loved grow wan. Of course right now I'm writing and searching for intensity and that makes me hard to please. That damn Russian though, *he's* got so much of it that he could reach you through the sound of a prizefight if you gave him half a chance. And speaking of prizefighting—Sugar Ray dug him up some religion and whupped hell outta Bobo.[2] His next role will probably be that of a preacher cause he's is simply gotta have that limelight. I can see him whipping the hell out of the whole sinner's bench and thus making a short work of converting everybody. Billy Graham would be nowhere. Certainly it won't be the first time that such has happened and I'm sure ole Sugar would do it with great style.

What are we going to do about getting together? It would have to be this year, since I've now been told that my fellowship is only for one year. (I suspect that writers are a bit too observant for the comfort of certain people here). So we'll have to see you during spring or summer. There is a possibility of my going to Madrid during March—which would put me closer. Spring isn't too far off and I'm told that it is a good time to visit Rome. Actually Fanny won't be able to travel until June, because her job will keep her tied up until that time. Let's make plans if we can.... As for the rugs, hold off a while if we get over there we could save you the bother and I'm sure that by that time

[2] Carl "Bobo" Olsen, middleweight boxer.

you'll have all of the best getting places nailed down. A couple here know of a place in Tangiers, but we saw samples of the designs and were not taken with them. I could use me some of those heavy leather shoes though, because all the floors here are tile and as cold as a well-digger's. No doubt the reason most of us are always full of cold. These I could use right now, having brought only a thin pair of traveling house shoes.... Glad to hear that things have quieted down over there, the French have had illusions of grandeur for so long that they can't believe all that crap about their being citizens of France. And looks like a lot of that talk about *absurdity* was desperately serious; those boys and their system just ain't nimble no more. A case where good old, even brilliant ole wagon done broke down. Look up a booker by Herbert Leuthy titled *France Against Herself.* He's a Swiss who has lived in France for a year and loves the country and from a piece published in *Encounter* knows it very well and spells out the nature of its crisis better than anyone I've read thus far. Here are a few excerpts...[3]

> *It is only with (France's cultural background) in mind that it becomes quite clear to what extent France has been driven in the past fifty years to an almost desperate defense against all the fundamental tendencies of our time. Here is an aristocratic, courtly, individualistic, and profoundly intellectual culture, in an age of industrial mass civilization in which the old cultured classes whose influences French cultural hegemony rested have been, in part expropriated, in part destroyed, and everywhere de-throned. In central and eastern Europe, one of the oldest and best orga-nized of France's cultural spheres of influence, the landslide of the last two decades has taken with it not only the entire network of French in-stitutions, schools, and cultural agreements, but the whole French-educated aristocracy. Even before the second world war, the eighteenth century style cultural diplomacy of the French, which sought to counter*

[3] Ellison's long excerpt from *France Against Herself* is included here because it is part of the letter and because it offers the reader clues to comments made in subse-quent letters by both Ellison and Murray about the state of France in the postwar era.

the commercial and industrial superiority of Germany with literary conferenciers *had in the end reaped nothing but disappointment. In the reaming zones of influences that still existed outside the teetering colonial empire, in Latin America, and in the Near East, French prestige is engaged in a hard fight not only with its old rivals, but above all with the industrial civilization of America. Which has a greater appeal to all "underdeveloped" countries than French literature and French Egyptology. And here too, that social resifting has come into play which sweeps aside, together with the old leisured classes, all sympathy with the French model of civilization. The age of social leveling, of the common man, the demand for well being and a share in the good of civilization for all do not favor the world hegemony of the French ideal of civilization... These are distant and underground processes which seldom reach the consciousness of the average Frenchman or even the average intellectual. But the calamities of the twentieth century, which has swept the ground from under France's imperium, are also clearly visible in the daily life of the motherland; in a multitude of small occurrences are the most visible—and most sensitive—surfaces of existence. The most obvious—and also, for the artist and literati of Paris, the most irritating—symbol of this change is the transformation in the social and cultural structure of tourism. Even in the between war period, which was itself only a dull reflection of the "Belle époque," the foreign visitors to France came predominantly from the propertied and more or less aristocratic classes of Central and Eastern Europe, Latin America, and even "good old England" then still in existence. They all had at least some tincture of French culture, and they made it a point of pride to speak French and to show that they were connoisseurs of wine and literature, gourmets and* hommes d'esprits *in the French style. This clientele has mostly disappeared. It is true that the worst crisis of the first postwar years has been overcome, but the new tourism of the "common man"—whose tone is set by the average American, the average Englishman, and lately by those tourists from what remains of Central Europe who are propelled throughout the country in busloads—possess fewer of these distinctions. The new tourist does not step piously onto the old soil of civilization, but visits France as he would any other foreign country, finds ruined houses not historic but wretched, the sanitary facilities of the middling hotels inadequate, and the horde of tip-seeking lavatory guardians oriental. He submits less and less often to the tyranny of the wine list and the menu and it is the hotels and restaurants that now must suit his barbarous taste... The little innkeeper, the dance-hall artist, the necktie seller and even the ladies of the Place Pigalle can see this "decline of the cultural level" in their own lives, and are only too quick to adjust to it. And the intellectual sees in it visible confirmation of what his "philosophy" tells him: in the day and night life of Montmartre as well as in the world-wide rear guard action of aristocratic taste, "Americanism" appears as the great enemy of the "French ideal." A good many really hysterical out-bursts, like the crusade against the "Coca-colonisation" or the anger at an American-sponsored cultural festival in Paris—"Messieurs sur le plan de la cultural, de la civilization, de l'esprit, La France ne recoit les con-seils de personne: elle en donne!" can only be explained by this irritation. Out of this deeply wounded sense of national pride there has sometimes developed an intellectual chauvinism which can go to the wildest lengths of persecution mania; in the last few years for example, writers and crit-ics of repute have repeatedly developed the thesis that Shakespeare or Goethe were never really significant figures and that their great names are the product of an "organized bluff" promoted by the Germans and the English in order to contest the legitimate preeminence of the French language and literature... From this perspective, the impasse of Simone de Beauvoir's* Mandarins, *and the tragicomedy of their search to replace their former certainties are perhaps more understandable. For them the prestige of France—which was their own prestige—remains bound to the Jacobin myth of the Great Revolution: although France had long be-come a conservative country, forced to defend an old way of life and an old cultural heritage against the industrial revolution of modern times. The "idea of France" whose once revolutionary message they wished to go on proclaiming, had lost all relations to the real France; and, at bottom, they wished to do nothing about it; it had nothing to do with their "French idea." It was only in the rejection of "Americanism" that they found a—purely negative—contact with the real problems of France, and this negation became the one fixed point of their position. None of them was*

*ever really excited or even genuinely interested by Russian communism,
even the fate of the working class did not occupy too large a share of their
thoughts. But frankly to oppose American civilization with the aristocratic and individualistic values of traditionalistic France would have
meant acknowledging themselves to be conservatives, which was intolera-
ble. And so they clothed their deeply conservative rejection of modern mass
civilization [in] the form of an ideological decision to take sides against
"American capitalism" in the Cold War—only to stumble against the insight "our values have more place in Communism." Nothing could do them
more good than to decide just once to apply Marxist analysis of the ideological to "their own ideological constructions"—or the revolutionary pose
of the mandarins is the very prototype of what the Marxists would call
"false consciousness"... But the Jacobin message is not the only message
France has and its old civilization is by no means on its deathbed. It is
passing through a crisis of adjustments to a radically altered world, in
which it has all the more difficulty in finding its bearings because it spent
the decisive years of the transition under the narcosis of Vichy—and the
years afterwards under the self-intoxicating myth of victory. It is by no
means inconceivable that a conservative idea of cultural reasonable de-
fense of aristocratic values against the frenzied technical and organiza-
tional development has reach[ed] its highest point and the rejection of
certain material vulgarity, which is all too easily caricatured as "Americanism" does constitute a kind of national common denominator for all
French intellectuals from Sartre to Andre Siegfried without necessarily
implying anti-Americanism, neutralism or pro-Communism...*

Man, it goes on like this and spells out his disappointment at length
and while you might reject his thesis he does make you think hard
about the state of French culture and about that which is still valid in
it. I guess the basic difference between French and American intellectuals is that Americans have always been aware of the flaws in our system and have never stopped raising hell about them while the French
have been convinced that they were the leaders and that they always
would be. One thing is certain and that's while you can argue about a
machine civilization that the only way you can beat it is to out pro-

duce it. What's more, the center of the world's cultural activities is no longer Paris but New York—art shows, music, opera, etc. and Louis Armstrong. That damn place generates creative tension and I never intended to be away too long—as much as I like over here. I plan to run up to Paris and get another look [and] see its kind of beauty before I leave. I owe a lot to France and despite my rejection of her intellectuals and their chauvinism, I'm not forgetting it.

If you have any word from Macon County, let me know... It's been raining here for two days and I made a big pot of chili for lunch and now my stomach is singing "the Wang Wang Blues." I've lost weight like a bastard, trying to eat this Italian grub. The French have them whipped hands down, both on food and wine. The Italians haven't recovered from rococo—although on New Year's we were introduced by [Alberto] Moravia and Paolo Milano to a traditional New Year dish which consisted of a stuffed pig's foot and peas and it was pretty straight, no fluff or cheese or wiggling... Tell Mokie and Mique we say hi and that we'd like to see them before long. Keep us informed of any changes and I look toward hearing from you.

As ever
[Ralph]

CASABLANCA
15 FEB 56

Dear Ralph,
Good to hear from you. Sorry to learn that you both have been ill. On that score we've been doing pretty good so far, only an occasional mild attack of the "Maroc trots" and a cold or so, and this goddamned rainy season is a bitch. It started in early November and keeps on off&on until March. Some wonderful days too very much like the Gulf Coast, but probably ⅔ damp&chilly or just plain monsoon rain. The really wonderful thing about it all though in spite of all the trouble of colds etc is greenness of everything. It started getting green with the very first few light showers back in late October, and now things are bursting out every way you look, flowers ever since late December, and they say you aint seen nothing yet. This is winter. Wait til Spring. Man, what soil! Fields that were rocky and barren back in September

are now greener than any golf course I ever saw in my life. And you never saw such vegetables.

We were down in Marrakesh in November. Berber town, Atlas Mts town, El Glaoui's capital. Some trip. Marketplace there called Djemaa el Fna (meeting place of the dead, execution place, from the days back when the Sultans used to behead the guilty ones there and display the pike-impaled heads all around the walls as a warning to all rebels). The Mainstem now: apothecaries & healers with foxes' teeth, stuffed lizards, dried adder power & the magic touch to cure illnesses of the mind and the body; barbers bleeding patients from the nape of the neck by sucking through a metal tube; venders of everything from water to camel shit; jugglers, the famous Berber dancers (boys); singers, instrumentalists, snake charmers, fire eaters and the completely fascinating Arab public STORYTELLERS. Man, I dont know the lingo, but you dont have to understand them cats words to know they blowing. They say them cats can blow a thousand & one riffs on each one of them 1001 nights, and I got to believe it because that's the way it's supposed to be. Talking about the role of the writer-artist etc, his ass *belongs* right out there among them healers, peddlers, dancers & snakecharmers. Jam or scram.

It really does look like the French and Europe have had it. It was good but it aint enough for now and it damn sure dont spell future. I too have learned from it, but you have to admit in the end that you actually find less and less use for it every day. That guy Leuthy seems really to have hit something. Have been talking along the same line. Must find that book. Man, seeing them American types on that culture kick when I was in Paris in '50 bounced me back to old Tricky Sam & chitterlings & the briarpatch immediately. Spent most of my time there arguing that we already knew stuff much more important than the crap they claimed that only Anouilh & Sartre & Co. could teach them. Sure there's plenty there that I got to see and get, but I got to use it in terms of what's back over yonder.

Also reread *The Royal Way* early last summer. Yes, it is thin. My reaction was that Malraux had just knocked it together as one would a detective story or an entertainment, using it as means of playing around with the place, archaeology and a few notions. I always viewed it as a sort of off shoot, say about on the level of Eric Ambler. Felt that *The Conquerers* still held up pretty good, ditto *Man's Fate*, but not *Days of Wrath*.

As of now our plans are as follows. Four or five days off around Easter to go either to Fez & environs or to Spain and the bullfights (not finally decided). Twenty-some days in June to drive to Italy and maybe Switzerland (via Spain, i.e., Costa Brava—Southern France etc.) Twenty days in September or October to take the Mediterranean Cruise to southern Italy–Tripoli–Greece & Turkey. Meanwhile as much getting around here as possible, got to get down to the blue country and also the Sahara. (Oh yes, the cruise is on the Air Force). Next year, summer of next year, that is, we intend to take our free flight to Europe. Plan to take it to Frankfort and then take the train to Denmark & maybe get up to Norway or Sweden too. Have to get in a motor trip to Paris and also the fine old Chateaux of the Loire. Meanwhile running up to Spain on short holidays.

Let me know your plans for this Spring and summer. June seems to be definitely our best time to take an extended motor trip, but the itinerary can be modified all sorts of ways. For example we could pass up Rome then because we plan to get off the boat in Naples on our way back from Turkey and come to Rome and then take the boat again at Leghorn. Only thing about that is that we caint be absolutely certain whether this will be in Sept or Oct & also you might not be there then.

Certainly hope we can work out some way to get you guys down here for a visit. Don't see why the hell not. From Spain or from touring with us this summer.

Looks like old Moque might be getting an expense free trip up to Germany next month. Air Force sending up representatives to a Girl Scout conference. She has been working with base program recently. Sure hope she does. Then I can get to hitchhiking around with a better conscience. Guys flying out of here to everygoddamwhere. England, Scandia, Turkey, Greece, Germany, Arabia, and it is not very difficult to get back to the States. All you need is either the leave time or a good stiff reason. Personally I intend to use my leave time digging this part of the world. However if we decide to take another assignment in Europe after our 2½ yrs here, we can zip back across for 30 no sweat.

My French is still coming. Almost ready to start Spanish & Italian. Moque is now taking French downtown. Mique takes it at school, but what with the situation as it has been she hasnt made the foreign contacts that she should have.

Things going very good in general. By now you probably have read about the officer who was killed here night before last. Knew him. So far hasnt been established whether accident or motive. Americans pretty shook-up. Man, talking about insecurity abroad, once out of them airships these cats for the most part are lost. And naturally they dont know what to make of the Arabs. Boy, that Negro-Indian thing obscures the whole situation for them. They're contemptuous of the French of course & are 100% for the theory of Moroccan self-determination in spite of the France-appeasing line of neutrality, but vis a vis the Arab they really dont know whether he's a mose to bluff or a scalp-hunting redskin that you better never trust.

Not a lot of news from Tuskegee. Letter from the Mitches the other day. Gwen & Byron back down there to live. Letter from Mann about renting my new house. No word from Mort.

Al

They say French Airmail is faster. So on your next letter use the address on envelope, address of one of our stenogs. Your letter was dated Jan 30 (inside) and I just got it yesterday—Feb 15. Got to be something plus rapide que celà.

Will have some interesting color slides to show you. Got myself that new Leica M-3 last fall and am banging away. Good way of taking notes since most of my quotebook notes continue to be about life in America.

AMERICAN ACADEMY IN ROME
VIA ANGELO MASINA V,
ROME 28, ITALY

MARCH 16, 1956.

Dear Albert:

Today I almost accepted a trip which, likely as not, would have brought me right down to Casablanca shortly after Easter, but I just couldn't make it. Anyway, it would have meant travelling without Fanny and using up the money which later on we may use together—perhaps when we link up with you and the Moque and the Mique. A painting fellow and his wife and baby are doing Spain and Tangiers and have been most persistent in urging me to come along: Easter week in the South of Spain, North Africa, the Prado again—everything I want to do. Perhaps if I'd been sure that you Murrays were going to be somewhere in the vicinity I would have taken them on—as Fanny urged me to. However a friend is driving down from Holland in May and I might get another crack at the trip. More on this later.

We've just returned from an interesting eight day trip to Ravello, where we visited the critic John Aldridge and his wife. They were very pleasant, rather famished for conversation, book talk, etc., after having fallen for the old American escapist dream of romantic Italian isolation up on a hill, only to discover that they need people in the worst kind of way. So that we spent the time talking and talking. Fortunately we had something to talk about, because after a sun so warm that we were able to sunbathe on the beach of the nearby Boitano, that blue sky upped and threw snow and sleet at us with all the Satchel Paige virtuosity of that dam eagle in Augie March which didn't even have to tense its anus in order to blast the unsuspecting air.

The Aldridges are living in an apartment in an old palace and have only one fireplace, a bottle-gas heater, and two electric stoves—so that it was drink like hell and eat like Virgil Branam or freeze. He was rather amusing in that he's been calling the institutionalized critics like Cowley and Tate bad names critically and is surprised that they don't pat him on the back and approve his doing what he says *they* were doing when they were his age. (Aldridge hell of a sentence, but you'll get it.) Anyway, they're fighting back and he's indignant.

Spectacular scenery there, little towns clinging to the cliffs, lemon groves terraced upon narrow ledges in the almost perpendicular stone; old houses stacked literally one upon the other, foundation on roof; white walls, green shutters—all looking bravely and precariously out across the bay of Salerno—from whence came the moors who shaped the architecture, the boat loaded with loot from the new New

World, and most recently, the Americans. It's a rough land and until the tourists crowd in in the spring the natives live a hard, hard life.

Aubrey Mennen, the Indo-English writer who lives at nearby Amalfi had us up for a grand style luncheon, with young waiters in white jackets and gloves, at his place where he lives with his male secretary-housekeeper etc. Intelligent and thoroughly British as are so many westernized Oriental gentlemen, he made us warmly welcome and invited us back for a talk on the American novel. This for later in the week, when several painters and an American poet from Wyoming were to be present. Fortunately, I was ill on the appointed evening, because Mennen used the occasion to bait the Americans and I don't play that hockey—especially not with Europeans who've never visited the States. He comes to a harsh, suffering country, where on the profits of his American sales he can live like a king (and without the social disapproval of his home life which he'd get in London) and in easy access of little boys, and comes on with an attack against the only country that gives a dam about the condition of this country. As Fanny says to me, I will eat a man's food and then give him hell if he thinks that a meal entitles him to my agreement to some crappy ideas. He told Fanny that there was nothing new in America (our writing is simply an imitation of the British!) and that India was the new thing in the world. Fanny told him, "Yes, and a good American industrial assembly line would blast away some of those 'new' caste lines and oil up his mama."

Aldridge has just finished another book of critical essays. Tell you about him when I see you. Look up a book by R.W.B. Lewis, AMERICAN ADAM; I saw it down at Ravello and it looks interesting.

Van Wyck Brooks is here as writer-in-Residence and we've seen them several times. Naturally I took Hyman's book off the shelf lest Brooks see it and bust a gut. He's very alert, despite his 70 years, and still writing away.

That market place jive sounds fascinating, I'd like very much to hear one of those public liars riffing, you think they'd recognize my standing in the guild? Old Cliofus and Love and some of my other studs—including old Mary—would really like to pick up on some of their stuff. I've been playing around with the ideas for a story about a one-eyed cook who is always fighting and lying and traveling—maybe a cross between Falstaff, Coutee Brown (Q.T. Brown) and Branam, he would be just the guy to feed on that Marrakesh jive, that *King and the Corpse* brew. He's a real fool, fights with everything from a baby to a bear—she turns out to be mechanical just when he thinks he's taking her to bed and when they get through fighting just about half of her is in one corner and the other half is on the floor. This is slapstick but there's much more to him, mainly comic, and that's the way he'll stay. Maybe the white folks down in Alabama won't let him though, because I've been getting clippings and some of them make me see red. But maybe not.

I feel a lot better about our struggle though, mose is still boycotting the hell out of Montgomery and still knocking on the door of Alabama U. So now the crackers want to withdraw their money from Tuskegee—which would be the best thing that ever happened—. Pat must feel like an ass because the crackers clearly reveal that their intention was to bribe the school into staying third-class. But hell, they forgot to bribe the preachers! I saw some photos of those brothers and some of them look like the old, steady, mush-mouthed, chicken-hawk variety; real wrinkle-headed bible pounders; who in the pictures look like they've been to a convention where they'd caught some son of a bitch not only stealing the money, but sleeping with all their own private sisters! Yes, man! But they're talking sense and acting! I'm supposed to know Negroes, being one myself, but these moses are revealing just a little bit more of their complexity. Leader is a young cat who's not only a preacher but a lawyer too, probably also an undertaker, a physician, *and* an atomic scientist. And they're standing their ground in spite [of] threats, assassinations, economic reprisal, & destruction of property. Dr. Brewer of Columbus was shot and killed by a cracker recently over some issue of police brutality to another Negro. Something is happening and its so very good to know that mose's sense of life is too strong to be held in by the Pattersons or any of the other clowns at Tuskegee. Mose is fighting and he's still got his briarpatch cunning; he's just been waiting for a law, man, something solid under his feet; a little scent of possibility. In fact, he's turned the Supreme Court into the forum of liberty it was intended to be, and the Constitution of the United States into a briarpatch in which the nimble people, the willing people, have a chance. And that's what *it* was intend[ed] to be. Bill Faulkner can write a million Letters to the North as he did recently in LIFE,[1] but for one thing he forgets that the people that he's talking to are Negroes and they're everywhere in the States and without sectional allegiance when it comes to the problem. The next thing that he forgets is that Mose isn't in the market for his advice, because he's been knowing how to 'wait-a-while'— Faulkner advice—for over three hundred years, only he's never been simply waiting, he's been probing for a soft spot, looking for a hole, and now he's got the hole. Faulkner has delusions of grandeur because he really believes that he invented these characteristics which he ascribes to Negroes in his fiction and now he thinks he can end this great historical action just as he ends a dramatic action in one of his novels with Joe Christmas dead and his balls cut off by a man not nearly as worthy as himself; Hightower musing, the Negroes scared, and everything, just as it was except for the brooding, slightly overblown rhetoric of Faulkner's irony. Nuts! He thinks that Negroes exist simply to give ironic overtone to the viciousness of white folks, when he should know very well that we're trying hard as hell to free ourselves; thoroughly and completely, so that when we got the crackers off our back we can discover what we (Moses) really are and what we really wish to preserve out of the experience that made us.

As for our travel plans, we'd like to make them fit with yours for the June period, because it seems certain that we'll miss the Easter in Spain. Fanny is working and I'm still tied up. If, however, I drive down in May, it might be possible to drop over to Casa even if I have to take a freighter back to Italy. As for June, we'd like nothing better than a trip with you [to] Spain, or to the north of here. Incidentally, I'll know

[1]In the *Life* magazine article Faulkner suggests that the civil rights movement may be moving toward desegregation and equality too rapidly, and advised the leaders to slow down and give white Southerners time to think about it.

in April whether we're to be here another year. It's being considered in New York and I'm told there is a possibility. After that I'll be able to make more definite plans.

I'm glad as hell to hear that you've taken up Photography; it's dam well time that those curious eyes of yours went on record. As for me I'm just like you, making notes on the U.S. and hitting and skipping here. But my camera went bad on me recently and I'm falling behind on my photo notes, I've just written the states to see what I can do about getting a 35mm job, so if you're dissatisfied with the Leica why not give me a chance to buy it; or if any of your boys is selling, let me know. That 3M is a sweet camera. Anyway if you know of something for sale please write me immediately because I've got to do something soon. Like to be loaded when I got to Spain, if I go in May. I'd take some of my travel allowance so don't worry about the dough, because I'm spending so much time on this dam book that it'll take a pictorial record to help us make the most of my year here. You know me, I have to have something between me and reality when I'm dealing with it most intensely.

Dam, I've talked myself tired, so now I'd better hang up the phone. I'm homesick for some moses for one thing, and I got no way to get any corn bread and these Romans think a chittling is something to stuff a sausage into. There is very little whiskey I can afford, *no* sweet potatoes or yellow yams, a biscuit is unheard of—they think it means cookie in this town—and their greens don't taste like greens. What's worse, ain't nobody around to speak the language. I'm up the creek. Fly up and see us. Tell Moque to drop off here and see us. Send Mique as a life-saving embassy. I know you won't, so give them our love and eat an extra helping of pie and real honest to goodness American ice cream just for us.

Ralph

CASABLANCA, MAROC
20 MAR 56

Dear Ralph,

You writin' good, boy, real good, blowing good, cutting good, keen & deep. If you gettin' any of this stuff working in there with old Cleofus & em you still swinging that switchblade and you aint got nothing to worry about. For my money you're *in* there with that shit, man.

Me, I've finally begun to get a few notes down for that jazz novel I've got to take a crack at. Only notes, no actual draft yet, but the people are coming on fine. Hope to get em cutting up by fall, maybe before. Plan to take my goddam time and have me some fun with them. Meanwhile I've still got to finish retouching some of those short pieces. Got some stuff in there that I just ain't going to give up on.

Enclosed clipping is for Fanny's French exercise. Took the hi-fi down to the American Library on the night of the 9th for the first of a two-part jazz session. Part of life in USA series, which includes lectures & films on everything from time & motion studies to atomic energy. Both the hipsters and the hot clubbers have been beating that path to my door ever since. Also sound & TV technicians! Very interesting and also good for my French. Also getting me into places I had no way of getting into before. Gotta have that contact, man. Also got me some keen young Arabs lined up for the near future.

Moque took off for Germany last Friday. Be up there approximately 10 days. Three day conference at Berchtesgaden, rest of the time for travel & sightseeing, flying back from Frankfurt. (Major Carter & family are at Erding just outside of Munich.) Should be a hell of a fine trip. Three gals from the base here.

Tentative travel plans go something like this, after studying some of those tour pamphlets: as soon as we can get Mique out of school in early June. Here around the rim of the Mediterranean, Barcelona, Cote d'Azur to Rome (6–7 days?) Rome, Florence, Venice, Milan, Switzerland, to Paris (10–12 days?) Paris, Chateau France, San Sebastian, Madrid, Tangier to here (6–8 days?). This is the route. No rushing, but careful planning of what we want to see & where we want to stop. Pick you guys up in Rome. (Notice that tour buses get down from Paris via Montreux & Venice to Rome in 7 fairly casual days, stopping at several places I'd just as soon miss). Tentative only. Where we go after Rome must also suit you. As I said before, no need to spend a lot of time in Rome since we'll be coming back when we take the cruise. Think the drive from Rome to Paris is definitely worth trying.

Know damn well you want to see that chateau country on the way from Paris to Spain. Paris we shall see again and we plan to be getting back up to Spain many times. So lets hear some suggestions. Camera news as follows: Can get new Leica M3 with 50mm F-2 lens for $212.00. can get Rolleiflex new with F-3.5 lens for $124.00, plus Releikin adapter for 35mm for $13.00. Plan to add a Rollei to the Leica myself. PX got a new shipment in today. Can get either one you want. Let me know right away so I can grab it and hold it for you. These damned SAC bomber wings rotate in and out of here pretty fast from time to time and they usually play hell with all the choice stuff. However, I just might be able to get that Rollei from the Navy PX up at Port Lyauty $10 or $12 cheaper. How are you fixed for film? Most 35 mm color is Ektachrome these days. Anscochrome for others. Plan to shoot a whole sack of color slides this summer.

Got to write somebody like old Andy Walker and find out how the Tuskegee crew is taking that Monkeytown stuff. Revs beginning to realize that they were the original riffers anyway. As for Marse Faulkner, he's good, but he ain't never come to terms with poro & straightening combs, let alone jazz and all that cadillac kick dynamism. Write soon about camera.

Murray

[ROME]
APRIL 1, 56.

Dear Albert:

I've been waiting for several days to hear from New York about a camera I was interested in there. It is a single lens reflex called the Hexacon and I hoped to get it new with a f, 2 normal lenses and a 135 mm telephoto and case for $165.00, but for some reason the guy hasn't written and that dam M3 is working on me too hard to resist any longer. Get it, please, so I can have some peace! I need a telephoto and a wide angle lens for inside work but they'll have to come later. I can't afford it but I can't afford to let this opportunity pass either. I'm enclosing a check on my New York bank to save you time and I hope it's no trouble. We don't have a bank here but I can send traveler's checks if you prefer. As for film I could use 35 mm Ektachrom and 120 color in any type you can get but how much depends upon the cost as now I'll really be cutting it thin. Here color's impossibly high and I just had to give it up. I'll also need a lens shade for the Sumicron, so send along the price for that too.

I notice that your letter was mailed the 23rd and arrived here on the 29th—which is longer than it takes to get to the states, I hope things move a little faster going over, though I swear you can never tell about Italy, these studs can be more casual than a Mose driving a white man's Caddy through a block where his boys are signifying at him from the sidewalk. I airmailed some galleys back to the states and two weeks later the editor was raising hell because he hadn't received them. I was down to St. Peter's this morning and heard the Pope and was in the crowd when he blessed everyone so maybe this will come through without delay. Anyway it was rather impressive, though I swear that if they'd just elevate them a mose, preferably one converted from one of the storefront cults—which would take a miracle—he would get in there and bring back some of the old vitality to the Church. He'd bring in some Negro Elks and Shriners with their drill teams and instead of having the platform at the top of the steps he'd elevate it up around the dome of St. Peter's. Most of all he'd have some real singing. Probably get old Bill Dawson out of retirement and that fool would have the whole city of Rome fighting to get up there to hear those righteous voices. Incidentally, I guess you know that Bill retired, I read it in the paper several months ago and forgot to ask you about it. Plan to write him soon, guess he saw himself getting nowhere fast with Foster.

That jazz lecture in French must have been something to hear, especially if you gave them Dry Bones in Parisian! Probably the first time many of those boys heard anything authentic about jazz. Keep it up because if we don't tell the story the fay boys will do to it what Stalin did to History. Better still is the news of the jazz novel. I've been seeing something of a fellow named Stanford Whitmore who has published a book titled SOLO which is about a jazz pianist. I don't know how it reads but if you see it around take a look as the British critics thought it had some importance as a study in individualism. Sounds bopish and Whitmore tells me that he derived something from me and I told him it's not what you derive from but what you make of it. Made

122 · Ralph Ellison & Albert Murray

me feel pretty good though to have him say that he was encouraged to
finish his book and to believe in what he was doing after he'd read
mine. He worked in the laundramat for 23 bucks a week, then when
the book was finished it was taken by a publisher *and* Hollywood—
50,000—just like that, and he got married and cut out. Stopped long
enough to buy him a Mercedes X.L. 190, which makes him enough
like a mose to warm my heart. Dig you later on that trip and other
matters, this is really about the M3. If, by the way, you have any idea
of how to get it to me before June, let me know. I'll try to learn what
the customs here in Italy think about it but I suspect that the duty
would make it impractical. I suspect that you'll have better ideas on
that end, perhaps someone reliable will be coming over. Anyway let
me know.

The couple who tried to get me to go to Spain with them might
come to Casa and if so I gave them your address and they'll probably
look you up. He's a good artist (name's Walter Hahn) who has just discovered the Golden Bough and is flipping over it and trying to get it
into his paintings, so blow him a few riffs. Take it easy.

Ralph

ROME
APRIL 12, 1956

Dear Murray:
Just a quick one to learn whether you received my check for $212.00?
I mailed it on the 2nd and sent it registered, but strange things happen
to mail here and I'd like to be assured that you received it. I have failed
to receive at least two packages of books sent me from the States and
thus far I can't even get an explanation, and before I wrote about my
camera problems I had written a salesman friend of mine back in the
states a letter in which I sent along a question & answer form so that
he would lose no time in getting some information back to me. There
was a good possibility that the guy would make a commission from the
sale but I haven't heard the first word. It's very odd and I'm getting annoyed. There is a censorship here with the legal right to open mail but
I don't think they have the right to hold my property without notify-
ing me, nor to stop my mail and I'm getting in just the frame of mind

to start writing about Italy in some of its less inviting aspects. I'd rather not however, as I'm too busy with my book to stop even for the money a series of articles would bring me. So let me hear as quickly as possible so that I can put a stop on the check.

Incidentally, I sent the letter to the address in the envelope, which was different from the first, being that of Melle Azoulay Reine/Rue de la Drome 22. I'm using the first address this time in case something was incorrect with the above.

It is still very confidential but I have just received the second year so it looks as though we'll spend at least part of next year in Europe. I'll let you know definitely later on, as I have also received a query from the President of Brandeis concerning my teaching there next year. They want a course in creative writing (fiction) and another in American Literature and have suggested that there would be no problem of Fanny's finding employment there, so you see I'll have to think about things. She doesn't want me to teach and I'd prefer to write books so most of the pressure is away from teaching. On the other hand however there is the security of the teaching job (I suppose) and the congenial atmosphere of the Waltham-Cambridge area. The only bad thing about this is that I've never been secure in an income kind of way and might not know how to live with it—especially in an environment in which there are no Moses. Maybe all I really want is a little house within quick driving distance of New York, good bird hunting cover and a trout stream. You would have laughed your ass off two weeks ago had you been here to see me trying to cook a mess of pigs feet here in Rome. Fanny found them easy enough but then she tried to find pickling spice—which just doesn't exist here. The poor girl walked her feet off trying to find them because she knew that I'd be an evil s.o.b. if I didn't have all the ingredients for this ceremonial dish, so that she came in late, with only some bay leaf and all-spice. And just as she expected I was fit to be tied. I wouldn't cook the trotters and spent the night cussing. Next day I set out myself. I must have covered every food store, market and drug store in Rome, trying to find the right jive. I went into stores and did everything from inventing new dances to standing on my head and pulling out my pecker trying to make them understand pickling spice and they dragged out everything from tomato paste to embalming fluid—everything and anything except *pickling spice*. Never in the history of the world did a mess of pigs feet cause so much exasperation. I returned to the academy beat to my socks and prepared to assassinate the first person who spoke to me and fortunately no one did. Fanny just looked at me and went and got me a drink—which calm[ed] me enough to cook the trotters, but they weren't right, man. They were the saddest and I threw most of mine in the garbage. The next time somebody says something to me about Roman culture they're going to have to get a cop to stop me from talking, imagine a city without pickling spice! I hope those Morocs have done better by you.

We're thinking and planning about the trip with excitement now and will let you know how things are lining up. Meanwhile let me hear about that check; our apartment in N.Y. was burglarized 2 weeks ago and I'm rather jumpy. Love to M. & M.

Ralph

CASABLANCA, MAROC
19 APR 1956

Dear Ralph,

You are owner of Leica M3- 785 222; Summicron 50 mm lens Nr.1278208. Got yourself something great, papa. Picked up your letter on the 6th. No difficulty cashing the check. Bought from the Navy at Port Lyautey, $212.50, same as mine. Air Force price when I got mine was $244.00, now $258.00. Still a hell of a good buy. But look at the additional money the goddam Navy saved us. Can get Leica Meter M, which couples into M3, for $13.00. Air Force beats Navy by better than $5.00 on this, strangely enough. Know you already have a fine meter, which is really sufficient, but the M is a good buy if you want it. PX hasn't been too well stocked on Leica accessories recently. Got my hood & screw-in haze filter in town. Moque got my 135 Hektor 4.5 in Germany. Can get what you want by friends flying to Germany all the time. Might even get up there myself. But don't really plan to go up until after the motor trip to Rome, Paris, etc. Can certainly have whatever else you want by the time we see you in June.

Now as to how I'm gonna get this boy to you. I've checked the guys in Flight Planning about our traffic into Rome, and find that we do get in there from time to time, in fact one flight has just gone in today. Might be able to come up myself, but will try to send the camera on the very next flight that stops there long enough. How can you be reached by phone? Is there some downtown location that could receive it for you? What's taxi distance & fare from The American Academy to down town?

As for film, we're now stocking Kodochrome again, 35mm rolls of 20, ASA 10, price $2.85 which of course includes developing and mounting. Currently no Ektachrome. Ansco for 120 price $1.50. Currently stocking new plus X black and white ASA 80, price .95 for roll of 36. Plan to be loaded for the trip. Starting to lay it in this pay day. Let me know what you want. You got to be loaded too. Send you some along with camera if possible.

Picked up *France against Herself* at the base Library today, getting it in tonight. Saw a piece by Leuthy on France in a December issue of a stateside Life, keen stuff. Checked out Kantor's *Andersonville*, but it doesn't move me. Seems to know the hell out of that shit as history, but I just caint get with the style for some reason or other, something a little too clever about it, no quotation marks … stream of JJ etc. Will give it another try.

Saw that Faulkner piece in *Life*. Sad, pitiful and stupid thing for a writer like that to do. That underdog shit makes me puke. How can a son of a bitch sit up and fuckup morality like that? The literary boys can give old Hemingway all the hell they want to, but he ain't never made no mistakes like that. Man, a motherfucker ain't got no business even sticking with the whole goddamned USA against *Freedom*. Son of a bitch prefers a handful of anachronistic crackers to everything that really gives him a reason not only for being but for writing. I'm watching his ass but close forevermore. Imagine a fatass travelling all around the world selling humanity for the State Dept and then going back home pulling that kind of crap at the first sign of real progress.…
Sounds like all of the other "safe liberals."

Murray

ROME, ITALY
APRIL 24, 1956

Dear Albert:

Man, did you take a load off my mind! Things got so balled up here postal wise that I thought maybe that check had gone AWOL. But now all the returns are coming in. I received six packages of books the other day, some of them a month over due, so now with your news and that little registration tag I feel a hell of a lot better, I can hardly believe it. I've been bugging the boys in the camera stores here by going in and looking at that job, examining it, pressing buttons, sighting, exchanging lenses etc.—just so I'll have some familiarity with it. Prices here seem to take off from the listed price and zoom. One of these dealers will ask anything up to twice the value and you get the feeling that they think you think money is confetti. One character thinks that I'm finally going to buy and has come down 15% from his 50% over price; next time I'm downtown I'll go in and play with the machine just to see how much more he'll descend.

As for reaching me here at the academy, it will be easy enough by telephone, the number is 588653. If the call comes before noon I'll be out in my study, so should be given time to run in to answer. All that is necessary is to tell the operator at the academy that the call is from you. As for the taxi fare from downtown, it's negligible, usually less than a thousand lire, and if I'm called I can be down in a hop, skip, and a jump. Rome is fairly small. Unfortunately I know of no place to leave anything down there. I might, by the way, be able to have a friend bring me on a motorcycle. Whatever you pitch I'll be there like Mays.... That Kodachrome price intimidates me, have they anything in bulk film? In the states costs are kept down by loading one's own cartridges. If anyone lands in Germany you could have them pick me up some cassettes for the camera and I'd be able to operate a little easier. The Plus X deal sounds fine. I'm certain that I can use a dozen of those boys.... Don't worry about lens shade and filter, will manage that later. If they have a neck strap could use. Plan later to get a 35 mm wide angle and a 90 mm long focus. Almost forgot the meter, get it; I'll send one check for the whole bunch of stuff, if it's all right with you.

Anyway I hope you shoot up here yourself, if only for a hot minute. Plenty of fly boys shooting through this town. Spanish Steps look like Broadway and 42nd Street most of the time. Not many in uniforms though, man, but you can pick em out.

Glad you got to Leuthy, I haven't located it myself though I've read the *Life* piece. Read a fairly engrossing novel about the Indochina situation called *A Forest of Tigers,* they speak of it in terms of *Man's Fate* and *For Whom the Bell Tolls,* but I'm afraid they're looking at it quantitatively, a little war a little novel and thus the three are war novels together.... Faulkner wrote a letter to TIME denying that crap he dropped on the world, but the reporter stuck to his guns and insisted that he reported true. Which I believe he did. Incidentally, he's the same young Englishman who came up to talk with me last summer and brought along a novel which he had just published. I didn't get to read it though. He told me some of the gossip of the royal family which was fairly amusing. Seems those two chicks were surrounded by capons all their lives as a matter of state policy. Shit, cried the King!... I've got to break this off because I want Fanny to put this in the mail today and she's giving me the rush. She sends the best, I send the best and my thanks.... Roethke's here lecturing, I lecture on Thurs night, American novel, ethical core blah, blah, blah! There's a guy here from Mississippi on this series (Fullbrighter) who did a book on Faulkner, I hope he's in audience when I open up. Not that I plan a blast but I will call a turd a turd and our boy is pretty full these days.

Take it easy.
Ralph

CASABLANCA, MAROC
15 MAY 1956

Dear Ralph,
Got your meter all coupled in and ready to read & click. No neck straps here. But of course you know the regular leather carrying case came with the camera. (Your case seems to be a later model than mine, and a slight improvement). As for cassettes, one came with the camera,

you can use the one that came with mine, and I might be able to scrounge another from a guy I know. Will have a dozen rolls of the new 80 ASA plus X for you as soon as I can find a way to get it to you.

We haven't had anything going into Rome since I started checking earnestly. Have one more shot before I go on to leave in mid-June. Can get to Greece via Tripoli without too much sweat. Can then try from Athens, or can try from Tripoli. Have four or five days of surplus leave to use up anyway. Only thing is that I'm trying to clear up several projects so I can definitely be free in June.

Looks like we'll be heading your way by car on the 14th or 15th of June, depending on the date we can get reservations on the ferry to cross the Straits. Looks like 10 days to Rome as follows:

Casa	Tangier	1st day
Tangier	Málaga	2nd "
Málaga Granada	Vélez Rubio	3rd "
Vélez Rubio	Valencia	4th "
Valencia	Barcelona	5th "
Barcelona	Montpelier (?)	6th "
Montpelier	Antibes	7th "
Antibes	Menton	8th "
Menton	Pisa	9th "
Pisa	Rome	10th with some to spare.

Which will put us there around the 24th or 25th, as it shapes up as now.

From Rome we are prepared to fit our course to your desires. Have the following suggestions for your comments and/or modifications: In as much as we shall be coming back to Rome when we take the Mediterranean Cruise this Fall, two full days there after the day of arrival is all we'll spend this trip, i.e. 3 nights, leaving on the morning of the 4th day there, or our 13th day out......

Rome	Florence	13th day
Florence		14th day
Florence	Venice	15th "
Venice		16th "
Venice	Milan or Como area	17th day
Milan-Como	Switzerland	18th day
Switzerland	Paris	19th "
Paris		20th, 21st, 22nd day
Paris	Loire region	23rd day
Loire	Biarritz	24th "
Biarritz	Burgos	25th "
Burgos	Madrid	26th "
Madrid		27th, 28th day
Madrid	Cordova	29th day
Cordova	Seville-Algeciras	30th day
Algeciras	Casa	31st day.

The only major restriction is that I have to be back here not later than the 30th or 31st day. Feel absolutely free to play around with the time from Rome on as you see fit. You got to figure pretty close though because you got to figure hotel reservations for some of those places. We are inclined toward Venice, Lake Leman & Paris, but the time allocation can be juggled to suit the situation. Let us know what you've figured out. We've already started trying to reserve our way across Spain. Not a hell of a lot of time left. Caint get away earlier because Mique won't be out of school until the 14th of June.

By the way, Mique picked up a pretty serious infection the week after Easter. Had to stay in for almost three weeks. Doctor felt that it might be rheumatic fever or something closely related and didn't want to take any chances. She's back in school now, and it's a hell of a job trying to hold down all that energy. Her 1st post treatment electrocardiogram checked out fine, but they want her to take easy until the 25th and then take another just as an added precaution. She seems OK so far and has had none of the after effects to date, and it is possible that it was only what they call "scarletina," but, man, I'm always for treating them for the worse, so I still got my fingers crossed.

Moque has also been having a little trouble physically. Sprained her ankle back in March. Cleared up for the trip to Germany. Then went bad again on Mique's last day in. OK now.

Goddammed rain finally stopped and now we have the beginning of Summer. They say this was the longest rainy season in decades. Spring has been more like New York than Alabama. Nights are still cool, a little windy at times.

Bought me a Mitchell fresh water reel in the PX the other day for $10.50. The Saltwater job goes for $14.50. Don't have anything to go with it yet, but had planned to get equipped while here. Also plan to stock up on British woolens before I rotate. Gibraltar seems to be the place to buy cashmere, tweeds and gabardines. We also have them here in the PX, but they're even cheaper on the rock.

Am not too certain that I can swing that Athens and/or Rome flight right now, what with trying to get cleared for June. If I can, will bring your stuff, if not will have to bring it in June. Meanwhile, if a Casa-Rome mission comes up I do have a[n] inside shot at it. Seems that most of the flights into Italy right now initiate at Tripoli. Caint afford to get stuck there or Athens right now. Athens run is very simple, but the rest would be a gamble. You caint tell tho.

Waiting for your tour plans & depending on you for Italian hotel information.

Murray

AMERICAN ACADEMY IN ROME

MAY 18, 1956.

Dear Albert:

With June leaping in on us it occurs that we'd better let you know our plans for the trip, which is truly simple because what it amounts to is that we're ready whenever you Murrays come up. The idea of going through Switzerland and then through the Chateau country sounds great to us and we've been putting some money aside in anticipation. If you've done your usual economic survey please let me know how much you think we'll need and by hook or crook we'll have it. As you see I didn't get back to Spain again and it's just as well, because if you drive down on your way back to Morocco it might just be possible to go along and take the boat back to Naples. Incidentally, Fanny is helping to organize an international conference which will take up the first week in June, so in case you get here during that period and want to keep rolling, I'll hop aboard and she'll catch us up the road a piece. What I'm trying to say is that we're ready and nimble, you just call the tune. We especially like the idea of doing Florence again, and Venice and Milan will be new worlds to discover. The North of Italy is wonderful country and I'm sure you guys will like it, bring your picnic gear along because we'll probably want to eat lunch along the road and fill eyes and belly at the same time; that's what we did on the nine day trip we took with the new fellows last fall. Fresh bread, cheese, meat and wine *and* sweets can be had in most of the towns and the air and the sights transform it into something almost as good as fried chicken on a Juneteenth ramble in the woods. So whatever you care to do we're with it. We'll gather road information and choice-spot data from some of the old Europe hands here and we have some guide books and will get others—which, with your information ought to nail things down. So let's shake, rattle, and roll. . . . Ran into Artie Shaw yesterday and he told me that he's building a house at Bagur, Provinzia de Gerona, which is on the Costa Brava. Swears that its to be his home from now on, so I guess he's here in Rome training to start through those Spanish chicks. Anyway, he invited us to drop in so it will be interesting to see him perform. Maybe we can dig him later because if I forgot to tell you, we're definitely going to be here next year. Got the official notice. . . . Was also offered Brandeis job teaching creative writing and one course in American Lit, which I had to refuse; but the cat wrote back and said he'd cool it for me until Fall, 57. Looks like they're ganging up trying to make an honest man out of me, a lo mo, natural born hustler! Because just about the same time The Man at Bennington wrote offering a job substituting for a cat next year at a take of $5500 plus housing. That one was right in my old briar patch, but looks like Brandeis will be the pitch because it's right in the Cambridge area and I'd like to operate among the Harvard brains a while so that I can see what they're really putting down. But, whatever I do, my main work will be writing novels and I'm making it plain to everyone. I'm thinking too that if I do go to Brandeis I'll get a critical book out of it, because I've watched you lit. teachers long enough to know how to put students to work on the problems by way of learning what they find hard to understand. So just as with writing I learned from Joe and Sugar Ray (though that old dancing master, wit, and bull-balled stud, Jack Johnson is really *my* mentor, because he knew that if you operated with skill and style you could rise above all that-being-a-credit to-your-race-crap because he was a credit to the human race and because if he could make that much body and bone move with such precision to his command all other men had a chance to beat the laws of probability and anything else that stuck up its head and if he liked a woman he took her and told those who didn't like it to lump it and that is the way true studs have always acted) here I'll also learn from your latest master strategists, the N.A.A.C.P. legal boys, because if those studs can dry-run the Supreme Court of the U.S. and (leave it to some moses to pull that one) I dam sure can run skull practice on the critics. Meanwhile I'm trying to get this dam book done so we can spend most of the next year traveling.

I've been looking out for the snapshooter since you wrote, but if it is troublesome to get up here I can jolly well wait until you come, I'm trying to get ready for it though and I've learned that the army was supposed to use an 85 mm fl.5 job called the Lithagon which is much cheaper than the Summerex and about as good. If you see one around let me know the price, I also know about the Nikor 105 mm f.2.5. which is very good, but it costs $152 stateside and that's a bit rough for the moment, though I need something for portraits and telephoto shots. As for film I can use a dozen roll of that 135 Plus X 80 and six rolls of kodochrome type Aldridge, if possible because I understand you can use it in daylight with a conversion filter. I'm having a bulk of film loader sent over from home and plan to pick up some M3 cassettes so I can operate within my budget... That's about it. A COUPLA SCALPED INDIANS is out in *New World Writing* No. 9 and I have a copy for you. Picked up abridged version of Kazin's *On Native Grounds*—which has a new postscript which mentions me. Also got Panofsky's *Meaning in the Visual Arts* (both Anchor books) which I understand is first class. Also reading Arnheim's ART AND VISUAL PERCEPTION and a new Mentor titled THE PAINTER'S EYE by Maurice Grosser. As you can guess I'm now trying to dig where Malraux dug his digging and as one of the art historians here pointed out to me, a hell of a lot of his stuff ain't French but German—and not just Nietszche either. I don't know where this will take me but it's dam interesting. Take it as you have to take it and as Louis said in his latest dispatch to the *Herald Tribune* from London, the Cats are still blowing and ain't shooting, and I hope that it'll stay that way—though I guess Louis hadn't heard about Cyprus. Tell them women folks hi! Fanny sends love.

Ralph

R*OME*, I*TALY*
M*AY* 22, 1956.

Dear Albert:

Your letter arrived yesterday and I'm answering right back so as not to lose your mailing address. I wrote you on the 18th so you should have received that letter by now.... Thanks for getting the meter, etc., and don't worry about any other accessories because Germany is the place for them, and as I said in my last letter, I can wait until June for film— both black and white and color. So don't gamble on Athens.

As far as the trip goes we'll be looking out for you on the 24th and will have a pensione reserved for you up here near the academy if possible. You can then have your meals with us here when convenient because the food isn't bad—if you can digest onion and some garlic— and you'll find the place interesting and a good place to relax after the hurly-burly of mid-town, tourist-crawling Rome. We have a living room where you can stretch out and there is my studio for general all out bullshitting.

The schedule looks O.K. to us, though I suspect we'll find that we'll want to linger here or there a bit longer, (Paris and Florence and no doubt the Loire region). Fanny says that she'll get to work on Italian hotels as soon as she gets rid of this conference she's running and meanwhile I'm checking with the people here, I've already arranged with a friend in Florence to use his influence to get us hotel rooms. We'll see who knows what about Venice—which we've been told is expensive as hell—and we'll write the hotel where we stayed in Paris to see what they have for those dates. So as for now we'll let the schedule stay as you have it.

Sorry to hear about Mique and I hope it's nothing too serious, especially not rheumatic fever. Friend's daughter here in Rome has had a similar fever but is recovering. I've got my fingers crossed too, so tell Mique that she'd better take it slow ... When I first read your letter I read "Back" before "ankle" and said oh hell! But now I see that Mokie has had the easier part of the sprain business. Probably got it doing one of those down-home struts on those Casa streets. She'd better slow it too because the Ellisons have had enough trouble for *all* of us.

Yesterday just as your letter arrived I got a call from a friend who is going to introduce us to Isak Dinesen. She's the Baron[ess] Blixen so when I autograph a book for her I'd better use that name cause I sure as hell messed the pseudonym up above. I'll send you a report and I admit to being delighted.

Good to hear about your Mitchell, it's a dam good reel. I know you can get the rest of the gear in France and perhaps the Swiss will have something. I just bought a light rod here which was reasonable, though I haven't had a chance to use it. But those British Woolens intrigue both of us and we'll discuss them with you later. Would it be possible to bring a few items when you come? If so, we could use 2 jars of Pond's dry skin cream (large); 2 medium jars of 5-A-Day deodorant pads; 6 cans of silex ground American coffee; some bourbon whisky and some Kleenex. Could also use some kidney beans, but don't let any of this weigh you down. I'm enclosing a check for $25.00; if it isn't enough let me know; if more, just apply it to the film etc.

It just occurs to me that we might make Pamplona for the running of the bulls if we juggle a bit, think about it and we can decide later.

Over to you; I'm cutting it so as to get this to you before the address goes. Give our best to the gals.

Ralph

Ralph Ellison in
Central Park, c. 1950.
Photograph by Fanny Ellison.

Fanny Ellison.
Photograph by Ralph Ellison.

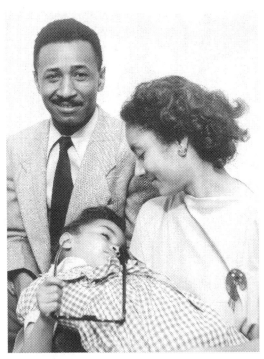

Albert and Mozelle Murray
with their daughter, Michele,
at the Ellisons' for New
Year's Eve dinner, 1947.
Photograph by Ralph Ellison.

Captain Albert Murray, U.S.A.F. (left), Ralph Ellison (center), and
an unidentified student in front of Murray's car on the
campus of Tuskegee Institute, 1954.

Albert Murray and his daughter, Michele, age twelve,
in his study, Tuskegee, 1955.

Writer Mary McCarthy and her son Reuel, by Edmund Wilson, c. 1955.
Photograph by Ralph Ellison.

New York City street
scenes, c. 1950.
Photographs by Ralph Ellison.

Fanny Ellison (left),
Mozelle Murray (center),
and Michele Murray
in Venice, 1956.
Photograph by Albert Murray.

Albert Murray interviewing Duke Ellington on a local radio program,
Tuskegee Institute, c. 1951. *Photograph by M. V. Stokes II.*

Ralph Ellison and James Baldwin at the Newport Jazz Festival,
Newport, Rhode Island, July 1958.

Albert Murray in his study, Los Angeles, 1958.
Photograph by Mozelle Murray.

Michele and Mozelle Murray leaving Los Angeles for
Hanscom Air Force Base, 1961. *Photograph by Albert Murray.*

TELS. 18001
18002
18003
18004

HOTEL VELAZQUEZ-PALACE
TANGER

16 JUNE 1956

Dear Ralph,

We're rolling. Arrival here yesterday. Cross the straits this afternoon heading for Granada. Taking the Madrid Zaragosa route to Barcelona. Should arrive [in] Rome as planned.

Am bringing what I could find of what you asked for but the 5-a-day deodorant pads n'existent pas à Casablanca. Should be able to get things at PX in Rome when I arrive. Bringing two kinds of coffee, skin cream, film, couple of bottles of bourbon, and red kidney beans. Am certain we can find some more bourbon at various American installations.

See you when we said or as soon thereafter as possible.

Murray

p/s Greece was something, man.

Al Murray

HOTEL COLON
AVENIDA DE LA CATEDRAL, 4 Y 5
TELÉFONO 22 87 7
BARCELONA

19 JUNE 56

Dear Ralph,

Still rolling and still on schedule. Granada, Madrid, Zaragoza behind us. Leaving here early tomorrow for France via Perpignan, Montpellier etc. See ya.

Al Murray

AMERICAN ACADEMY
VIA ANGELO MASINA 5
ROME 28, ITALY
JULY 31, 1956

My dear Mokie,

I hope that all went well in your travel back to Casa, and that you all enjoyed the Loire Valley which we hated so much to miss seeing with you. As for us, there began that Sunday morning as we departed for Paris a most varied order of experiences from the irritating and ridiculous to the most astonishing pleasures. First we found ourselves at the air terminal with nine kilos of overweight luggage, which we were to pay for each time we boarded a plane in amounts of $9 to $10. However, we found that we needed every ounce of clothing and when we finally returned to Rome, we'd used everything except Ralph's bathing suit and my bathing cap. There were times when we could have used that too—I borrowing his suit for my cap and vice versa.

Secondly, upon arriving at the London airport an overly conscientious little bureaucrat held us there for 40 minutes or so because we failed to renew our passports before leaving Rome. Ralph fumed and stamped and told them he wasn't interested in entering a country with such Fascist attitudes anyway, that he had only come because he was invited by P.E.N. anyway, and in so many words they could "Up it." They asked if we had a letter of some kind showing that we were invited to London and we were able to produce a most cordial and enlightening one which the president of the Congress had sent Ralph. They then called the American Consul, who apparently said, "For Christ's sake why are you holding them; yes, let them in." So with a much softened attitude and some apology they passed us. A few days later when we went to the Consul there, he said, that the whole thing had been unnecessary and although the passports were due for renewal there was no reason why we couldn't have done it upon our return to Rome. So very much out of sorts we proceeded to our fancy hotel—the Ritz.

Our room was fairly elegant, with at last a bath. And what a bath! Big enough to swim in, with towels as large as tents. We thought, this is going to be very nice. But lo and behold! on the second afternoon when we had returned about four hoping to take a much-needed nap before the evening's activities, we heard such a banging immediately outside our window that we thought the place would fall apart. Outside was a scaffolding with six or eight men working, hammering and yelling, repairing or building a new wing onto the hotel. By then we had un-

packed completely, with clothing deposited in the two closets and numerous drawers. We debated whether to ask for another room or try to stand it, since we were to be away for most of the day at the Congress. We stayed but complained to the P.E.N. that they were paying an awful lot for a very unsatisfactory room, the P.E.N. called and gave them the devil but all the hotel did was prevent the workmen from starting before nine in the morning.

Hotel service was the ultimate but the substance was ordinary. For instance breakfast—rolls, toast, marmalade and coffee—were rolled in each morning on a very high table covered with linen table cloth. There was much silver and always huge stiff napkins. There was a pitcher of hot milk, and one of hot water to whiten and thin the pot of heavy black coffee. One morning I departed and ordered in addition a bowl of corn flakes. There was hot milk for that too and the corn flakes become glue. Ralph said that that was the English way. There were three buttons in the room—one for the maid, one for the valet and one for the waiter. Without your iron to borrow we had to have the valet press all of our clothes. Had we known that this would cost us the price of a suit of clothes we could have gone out and bought an iron.

When we'd ask the clerk at the desk where such and such a place was, he'd make a feeble effort at finding it on the map but end by saying, "It isn't far, why don't you take a taxi." It would turn out that the place was several miles away and, which was more, had more than a dozen buses going right to its door. Finally at the end of the week we applied for our bill (we knew we were honored guests and therefore not paying for the room but we wanted the extra charges) and much to our astonishment we were handed a bill for $70. When we protested they informed us that P.E.N. was not paying all but for half the room. We gulped back our embarrassment and rage and went off to find an official of P.E.N. We found someone who told us that not only was P.E.N. paying for the room but that it had been paid for in advance and that apparently the hotel management was confused. So we went back later that day again and asked for our bill and this time it was $40. We had made the mistake of staying a day beyond the week paid for (although we had asked them when the week ended and been told we were not overstaying); we were paying also thereby for two extra breakfasts (rolls, jam and coffee); for the pressing; for a cheese sandwich and two bottles of beer, and a steak dinner we had recklessly ordered one night after drinking too much champagne at a party. That, plus tipping the maid, the valet, the elevator man, the desk clerk, the doorman, gave us heartburn.

But we weren't on our way to the airport when we left the great and mighty first-class Ritz (merely a gip joint in fancy dress) but on our way to a room gotten for us by a young Britisher writer and his wife at their Apartment house so that we could see a little of London as individuals and not as part of the P.E.N. Congress. At this place the rooms were $2.00 a night but we each had to take a separate room. Ralph was in Keyes House No. 59 and I in Hood House No. 74. We communicated by telephone or otherwise visited each other in stealth, the rooms were very much like those in a "Y"—small, plain and rather grim. There was a wash bowl in each room and all up and down the line they fought with each other, moaning, gurgling, throbbing when one was in use. When the party next door pulled the stopper from his bowl I thought my bowl would jump off the wall. But our friends had us in for dinner on the two evenings we lived there and she turned out to be an excellent cook, feeding us a pork roast which we'll always remember for its succulence and flavor.

I realize that in all this ghastly detail about accommodations I'm leaving out the main event—which was the P.E.N. program itself. On the evening we arrived we had just time to bathe, dress and get to the opening reception. Imagine our consternation when we arrived and found 750 milling around. There were that many attending, from all over the world, each supposedly a writer of some sort. The reception was held at the Tate Gallery in the room given over to Rodin sculptures. People stood around munching (or wolfing) canapés and drinking wine in and among the passionate lovers of Rodin's world and searching for a familiar face out of the sea of faces.

That was the beginning of a fantastic series of social affairs with a few literary and business sessions thrown in for good measure. We drank champagne at the Lord Mayor's reception; had lunch with the American Ambassador; Lunch with the Mayor of Brighton, Tea with the president of the House of Lords on the terrace overlooking the Thames. At the main banquet Ralph and I sat at top table with Charles and Mrs. Morgan (The Fountain), J. B. Priestley (whom I "charmed" for the evening as we sat next to each other), Mrs. Priestley who is Jacquetta Hawkes, Stephen Spender, Sholom Asch, Kate O'Brien, Storm Jameson, Veronica Wedgewood, André Chamson, T. S. Eliot and all-a-lika-that. We went to a small buffet supper party at the Priestleys' the following evening, and sometime during all this Ralph with a few chosen others had been received by the Queen Mother and Princess Margaret. On the second evening a 74 year old man had approached

Ralph for permission to kiss my hand and every time thereafter he was telling me that I had won his heart.

As the days went by he became a kind of shadow and I couldn't escape him. Sometimes when he couldn't contain himself a funny smell would permeate the atmosphere, once like mothballs and another time like something else, for Ralph made the improper remark, "God, I think he's pea-d on himself!" I tried to be a stoic but I was saddened and not a little revolted. On the final day he gave me what he said was a previous memento of his—a letter opener which George Bernard Shaw had given him many years ago. It is about five inches long, silver metal with the rose of England on its head. It is neither pretty nor distinctive looking but I must say, it is significant.

There were Lords and Ladies all over the place, whom we were told have invaded the world of letters with much success, materially if not literarily, mostly writing romantic fiction, historical romances, children's stories and society columns. There were a couple though whom we'd like to see again. Real old salty gals with fine humour, sophistication and a devil-may-care temperament.

So much went on that it would take pages to tell you. But I'm sure that you can understand why we had to rest and get our balance before we could fly out of London.

We made reservations to leave on Tuesday. Because we wanted to fly early to Munich we were advised to book through Zurich. When we got to the terminal we found it was going to cost extra to go through Zurich, although I had asked the girl this when making reservations by telephone and she had said no extra charge (thank heavens Ralph was there as a witness). So we raged and fumed at the terminal and said we would pay no more and preferred to wait for the late flight directly into Munich.

So we waited in the station from 9:30 A.M. until 4:30 (again there was the awful tax for overweight baggage) to leave on a plane which would stop in Frankfurt, but we were assured we could get space out of Frankfurt to continue our flight to Munich. We were told several times that "it looked very good." Of course, when we got to Frankfurt we were bumped and had to stay at a hotel near the airport to await a flight out the next morning. This time we were told we could go via Vienna without extra cost and we thought fine. But the next morning we learned that to go via Vienna would cost extra so we cancelled that flight and were for a worried fifteen minutes without means to get out of there.

We were finally booked on the Swissair which left at 1:30. We tried to find out why we had been told we could go to Vienna without extra charge (this had been negotiated by phone from the hotel also), but the BEA blamed Lufthansa and the Lufthansa blamed the BEA. Both representatives talked in earshot of each other. But that was the most satisfaction we got as to why.

Finally we landed in Munich in late afternoon. The bus left us off in front of the Banhof and Ralph walked across the street to one of the numerous hotels in the block, walked into the nearest and booked us for a room with bath. The Hotel Wolff looked seedy from without and in its lobby but when we were taken to our room, it not only was bright and cheerful but absolutely new. The maids were pushing the last bit of plaster into their dustpan and not a fixture in the bathroom had been used. Even the towels and rugs were new with labels still affixed.

We were delighted by this novel turn and immediately felt better. Then we began to walk around the town, which turned out to be exceedingly lovely and the people were all so nice, treating us not as tourists but strangers whom they wished to feel welcomed. The beer and the food [were] the best we'd had on the trip (except of course for Auxerre where you and Ralph and Mique feasted and Al and I sat there too full to eat). Only a few places were there signs of bombings and most of the rebuilding had been designed to harmonize the old and the new with great feeling for grace and space. There are few high buildings and frequent use of the arcade. Most small shops are to be found in arcades. There are parks and fountains and statuary, not hideous like what we saw in Paris. The Isar River runs through the city. And not the least, Ralph was able to buy his wide-angle lens at the saving anticipated.

One day while walking down a street in Munich, who should we meet but the one *person* we know in Munich. It was quite a coincidence because he himself only happened to be in town since he now works at Bonn and gets to Munich only once in a while. He took us out the following evening—and since he is young, perhaps 23 or 24, we were carried to the places where the students and the young people go. First, to a restaurant in a cellar for a good and reasonable dinner where the young people go each evening to drink wine; then to two nightspots.

The first was real funky and crowded. The couples slowdragged on a small dance floor hardly able, and barely wanting, to move as they danced to a band trying very hard to imitate Geo. Sheavana. At a second night club less crowded and a bit more elegant a little singer was trying to warble like Sarah Vaughan. Other than these two startlingly brass attempts at imitation and our drinks of *gin with beer chasers (we were told that was what to drink) all was familiar and uneventful. The next morning we woke with hangovers but managed to pack our bags and leave on an afternoon plane for Rome.*

I'll go back to work tomorrow and Ralph is trying hard to get back into the swing. Taking our full trip into account—the Murray half and the P.E.N. half—we can say it was a very eventful 27 days. Do write and tell us how you are. We both send you all much love and warm wishes. Special kisses to Mique in her pink toe slippers.

Fanny

CASABLANCA, MAROC
11 AUGUST 1956

Dear Ralph & Fanny,

Know damn well this is long overdue, but what with the satisfaction of the trip and catching up with several major changes that went into effect while I was away, the time just got away from me.

The rest of the trip went as smoothly as the part before. Took in the Chateaux at Blois and Chaumont, had wonderful meals at Chaumont and Barbezieux and drove on to Bordeaux that Sunday. Burgos the next day with no sweat. Madrid by noon the following day. There for three days, the Prado & the bulls. Seville in one day in spite of the terrible road after Cordova (Definitely must get back to Seville when that stuff starts next Spring. Don't miss that Andalousia if you can help it, man.) Seville to Gibraltar in time [for] the midday ferry but spent the rest of the afternoon window-shopping around Gibraltar. Crossed over to Tangier that night and drove on to Casa because there was no hotel space. Car was fine all the way. No trouble with the Spanish gas.

Got all of the color slides back now except the roll that has Seville & Gib on it, which I just completed and mailed last week. Last half of the Pisa and Rome stuff on that roll I had doubts about in the Forum. All in all pretty good. Kodachrome came out much better than the Ecktachrome. All of the rest are from passable to very very good, the errors mostly in light readings. Several very good ones in Venice. Very pleased with Ansco. Shot fifteen exposures at the bullfight (beginning at 630pm) and got them all. Used the telephoto and pulled it in like in the movies. All good but I left out two phases: the banderillas and the pic-ing. Moque & Mique were downright enthusiastic about the bull-fights, by the way, and are looking forward to going again.

It was pretty hot here for several days, but has been very very pleasant since, even a little chilly. Bound to have a sirocco or so tho before it's all over.

Getting ready to move on base. The housing project being completed much faster than most of us thought. Four hundred units by 1 Oct. We'll probably be moving out there around the 15th, but certainly before Sept 1st. The facilities are better of course; it'll be less expensive and I'll gain time. Also it'll be easier to get away on trips without having to worry about that goddam evacuation plan, or the housebreakers, or the family when they are not with me. Been very interesting here in town, but I'd just as soon get on out there and use that time on this manuscript that's beginning to take a little life recently.

Received Fanny's letter this morning. Glad to hear that you got that wide angle lens. Definitely my next buy, unless they get that new Braun Hobby electronic flash in the PX before the next shipment of lens comes in.

Really had fun batting around with you guys.

Al Murray

Note current address

THE AMERICAN ACADEMY
ROME, ITALY.

SEPT. 15, 1956.

Dear Albert:

I'm getting this off at the last minute for I've been hung up with a piece on desegregation which I'm doing for ENCOUNTER and just haven't been able to write anything else. It seems that the trip up to London was just the beginning of a spell of dashing around for after Wright's inviting me to come up to take part in the conference on African culture, I've been approached by two other groups to represent them there. One was the *Encounter* bunch, who wanted me to do a report and the other is an American group on Race and Caste, which offered to pay my fare there and back and to take care of expenses on a $35 per diem. At first I was willing to go for this group, only to learn that they wanted me to speak, to have a paper for publication, to write them a report and to be there a couple of days beforehand so as to hold conferences with the State department and others. Which was just too much for me, so I refused, withdrew; and the guy is still cabling me to change my mind. I guess the son of a bitch thinks I'm impressed by the little money he offered me, certainly he can't understand that I place my work above all that he holds important, or that I'm simply not interested in racial approaches to Culture. Let him get hold of Dick Wright, *he's* on that kick, not me.... Well, as if this wasn't enough, here comes a letter from the Congres pour la Liberté de la Culture asking if I'd be a member of the American delegation to Mexico City Conference on Cultural Freedom in the Western Hemisphere, with first-class air passage and expenses, and this time I've said "Yes." This is something I'm interested in, know something about, and which seems to hold some real promise. Besides I need to see my dentist and to take a look at the apartment in N.Y. so I'm off tomorrow and will be gone until the third week in October. I'll try to write from some point on the trip, which will give me some time in Paris on the way back, otherwise I'll write to you from Rome.... I guess Fanny gave you the dope on the trip to London and I have little to add. It was exhaustingly exciting and we were given special treatment: $21 per day rooms at the Ritz, platform seats on all social occasions, guided about by rump-sprung ladyships and slightly rummy ladyships; drinking the Lord Mayor's champagne, and Her Majesty's champagne, and the Mayor of Brighton's martinis, and J. B. Preistley's liquor and God knows who-all's scotch and eating everybody's food. I was one of the lucky ones who were received by the Queen Mother and Princess Margaret, two very charming ladies indeed, the Queen Mother actually reads books and knows how to talk about them and Princess Margaret is the kind of little *hot* looking pretty girl that our girl Laly[1] only *thought* she was and who could upset most campuses, dances, club cars, bull fights, and three day picnics even if she had no title. No, I'm not about to do a Henry James but I was impressed by

[1] Miss Tuskegee, 1935.

those two. I was also impressed by some of the writers I met, especially by Eliot, with whom we shared the guest of honor table the night of the closing banquet. I talked with him very briefly however because he was just recovering from a heart attack. All in all London was impressive and is, I think, the only city which in its massiveness and harsh sprawling conveys the idea of power. It is simply huge, a monument to empire which will remain long after the empire is gone. Full of art too, those damned Englishmen really have their share, with many private collections rivaling the Louvre in many types of art.... I must say, however, that despite the language the only time I didn't feel exactly alien was one afternoon while we were having tea with the President of the House of Lords on the terrace of that House, and I looked across the Thames with its bridges and boats, to Westminister towering in the haze, and suddenly I was a child again and nursery rhymes were singing in my head. So London *is* a sort of literary possession, but all the public ritual, the fading pomp and circumstance constitute a wall that's far thicker, because I understand the language, than anything I've found in Italy or France. To be an American is to be many things but only the slightest bit English... We left there and went down to Munich to rest, to stuff ourselves with food (the British still ain't cooking) and beer. Stayed a week. I got the wide angle which I find very useful and I shot some of the anschrome, which pleased me very much, so I'm buying some in 35 m.m. bulk film so that I can load my own cartridges. $9.95 buys enough for eight rolls, which is much cheaper than Kodachrome. My Kodachrome came back fine, but I wonder how that roll came out that you started? The black and white was O.K. and I'm very impressed by your telephoto lens, which will be *my* next buy. Indeed, I wish I had it for this Mexico City trip. Don't, by the way, forget that I'm interested in an Omnica bag for this stuff, as the one I have is simply too heavy and incapable of being handily arranged. Right now I'm using a little plastic bag to hold a couple of rolls of film, my wide angle and some lens tissues. It's much easier to carry and it makes you less conspicuous. Some of the Venice stuff came out quite well, both in Kodachrome and Anscochrome.... All in all the first part of the trip with you guys was the best and we're sorry that it couldn't have lasted longer. I still want to explore some of those towns we had to shoot through and to do the chateau country, so come on up next year... Picked up a Hemingway picture story in the barbershop the other day and was struggling to translate it, only to find it the next day in *Look*. He's still in there and I'd like to run into him now that he's doing Europe. I'm using that bit of dialogue from THE SUN ALSO RISES, wherein Bill tells Jake that Lincoln was a faggot who was in love with General Grant and that he freed the slaves on a bet etc., in this essay I'm doing. The thing is beating the hell out of me because I have too much material, too many fleeting insights keep popping up which cannot be used in the short piece. I'll send along a carbon when I finish it as I'll probably extend it into a longer study of late 19th and early 20th century writing. I got to get the stuff out of me before I can have some peace. In the meantime I've written enough stuff for at least two further articles in the subject which I hope to sell. It is very odd how Mose seems to have thrown up his hands before this subject and here it is in the headlines. You look in the Italian press and one day you see Egyptian belly dancers posing with rifles all set to blast at the French and the British, in fact at all Christians, white folks and Jews, and the next day you see those crackers in Tennessee being stood off by the fixed bayonets of the all-cracker National Guard. Thing about it is that the Egyptian belly dancer looked like Althea Gibson, the Harlem tennis champ, French tennis champ, and about sixteen other champs. What the hell do those crackers think they're doing? Mose is the only darker group who doesn't want to blast his kind from the face of the earth, who make any kind of allowance for their form of insanity. There was a time when the cracker's madness could be rationalized but now they're acting like a maniac chasing hell in an airplane loaded with the atomic bomb. Somebody, the Federal or State governments, I don't care which, had better strait-jacket those fools before they wreck the plane. *Life* is running a series on desegregation but it hasn't appeared over here as yet... Man, that coffee which you brought us has certainly improved our breakfast a hell of a lot. I don't know what the hell we'll do when it runs out because we've nearly been spoiled.... There's no news in the States worth relating except book news. Vintage is bringing out two editions of James's essays, one on European and the other on American themes and Stravinsky's *Poetics of Music*. There will also be a two volume edition of

Gide's *Journals* and Hyman's anthology, THE CRITICAL PERFOR-MANCE. Faulkner is working on a sequel to *The Hamlet,* one part to be called *The Village,* the other *The Mansion.* When we got to London we found a copy of Wright Morris's THE FIELD OF VISION which is quite a good, quiet novel. That Morris is probably the most skilled of the younger novelists, he just won't open up with all he has.... This is it, man. I'm getting packed to take off and by this time tomorrow plan to be heading to Paris. Tell Mike that I've learned to make more reasonable sounds on that recorder and that I promise to cook up some chitterlings just in case I find my way down there in the spring. Maybe with a belly full of that righteous cuisine—con corn bread, con butter milk, con mustard greens. Speaking of which, reminds me that I've forgotten to tell you that old down home Mose and his wife have found Rome this summer and are walking over these ancient streets with the same deliberation with which they walk along an Alabama Road. Man I liked to laugh out loud, I looked out of a shop on the Corso and there is old Mose wearing a billed cap, and his high-assed sport shoed buddy was wearing a cream colored silk shirt with a cravat that showed grimly beneath his round head. That mister was grim, taking no shit and seeing everything. In fact they were arguing with the women for getting tired just as we were arguing with Mokie and Fanny a few months ago.

You can't hold him man, he's on the move, all he wants is for the dam crackers to get the hell out of his way. I don't know where they got the money, but Brother, they are over here! See you. If you need anything from over yonder write me at 730 Riverside Drive or until the 26 of Sept at the *Hotel Frimont, Calle Jesus Teran No. 35, Mexico City.*

Ralph Ellison

[POSTCARD FROM MEXICO CITY]

SEPT. 24, 1956
CPT. A.L. MURRAY
CHEZ M. RAZZ
75 RUE DE REINS
CASABLANCA, MAROC

Dear Albert,

Been trying to see as much of this country as possible with all the yak yak coming from these Latin intellectuals. Mucho modern, this city and as interesting as Italy. Rich past. Been going around with Dos Passos who knows the country from 30 yrs. ago. I'll write from New York. Love to Mokie and Mique.

Ralph

CASABLANCA, MAROC
23 OCTOBER 56

Dear Ralph,

Sorry we missed you on the 2nd & 3rd, but the news of where you were was very good. Some deal, man. I don't see how you could've come out any better, even using the old con game. Boy, I guess you just about shot up that Mexico about something near 'bout as bad as old Pancho Villa did. Hope you were loaded. With film, I mean. Know you were loaded otherwise.

We left a day or so before your letter arrived. Cruise came through on schedule and was quite a nice thing. It was a very fine boat with excellent food, and the weather was perfect. Eighteen mellow autumn days on the Mediterranean, pulling into a port on an average of every two days. Livorno, Napoli, Tripoli, Piraeus-Athens, Istanbul, Izmir, and then Naples again where we took off for Rome, rejoining the boat again in Livorno three days later. Cost: a nominal fee of $26.00 each for meals, since the gov't provides us subsistence already. Expenses ashore determined by the amount of shopping involved. Not a whole lot of time in any one place, but enough to see all the highlights and shop etc. We almost always pulled into port in the morning and stayed at least all day. Overnight here, a couple of days there etc.

Got the last batch of slides back today. Total of about 220 for the cruise. Not bad. Generally better than those this summer, which were not bad either, except for that goddamned Ektachrome in Paris. Shot four rolls of the new Anscochrome (processing included). Very good when you're right, but doesn't give you much leeway for mistakes with that meter. A half stop off and you've had it. I find that I'm much more consistent with the old Kodachrome standby. However, I did get some pretty nice Anscos at the bullfights in Madrid this summer. Fifteen out of fifteen, and you know what time of day that had to be. Maybe I'm better with it when the light is not so bright.

Guess you've seen the ads of the new m-3 accessories by now. Now that new wide-angle attachment is just what I've got to have. I don't expect it in the PX soon, but I intend to have it from the getting place in a matter of weeks if possible.

Saw Warren's piece in *Life*, and have also been following the *Life* series on segregation. Did you see Theodore White's piece in the August 17 *Colliers*? Magazines generally doing pretty good, except for *US News & World Report* which is doing its damnedest to put stuff in the game in a subtle way which ain't in the least bit clever.

Look, those tapes I left there, erase them and use them. I don't think that stuff put on them was put on very well. It was taken from a GI transcription last year before I sent to Sam Goody for the original. What speed do you prefer? I have several things you might want to hear, and I'm sending for another stack next week. By the way, they have those Omnica bags in now at $17.00. Can get when ever you say. Had mine for the cruise. Very handy when you have to carry all that extra stuff you have to have.

Pictures you mentioned enclosed. Will send negatives as soon as additional prints are made.

Murray

New Braun Hobby Ectrome flash in PX $44.00

AMERICAN ACADEMY IN ROME
VIA ANGELO MASINA, 5
(PORTA S. PANCRAZIO)
ROME

CABLE ADDRESS
(AM ENCLOSING CHECK FOR IRON).
"Amacadmy"

Nov. 7, 1956

Dear Albert,

I found your letter waiting for me when I returned on the 30th. I left N.Y. on the 27th and spent the 28 & 29th in Paris, where I gave my impression of the Mexico congress to the people who sent me over. Winter had come to Paris and I was tired so I described the ten days of Latin-American hot air, clichés, the strutting and posturing as great intellectuals that went on there, and came on down here to see Fanny and catch up on my home work. Those Latin Americans are wild and even the writers had nothing better to talk about than blame the U. S. for everything negative in the world and to mouthe worn out Marxist slogans as the latest wisdom, there in one of the cities most given over to modern architecture and in a country in which there's an ocean's width between the rich and the poor, those bastards are fighting the machine! They, they say, are spiritual; concerned with personality, value, distinctions (subtle, of course) and hierarchy; while we North Americans are materialists and concerned only with building roads, bridges, machines, and in out-doing ourselves, so as you can see, I had it up to my ears. New York was such a relief that I was filled with a burst of energy. I felt like that middle aged mose you met in Paris: it's a dam good town. I stayed a month, having teeth repaired and cussing the bitch who made a pig sty out of our apartment. But what a bitch! Not only were things broken but she didn't replace a single light bulb, or, from what I could tell, dust a single piece of furniture. Blinds were busted and rusting, expensive plates, crystal cocktail pitcher and wooden salad bowl busted and cockroaches in everything. Even up front. So again I had it. But I did see a few movies, ate ice cream and was entertained by our friends until I was bowlegged. In Mexico I ate biscuits every morning until I saw the Mexican woman pouring hot cakes, and brother—they are the largest and the lightest I've *ever* had. Those tortillas had prepared the Mexicans to really romp with Aunt Jemima! We'll have to jump down there with a car, man. That place is easily as interesting to me as Italy and in many ways with enough cultures rolling around under the surface and with a decided flair for things modern.

But back to New York. The changes in the city can be seen with some distinction after a year. More attention seems to be being given to neighborhood planning; 3rd Avenue sports the new fluorescent streets lights, is being paved and promises to become the most interesting street in the City. That El was messing up a hell of a lot of good space. The new Seagram's building on Park has been designed so that it offers a wonderful frame for the Lever building, which it faces at an angle. It's jumping and it's the liveliest city in the world.... Well, that bastard Stevenson didn't even take the solid South. I hope that's the last of him—and I'm still a Democrat. Maybe now we'll get rid of some of those crackers in Congress and the next time we'll get a statesman and not a jackass.... Forgot to mention that I saw a lot of Norman Thomas, Roger Baldwin, & John Dos Passos in Mexico. Part of American delegation. Called me the 'Kid.' Boy, if we could only get in the position to use what we know and have learned by living in the groove of our circumstances! They're O. K. but they know the issues no better than we do and often not so well. I'll write more on this later.... I was so busy down there that I didn't shoot up the place like I wanted to but did quite a bit. But brother, I picked up a Nikon 105 m.m. telephoto and have been reaching and gittin' it for a fare-the-well around Rome. A beautiful optic which you'll have to try next trip up. I think I like the Rollie better for color although I brought back Anscochrome in bulk and am loading my own 35 m.m. at 8 20 exposures for less than $7. I find it better than EK and Gordon Parks uses nothing else. Sorry you didn't see the stuff from the summer, it was right there in the top drawer. I'll be sending you the money for the Omnica soon, because the bag I have is too heavy. Will the Leica bag hold a Rollie too, or will I have to have the larger size? Prefer the smaller one for its compactness. I don't expect to be buying any more lenses even though the new wide angle with the attachment looks very good. Just wish I'd waited to get the new meter, cause I'm traveling light as possible... Thanks for the tapes; they were equalized badly for my machine but by adding bass they sound good enough to hear until I can do better. Most of the stuff is good Duke and I'm starved for more of it. Missed him while in N.Y. but saw Ruth, who had a good down-home meal on the table—Yams, man! I told her I *knowed some*body knew I was coming! Greens too, and all the fixings. That chick ain't Duke's sister for nothing. Anyway, if you can send more tapes, please do. My machine only plays 7½ inches per second and I suspect that the trouble with these is that the tape you used has different characteristics from the M.M.M. tape for which Ampex machines are equalized. *Scotch* is the brand name. I picked up the components for a sound system for the Academy while in N.Y. but they haven't come over yet; when they arrive and I've set it up I'll have the problem of classical music licked, but the jazz will still be missing. So send along anything that's good to you. Heard some Chico Hamilton out at Kenneth Clark's and liked it. They tell me he challenged Duke at a festival last summer and shook up those bored Ellington cats so much that they came storming back and outdid themselves. Which is pretty good for a five piece group of so-called modernists. I only heard two discs, is he consistent? The Clarks send regards to you and Mokie. He's been advising Luther and still can't understand the place. He's also been asked to keep an eye on Derbigny's little blue-gummed gal[1] and is puzzled by her strange blend of naïveté and sophistication (mainly verbal about sex and extra-marital affairs). Sounds like a campus raised kid to me. What kind of person is she?

The Brandeis thing is all over; I turned it down after they only offered me $6500 and academic status. To hell with that; I could bring them that much in publicity—which they counted on—*and* I have a point of view which is fairly original. I certainly don't plan to go anywhere and start fighting with someone like Irving Howe at this late date. I'd rather go to a mose school where I might keep some of the stuff in a briarpatch. For $8000 I'd have taken it and would have worked like hell—which I've been avoiding all my life. I guess the

[1] Daughter of Tuskegee's administrative dean.

man thought I would be taken in by the ofay set up, but hell, if I've got to have children I want 'em to look like me, they'd have some of the same things to write out of. The Man up there might not know it but there's a hell of a lot more knowledge and discipline in writing a novel than it takes to get a Ph.D. or at least *most* Ph.D.s and if he can't see it *I* can. Anyway I've been living poor and avoiding the nets so that I could write and now [it] is too late to sell myself cheap; I'd rather write ads—which in its abuse of words is as low as whale shit.... Writers around here at the moment: Warren and his wife, Eleanor Clark are here; old Albert Erskine will be back from Madrid in a few days; William Arrowsmith of the *Hudson Review* is here on fellowship (he's a classicist who wants to write novels); Blackmur will be here to have drinks and dinner with us tonight; Allen Tate came in the other day; John Cheever is to be In Rome for a year, so it looks as though I'll have a few people to talk with during the winter. I didn't get to see Kaplan[2] in Paris, but heard his wife is seriously ill. Baldwin's down in Positano; Wright was still het up over the Presence Africaine conference, which he feels is of great future importance; says the American Negro is in the position to help them, which perhaps we are. But who the hell wants to live in Africa? Which reminds me, I hope no fool pulls the lid all the way off the mess we have in Egypt and Hungary, because I'm as sure as I'm setting here that the British will drop a bomb—if they have one. The Russians are threatening them and I think they've been pushed too far to give a dam, U.S. or no. Nasser is gambling too hard and too fast unless he intends to involve every-body. One thing is certain; he ain't the Jungle King. Poor Stevenson, he starts talking about the draft and bomb control just at the moment hell pops. We'd better prepare to jump and jump fast if that bear keeps farting because he'll head in our direction in spite of hell. If he does I hope we'll go for broke on his ass.... Take it easy and give our regards to the girls.

Ralph

[2] H.J. Kaplan, friend of Murray's, *Partisan Review* Paris correspondent.

Dear Ralph,

Am sending the Omnica by a Miss Ruth O'Dell, who will be up there for the holidays. Mose chick who is teaching in the elementary school here this year.

Things going pretty good here. Writing beginning to come along somewhat better now. Think maybe I've finally settled on a form for this jazz thing. No really big explosions yet, but my head is beginning to buzz continuously with ideas some of which are bound to hit the fan sooner or later. Meanwhile the few details that I've been able to put down so far stand up well enough to keep me in the mood without too much struggle in spite of all the interruptions. If I can keep it up I should have enough for somebody to see by Spring.

Weather has been completely wonderful. Only one week of rain this fall. Normally the rainy season would have begun by now, but so far we've had nothing but cool nights, chilly mornings and warm days and bright, blue cirrus sky.

The gals are fine. Drop you another line during the holidays, meanwhile y'all have a good Xmas.

Murray

CASABLANCA, MAROC
11 MARCH 1957

Dear Ralph,

What's happening chez y'all these days? Nothing much to report from here. Mostly we've just been biding our time and waiting for the winter rains which didn't quite make it this year. Only rain we've had recently was the one that Nixon brought, and with the number of scobes that cat was hauling around with him he could have brought almost anything. Mose just about fifty-fifty, both on Nixon's plane and on the one with the newspapermen. What with all the rain and the VIP treatment the base staff was putting down I didn't get a chance to check any of them out (the troop ceremonies, my part of the program, was weathered in). Funny thing was that the wheels had all the names and were planning balls out, but they really didn't seem to have any idea at all that except for the Nixons just about all the rank was old Mose, who was naturally dead in there with all them embassy lines and that protocol. The Air Force of course handles stuff like that without turning a lash, but *that* many scobes wheeling and dealing from that high up caught them napping to say the least. Maybe some of them will still be in the party when they come to Rome later on. You better check up on them, man, seems like old Ike is beginning to use this shit for what it's worth.

Haven't been anywhere recently, but I'm just about ready to get moving again. Got to get back down to Marrakesh to get some pictures. Got to get up to Fez. Plan also to get up into the Atlas Mountains and down to the Sahara. All this I can do without too much trouble. I just don't want the time [to] get away. After all, we'll [be] the hell out of here this time next year. Right now I'm checking into the possibilities of getting into Seville around Easter. Looks as if I might have to fly commercial. I can get to Madrid at almost anytime, but we don't have regular runs into the base in Seville. No direct commercial flights from Casa either. Tangier, yes. May have to go Air Force to Madrid and come back down to Seville commercial. Caint spare but just three or four days. Hoarding leave time against summer, but I sure would like to shoot that bull festival. Will probably get a short trip up to Germany (Bavaria) around 30 April.

Tentative summer plans as follows: Morale flight to Frankfurt and then on our own to Copenhagen, Stockholm, Amsterdam, and London by surface transportation before settling down in Paris for ten or twelve days. Very tentative as yet, but this is what we're playing around with. What have you guys got up? It's a damned good thing we got that motor trip in last year, in light of what the goddamned Nasser has done to gas. We can travel around down here without too much trouble again now. GI gas hasn't really been affected, but they had us restricted here for awhile for good will reasons, which nobody knew about but us. Now that that is off, most of the places are within reach if you take along a couple of extra jerry cans. We are still not supposed to buy gas on the local economy, as if who the hell wants to at that price.

Let's have a report on your activities and plans. Whatcha been shooting, whatcha writing, whatcha articling? Me, I'm still laying out this thing of mine. No leaps and bounds, but I'm still plugging away at some of the more functional scenes, setting up character material etc. You said some time ago that you were working on a piece or so for the magazines, have you anything in print recently? Let's have that goddamned report, cousin.

You mentioned Chico Hamilton in your last. From what I've heard of him I'd say he could really go if he settles down. Had old Buddy Collette, who could play anything on anything and has written and hack written himself into one of those studio music directors job with some radio station out on the Coast. The young mose who keeps the fay boys all shook these days is a bass fiddle player named Charles Mingus, who can out talk, out analyze, out intellectualize, and out fiddle just about anybody around. His best stuff is straight out of Duke, of course, but he also seems to be out to out conservatory all the post-boppers and Juilliarders and Milhauders together. He is really the wildest Academician going these days. I don't think he's really hit it yet, but I'm just dying to check out what goes with all the spieling. By and large, I'm afraid that too many of these cats, some of whom have real potential, get so carried away with being MODERN and EXPERIMENTAL and SERIOUS that they not only forget what jazz is they don't even remember what music is supposed to do anymore. In the end I suppose something good is bound to come of it all, and I'm not against it, but I do wish to hell they'd get on with it and stop fucking around with that goddamned "Indian."[1] Reminds you of the time when young writers thought that Joyce and Kafka had changed the whole FUNCTION of literature.

Anyway, Duke and Count are still the bands to hear these days. They have assimilated about as much of the so-called Modern as will probably last anyway, and they still have the old identity and the old drive. A master is a goddamned MASTER, man. It's just as true now as it ever was: when you start fucking around with that goddamned Duke Ellington, you're subject to have yourself a new asshole cut.

[1] References to Ralph's yarn about a dark man who becomes so involved with disguising himself as an Indian chief in a futile effort to trick the station machine into changing his weight and fortune card that he almost misses his train connection.

But seriously, old Duke does seem to be out for blood again these days. I have the Newport album and several other recent things which hit a high %, and I'm checking the mail daily for this newest extended thing, called A DRUM IS A WOMAN, which is supposed to be a very ambitious piece of Ellingtonia, augmented with Joya Sherrill, Margaret Tynes and a lot of others. If I get a chance, I'll have some of all this new Duke and one or two of old Count and Joe Williams taped up and send it up next time I catch somebody coming up that way.

Picked up a copy of BIG BILL'S BLUES the other day. Some character with the improbable name of Yannick Bruynoghe helped him and did a pretty good job of it. A hell of a lot of the old down home stuff gets through. As you know Old Bill Broonzy has very definite affinities with old LEADBELLY and old Luzana Cholly. Published London 1955 Cassell & Co. Ltd. Snapshots of PEETIE WHEAT-STRAW, Big Maceo, Tampa Red, Memphis Slim & Washboard Sam. Just 139 pages. Stuff comes through, pretty much in the raw. None of that phony hype they ruined Louis's SATCHMO with. Have a look at it if you get the chance.

The gals are all right. My only problem is getting Mique to buckle down to 8th grade math. By the way did you hear that the Chapel burned down? Lightning struck it. Tuskegee was never so shook up before. Now how in the hell is Foster going to explain THAT to the trustees when them Negroes are supposed to have had the weather down there under control for all these many years.

Albert

Note change of address on envelope.

CHECK ENCLOSED
AMERICAN ACADEMY IN ROME
VIA ANGELO MASINA, 5
(PORTA S. PANCRAZIO)
ROME

CABLE ADDRESS   *APRIL 4, 1957.*
"Amacasmy"

Dear Albert:

This has been one of our longest silences, which means that the world has really been too much with us. I've been up to my ass in typescript and have only just climbed out of one level of the mess after another back to my novel. Last year I made the mistake of agreeing to do an essay on the novel for an anthology edited by Granule Hicks and which will include people like Bellow, Wright Morris & Herb. Gold and which Macmillan will publish. But I got bogged down on the damn thing for two months, perhaps because I was resisting the necessity of leaving old Bliss and Cliofus and Severn and Love to deal with The Novel and those who say the form is dead. Fuck Trilling and his gang, I know that a novel is simply hard to write, especially during this time when you can't take anything for granted anymore. Anyway I've finished that piece and I hope they use it. The other piece I probably mentioned is a piece on desegregation, which is still in the works. It deals quite a bit with literature and I'm hoping to make a short book of it at the suggestion of Robt. Penn Warren. I've begun to look closely at the novels of the twenties through the frame provided by today and the Civil War period and have dredged some interesting stuff out of Hemingway and Fitzgerald. The other writing news is that the Battle royal scene has turned up in *A Southern Harvest* along with all those Southern big names, which amuses me to no end because it must mean that I've sold my soul to the crackers! *Flying Home,* that long and not too smooth story is appearing in an anthology of writing edited by Charles Fenton of Yale, to be published by Viking (W. W. II, that is). I picked up a book on criticism published in England under the title, *Catastrophe & the Imagination,* which gives *Invisible* lots of space and picks it for a short list of novels which that wild stud thinks will be of interest a century from now. Surely the man must be on the weed. The other project is an interview of Warren for the *Paris Review*, which, if they don't cut it too much, should be one of their most interesting. Eugene Walter (Mobile white boy) an editor of the mag, helped me and we all got tight on some Pernod that Warren brought up to our place and we taped the whole thing. Sounded like a bunch of moses drinking corn and I wished you could have taken part because for all the drinking we were axing straight through a lot of marbled-hard bullshit. I'm holding the tapes as long as I can so if you zoom up here you can hear them. Got to see Warren and Eleanor two, three times a week for two months and we became very fond of them and they of us. We knew them before but it took Rome to let us discover one another—which might be the most important thing to happen during these two years. I got to measure my mind against one of the best Southerners and its just like we've been saying, if Mose takes advantage of his own sense of reality he doesn't have to step back for anybody. Anyway, Warren is a man who's lived and thought his way free of a lot of irrational illusions and you'd like him. Maybe I told you that R. P. Blackmur was here most of the winter after being evacuated from Egypt. We saw a lot of him also and he has a capacity for night-owling and drinking that is appalling; and an elder statesman's tendency to dominate conversation even when he has nothing interesting to say that can sometimes be boring. Too much teaching and undergraduate worshipping, I guess. Nevertheless, when he's really riffing he reminds you of Buck Clayton, no straining and grunting just smooth, hot sound..., MacLeish is here just now but I'll write about him later. Have talked to his wife about Hemingway during the twenties in Paris and it was dam interesting. So you see that writer-wise this has been a year more interesting than the last.

That picture you give of Nixon and old Mose knocked me out and I'm sorry I didn't get to see them when they *hit* here. Not only the air brass but plenty moses back in the states must wonder what time of day it is. And the Democrats! If Ike wins the next election even Bilbo will rise up out of his grave and tell his boys to 'forget about white supremacy and git those damn nigras on our side' which reminds me that I've seen the Isaacsons twice since we visited them in Florence last July and each time he's given me a hurt puzzled look. I guess he's still puzzled by your little comments on Ike, politics, and the election. He still doesn't know whether you were just kidding or were damn serious and, I suppose, since I agreed that Stevenson couldn't win he doubts that I'm a Democrat, which I still am although I didn't vote for that weak sister.

As for travel we haven't been anywhere either and I don't see us going. We've just investigated getting down to Barcelona for Easter but found the fare too expensive. I did have the use of a car for a few weeks and we got to see a bit of the Roman country side this lovely spring, but no Florence, no Siena, nowhere. We're waiting to hear from the freighter line about passage home. We want to leave here in Sept and wander back with the tides, thus saving our dough and staying here to the very end. Thus far see no possibility of taking a summer trip. Incidentally, the gas situation here is O. K. Tourists get 300 liters a period, same as before. Don't worry about France, if you can bounce in here for a second before you start moving we'd like to see you. I haven't heard the idiom since Harlem in the fall.

Thanks for the bag for which I'm enclosing a check; it's the best ever and you may tell the young lady that I want to send her a book when we get back home, she was very nice and I'm sorry she hit here when I was a bit under the weather. But the bag has brought order into my equipment and beginning to get the hand of the Leica and the extra lenses. The 105 Nikon is a fine piece of glass and I've been using it to pick faces out of crowds as well as to do detail work on buildings etc. Fanny, by the way, is shooting some nice color with her old Rollei, in fact much better than most of my recent stuff. I've been giving my attention to black and white and having great fun.... Those tapes you sent are still sending the Academy. Sometimes I play them and open the door to find guys standing there bending an ear; so I say come on in, what this place needs is a little more Ellington. And man, we gave a party with another couple, got hold of some cheap but excellent French-style champagne to start them on before serving the martinis (we were celebrating the good fortune of those who were given a third year) then I put on Basie and Joe Williams and the whole building took off! People who had never danced before were trying to move and I was yelling never mind your feet, just bounce and let the rhythm tell you what to do! And some were doing it too. We went out to eat and they kept dancing in the restaurant to a guitar played by a Neapolitan character who must have gotten rich off of our party, then we came back and danced to Duke until everybody started falling down. As soon as the cartridge comes, I plan to assemble it and then go find A DRUM IS A WOMAN as I need something new to help me through the summer. If you have anything new you think I should have I would gladly pay for the tape and the cost of having it recorded. Let me know.... I have just received *The Town*, Faulkner's book on the Snopes, and Steegmuller's translation of *Madame Bovary*. Too busy to get to them at the moment but look out for them.

The news about the chapel was rather shocking; I guess I loved the old place; so much of what I hated about Tuskegee took place there as did so many of its lost possibilities come to focus there. Perhaps the burning is symbolic. I had hoped to see it again, now it will become the occasion for some more stealing and more bad design and construction work and a hell of a lot of self-congratulation and pious bullshit when the new chapel is completed. One of these days I'm really going to put the bad-mouth on those scobes; here Africans and West Indians are taking over governments and Montgomery Negroes are showing their quality and *they* continue to act like this is 1915. Foster should be ashamed of himself. Well, man, world events are justifying our position and interests of the thirties, not those of the administration or the campus heroes and politicians; we are operating out of a different sense of time and on a different wave-length. Maybe Foster will see the light and be a man.... Love to your girls from Fanny and me—Say, when do you go home?

Ralph

Casablanca, Maroc
5 May 1957

Dear Ralph,

I mailed you two fifteen-minute tapes last Friday (3 May). I mailed them through APO, so it just might take ten or fifteen days for them to reach you. Didn't have time to be bothered with French parcel post crap. They fly APO stuff directly from here to Germany and put it into the international mail stream there, and the guy here claims that the time is not bad.

The tapes are as follows:

1) *Diminuendo & Crescendo in Blue* from ELLINGTON AT NEW-PORT. This is one whole tape. Interesting for several reasons. This is the piece that broke it up. They say the first ones to start cutting loose that night were not the groundlings but the native Newporters, who suddenly realized that they got some of that kind of blue in their blood too. You hear old Duke in there sic-ing that stuff on just as if it's all happening somewhere in a tobacco shed or a corn likker joint, and there's that fancy fingering in there treeing squirrels and running rabbits all over 27 counties and choruses. And as if that new suped-up rhythm section weren't enough in itself, there's old JO JONES standing down there beating on the edge of the stage with a tightly rolled copy of the CHRISTIAN SCIENCE MONITOR! Sorry that I wasn't able to include the new thing they did up there called Newport Jazz Festival Suite (Festival Junction, Blues to be There, Newport Up), which contains some very fine new writing, but this is a lot of fun and it also holds up pretty good.

2) *The Comeback,* Joe Williams and Count. If this doesn't rock that Academy, it must be time for Nero or Atilla to take over again.

My Funny Valentine, in which old Duke redoes a pop watercolor in oils.

A Very Unbooted Character, the new Duke band doing one from the 40's. I just think that this stuff is very very fine Ellington indeed. I don't think you write this kind of stuff for money. Man, this stuff comes from down there where that cat *lives,* and he's got 14 outright thugs up there voicing that shit as if [it] was a certified symphony, and you and I know good and damn well they don't have to *think* symphony at all.

Rhum-bop, from A DRUM IS A WOMAN. This is a three-minute excerpt. The whole thing is a 12 inch LP. I don't think it really comes off. It's a sort of Peter and Wolf story about Jazz (Madame Zajj and Carribee Joe). Duke narrates, and in several places he works in a down home signifying grunt that is gassed no end, but the overall scenario strikes me as being slapdash. In some parts it seems that he's about to

do some thing all his own and in other parts he just seems to be knocking out a musical comedy routine. The possibilities are all there, but
he does just enough to let you see how much he probably could have
done if he had really buckled down. Am sending this particular part
because I like the beat and also because it has old Joya Sherrill singing
again (who was as right as Ivy). She's married and settled down but she
came back to do Madame Zajj and she's up to par on all of her four
numbers. Man, you should see the cover of this thing: two tall drums
and a sock cymbal and a blonde in a red union suit (facing the other
way) with her flat ass spread all over a little bitty talking drum!

"*The Birdland Story*" tape (Incomplete) is old King Pleasure singing
one of James Moody's tenor sax solos. What the hell does he care
whether it's poetry or prose, if it'll fit it'll swing.

Say, what about that goddamned Sugar Ray! Now there's a cat making "history" in the Eubanks sense, meaning myth & ritual and all that
hero stuff about the dying god of the repeating birth. Back in January
when Fulmer[1] outpointed old Sugar, a guy named Martin Kane wrote
in *Sports Illustrated* as follows:

"So passes the brightly lighted Robinson era. It ended in the fifteenth round, when the plodding tortoise beat the flashy hare once
again, as he always does in the fable. Sugar Ray Robinson thought he
was living another fable, which is what the hare always thinks."

So much for Mr. Martin Kane's knowledge of Mose & Myths. On
the other hand you always have to watch out for guys like Hemingway's favorite boy, Red Smith, who in an interview with one of the big
league managers a week or so ago was talking about some of Robinson's prefight faith talks. The manager wondered if Ray really believes
all that stuff about positive thinking, and old man Red Smith told him,
Man, Sugar Ray Robinson is Norman Vincent Peale with a left hook!
And where the hell is that character who wanted Fulmer to "bust him
in his pink Cadillac?"

So now they will have to console themselves by talking about how
much income tax he will have to pay, but they're kidding themselves

---

[1] Gene Fulmer, a very popular contender for the welterweight and middleweight
boxing championships.

again just as they do when express[ing] their sympathy for Joe Louis' income tax problems. (Man, I tell em as long as a sonofabitch is still making around 50 grand or better a year he don't need no sympathy from no body in my income bracket). Income tax hell, I say watch out for Old Man Mose of the Mountain. That's just the thing about old Jack the Bear, he's both hare AND bear.

Things all right here. Getting some of that rain that didn't get here during what [was] supposed to be the height of the rainy season. Didn't get up to Seville for Easter because all hotels were tied up over a month in advance. Have put in for reservations in Copenhagen, London and Paris for this Summer but haven't heard from them yet. We plan to take leave from about 20 June to about 20 July. As I probably said last time, we fly from here to Frankfurt and fly back from there. So we plan to get in some Rhine areas too.

We don't rotate to the States until next February. After that I'm not too firm. Have been playing around with the idea of trying to get a year at some base near San Francisco and then trying to get to Japan before the Japs get completely fed up with us, but I don't know.

The check you mentioned was not enclosed. That bag was a Christmas present anyway, so I hope that you haven't lost your money. Hell, man, I can always get $17.00 worth of free books from you when we get back to New York.

Murray

p/s Before I could find somebody to take this into town and mail it, I had to come into the hospital for a few days of rest and observation. My electrocardiogram didn't turn out so good during the annual (over 40 years old) physical last week. I don't feel any pain or tired or weak but these guys don't take any chances and I'm glad all for it. I *do* seem to be feeling the effects of the weight I've been putting on.

ROME,
JUNE 2, 1957.

Dear Albert,

Tapes received and everybody knocked out. With both Duke and Basie I couldn't hope for better word from home; and if they weren't enough, that character who calls himself King Pleasure is about to drive me crazy. The idea of him breaking off the story at that point. Did Moody blow everybody out of the place or did it go limp on him, or did everybody blast everybody else? Well, however it came out that King Pleasure sings more bop rhythm than anyone since Anna Randolph, who was singing it and improvising her lyrics during the days when Dizzy and Monk were confined to Minton's Playhouse. Here's a fool who doesn't know you aren't supposed to sing prose, so he gets away with it. . . . As for the bit from *Drum,* I like, but suspect that here again Duke fails to make the transition from the refinement of his music over to drama—or even over to words; so that what in music would be vital ideas comes over with a slickness and hipster elegance that makes you want to go and tell the man how really good he is and that he should do anything with that Broadway-hipster-Mose decadence but get it mixed up with his music. He should leave that element to Billy Strayhorn. Well, if we have to have that in order to get those diamonds, very well.

As for that Sugar Ray, I won on him against Bobo, would have lost on him when he lost to that meat-headed Fulmer, only the guy who bet me wouldn't bet, and I would have won on him this time if the guy hadn't gone back to the states. Somebody will have to whip Sugar Ray some day but I'll go along with him because he is an artist and I'll bet on grace and art when its coupled with strength before I'd ever bet on simple youth sans these. And you never said a truer word about Jack, he is indeed both hare and bear, and he's bound to get you one way or the other.

Which reminds me that that heart thing worries me, I hope it's nothing serious. As for the weight, you can lick that by walking. I'm down to 181 with my clothes on, which means I'm lean and mean. I think I'll have a physical soon myself just to keep in touch with myself for this spring hasn't been too easy on me. I wish you were stopping here for a day so that I could talk about it. Fanny and I are in a state of crisis at the moment and I might just be acting like a fool in his forties. That's as much as I can say now except that it's painful and confusing. . . . I don't know what our plans are at the moment. Fanny has to go home at the end of next month and I'm still waiting to hear if I'm staying here another year. A. MacLeish is doing something about it and

I've been asked if I want to go to Tokyo & Kyoto in Sept. for P. E. N. I think I'll say yes but I don't know where I'll end up but it'll either be to Trieste, Milan, Turin, Genoa, Florence, Naples, and Bari—which promises to be the extent of my travel this summer. I go through the ordeal of a lecture here in Rome on Friday and that'll be the end of that mess. It's worse than playing one-night stands and there is nothing amusing about it, because these people won't blow back at you.

I suppose you've gotten the check by now, Fanny had sent it along with a letter to Mokie which was returned but we used the last address you gave me, thanks for the bag, and as for the books, I have an extra copy of Faulkner's THE TOWN and one of Steegmuller's translation of *Madame Bovary.* If you haven't picked them up yet, just let me know where to mail them. Faulkner has some amusing things, mostly re-worked from some of the Snopes stories, but I haven't gotten around to the translation. I've really been too busy battling with myself and with this novel-of-mine-to-be to get much reading done. I'm going to whip the dam thing but it [is] giving me a tough fight; it just looks as though every possible emotional disturbance has to happen to me be-fore I can finish a book.... By the way, Hyman sent me a lecture he gave on Negro writing and the folk tradition, in which he writes about the blues, but it was a very disappointing piece. He's so busy looking for African myth in the U.S. that he can't see what's before his eyes, even when he points out that African and Greek myths finally merge in that similar figures appear in both. He sees what he terms the "darky entertainer" i.e. characters like Stepin Fetchit—intelligent men hiding behind the stereotype—as the archetypal figure to writ-ing by Negroes—including mine. This figure, who he also terms a "smart-man-playing-dumb," he sees everywhere in Negro writing and I pointed out to him that that wasn't African, but American. That's Hemingway when he pretends to be a sportsman, or *only* a sportsman; Faulkner when he pretends to be a farmer; Benjamin Franklin when he pretended to be a "child of nature," instead of the hipped operator that he was; even Lincoln when he pretended to be a simple country lawyer. But Stanley, being Jewish and brought up to wear his intellect like a crown of jewels can't see this at all; he thinks mose had to get this mess from Africa when all he had to do was breathe the American air and he was ready to teach other Americans how it was done. But even as sheer method Stanley's approach is weak because he tries to discuss the novelist and folk tradition without discussing the novel, the form which is itself a depository of folk and other traditions reduced to formal order. I knew mose lore yes, but I didn't really know it until I knew something about literature and specifically the novel, then I looked at Negro folklore with a shock of true recognition. I was trying to write novels in the great tradition of the novel, not folk stories. The trick is to get mose lore *into* the novel so that it becomes a part of that tradition. Hell, Hyman don't know that Ulysses is both Jack the rabbit (when that cyclops gets after his ass) and Jack the Bear, Big Smith the Chef, John Henry and everybody else when he starts pumping arrows into those cats who've been after his old lady. Or if he does recognize this, it's only with his mind, not his heart. I was especially disappointed with his treatment of the blues, for while he lists a few themes he restricts their meaning to a few environmental circumstances: Mose can't rise vertically so he's restless; he can't get a good job here so he goes there—missing the fact that there is a metaphysical restless built into the American and mose is just another form of it, expressed basically, with a near tragic debunking of the self which is our own particular American style. I really thought I'd raised that boy better than that. But hell, I keep telling you that you're the one who has to write about those blues. The world's getting bluesier all the time, as Joe Williams and Count well know, and even though those Africans have Ghana they still haven't developed to the point where the blues start. Well, what bothers me about Stanley's piece is that after all his work and insight it seems to reveal a basic failure to understand the nature of metaphor, thus he can't really see that Bessie Smith singing a good blues may deal with experience as profoundly as Eliot, with the eloquence of the Eliotic poetry being expressed in her voice and phrasing. Human anguish is human anguish, love love; the difference between Shakespeare and lesser artists is eloquence but when Beethoven writes it it's still the same anguish, only expressed in a different medium by an artist of comparable eloquence. Which reminds me that here, way late, I've discovered Louis singing Mack the Knife. Shakespeare invented Caliban, or changed himself into him—

Who the hell dreamed up Louie? Some of the bop boys consider him Caliban but if he is he's a mask for a lyric poet who is much greater than most now writing. That's a mask for Hyman to study, me too; only I know enough not to miss my train[1] by messing around over looking over in Africa or even down in the West Indies. Hare *and* bear [are] the ticket; man and mask, sophistication and taste hiding behind clowning and crude manners—the American joke, man. Europeans dream of purity—*any* American who's achieved his American consciousness knows that it's a dream so he ain't never been innocent, he's been too busy figuring out his next move. It's just that the only time he ever comes out from behind that mask is when he's cornered—*that's* when you have to watch him. Unless, of course, he's Mose, who has learned to deal with a hell of a lot more pressure. Write about those blues, and love to the girls from me and Fanny.

Ralph

Watch that heart!

CASABLANCA, MAROC
6 JULY 1957

Dear Ralph,

I've been here in the hospital since the 6th of May. I feel fine now, and I've been feeling fine all the time, but as I told you they didn't like the electrocardiograph pattern I came up with on my annual physical. Well, they slapped me in for twenty days of complete bedrest followed by a very gradual reactivation, periodic electrocardiograms all along. The verdict: sometime since my last year's EKG I had a mild heart attack, so mild that I must have passed it off as indigestion or upset stomach and just forgot all about it. There seems to have been no other symptoms or evidence other than the EKG. No pain, normal blood pressure, normal pulse, no shortness of breath, no noticeable fatigue. Man, I thought I was just about fit. I knew that my waistline was beginning to go, that I needed to lose about 10 or 15 pounds, and that I needed more action, but other than that I figured that I was just 41, and so did the Flight Surgeon until he read my EKG a few days later.

[1] Ellison yarn, see footnote on page 155.

So it's just one of those unusually lucky cases where you just happen to take your annual when it really can do you some good. The Air Force Cardiologist for Europe has been down, and he said the doctor who called me in really did a brilliant job of diagnosis, because very few doctors would have spotted a case like this one.

So now I'm still in the hospital, but I spend the afternoons at home. Looks like it'll be about two more weeks of this and then they'll put me on convalescent leave, and then they say I'll be able to return to "normal" duty. So that's what's with me man, and it's all news to me so I'm just rolling with them.

Been doing a lot of reading, including Faulkner's *The Town,* which I thought was pretty good but not very good. Very amusing little book by Russell Lynes called *A Surfeit of Honey.* Schlesinger's *Age of FDR* vol. 1. Some stuff by a guy named Richard Bissell. Etc. Wish that I had been able to use some of all this time for writing but reading was about all I could manage between sedatives. Did sketch a couple of pretty solid episodes tho. Maybe I'll be able to write them during convalescent leave.

Man, old Duke just keeps hacking at it and keeps me busy sending to Sam Goody for his latest. His latest this time is a suite commissioned by some Shakespeare Festival group in Canada. It's called *Such Sweet Thunder* and seems to be based on a survey of S and includes such elements as Henry V, Sonnet for the Moor, Romeo and Juliet (Hodges), Lady Mac, Sonnet for Sister Kate, Anthony and Cleopatra and Puck. I had recently read in a French magazine they took this stuff into Town Hall on a program called Music for Moderns (which included a tonal concerto by Kurt Weill conducted by Mitropoulos) and broke it up. I'm sending for it today. Old Duke is subject to hit that shit yet, man.

Don't know when I'll be able to get that European trip in now. Really the best time would be late September and early October, but that will interfere with Mique & school. I wouldn't mind that so much, but since we rotate in February that means she would have to be out twice in one year. And if Mique has to stay here Moque has to stay too. Don't know yet how I'll have to work it out the main thing now is to finish this recovery.

Murray

Dear Ole Albert,

Here I was thinking that you and the girls were sweeping over Europe and you've been grounded all the time. That business of a *mild* heart attack makes me feel like the time I got in the fight with that Ringer character down at Tuskegee, I was so busy hitting him and trying to knock him out that I didn't realize that what he was hitting me with wasn't his fist but a 12 lb. lead pig. What's more, I didn't realize that I was bleeding until my roommate came in and said, "Man, leave that sonofabitch alone, you're bleeding like a stuck pig." Well, I hit him again and left him alone and I'm lucky that I did because he just might have got my true range. Anyway, the sight of my own blood was a surprising sight indeed. Actually, it sounds very typical of you to be hit by a heart attack, confuse it with an upset stomach and keep on jumping. I'm glad they caught you in time because I couldn't see you keeping still otherwise unless of course they broke your leg.

Things here are slack for the moment. Fanny sailed on the 23rd and most of my crop of Fellows have taken off for the states. This morning I'm going to get visas for my trip to Japan and it looks as though I'll stop in India in my way back here to give a couple of lectures on American Lit. before some Congress for Cultural Freedom groups in Bombay and New Delhi. It makes me tired just to think about it but I am fascinated as any mose by the Japanese. I'll take off about the 28th and will be there for 10 days but don't know how long I'll spend in India. Incidentally, if there's any camera junk you're interested in in Japan let me know and I'll try to bring it for you.... I'm still shooting but I've just about used up my supply of Plus X and I'm trying like hell to get a fresh supply before I leave here. Colorwise I'm not doing so good; this Roman light is red as hell and I haven't been able to get the proper filters to cool it down. The other thing is that I want to control my color shots more than I'm able to do now and I have neither the time nor the money with which to experiment.... I agree with you about Faulkner's THE TOWN, the stuff was much better as separate stories. Here ole Flem Snopes has become as respectable as Faulkner. I've been reading the papers of Dean Christian Gauss and have enjoyed his correspondence with Fitzgerald and Edmund Wilson. The correspondence with Wilson spans over thirty years and all of it interesting. We just didn't have teachers like that, man; and when I think of trying to write of some such relationship between a Tuskegee teacher and student, my mind, once M.D. is excepted, flies swiftly to satire, to the Impossible Interview caricatures on the old *Vanity Fair,* to burlesque. Old Gauss must have been an unusually warm and intelligent human being. Been rereading *Moby Dick* again and appreciating for the first time what a truly good time Melville was having when he wrote it. Some of it is quite funny and all of it is pervaded by the spirit of play, like real jazz sounds when a master is manipulating it. The thing's full of riffs, man; no wonder the book wasn't understood in its own time, not enough moses were able to read it!... Speaking of Jazz, I'm still knocking myself out with the tapes you sent. Indeed, more than ever, now that Fanny's gone; it's my only true atmosphere, yesterday the girl I grew up with from birth (she's the granddaughter of the old man in whose house I was born) showed up with her husband and thirteen year old son, and we spent the day talking about old times. Here some twenty-five years later she's trying to understand Charlie Christian and Lips Page and Pres,[1] who were all out there in the old days. She felt that their importance was an accident and thought that they didn't understand their influence, and I tried to explain how important they really were and how they were highly conscious artists. By birth and social status in the town she tends to look on jazz in terms of status, so I tried to get her to look at it as art and a universal language. Her husband, who is a physician and a good joe from Arkansas, can't understand Louie's appeal, was nevertheless impressed by the fact that everywhere he's been in Europe he sees big photographs of Louis and hears Europeans trying to play like him. So I lectured him about the universality of the jazz language—really not trying to impress the father, but to get the thirteen year old son moving in the right direction. It was quite amusing and you would have appreciated the irony. We were having dinner under a trellis where there were several Italian families having a lomo down home go at the vino and the food.

[1] Lester Young, who became famous as a tenor saxophone player with Count Basie.

There was an accordion player and several cats who thought they could sing and sometimes the family joined in and sang folk songs, and once in a while one of the young fellows ripped up the summer quiet with an aria from Verdi. Posturing like a non-bullfighter before a paper bull—all very local color and, with the laughter and family togetherness, pleasant to observe. But there *we* were talking about jazz and the world of music in which they'd lived but of which they'd been unaware. It's all the more ironic because she was a music major at Fisk and strove like a pilgrim striving for a piece of the true Cross to master that same music which the Italian family, including the little boys and girls, were throwing around with the same familiarity and impiety that you and I used to sing Before I'd Be a Slave I'd Be Dead and In My Grave—or Funky Butt. Dignity lies at home, and that's a fact. Well, they have loads of money—not n-rich, but *rich*, though you'd never know it by looking at them—and they're traveling and they have curiosity and are fast measuring their lives against what they see over here. That's all to the good for their lives will have become just a little more real. I spent the evening after they left playing Duke and went to bed feeling just a little less lonely. I'd heard the idiom and relived a bit of the past—which is really the same thing. One of the pleasant things I look forward to when I get home in late Sept. will be the chance to buy all those latest Dukes you've been writing about. The Shakespeare suite sounds intriguing. You know, one of these days I'm going to get ambitious and write an opera libretto and submit it to that guy. All the elements are floating around and I just might be able to write something wild enough and attractive enough to catch his attention. *Somebody* should do it because I'm sure that with a form to keep his imagination in bounds old Duke will surpass himself. *You* might think in those terms too. I'm going to give Weill a good hard look just to see what was really happening and I'm planning to get back to my old preoccupation with the ceremonial form of the Negro church to see if there's anything usable there. Recently I've been listening to a bit of Stravinsky every day and a bit of Webern and the younger boys who are on that kick. Listening to the latter it is easy to see why guys are trying to compose with tape recorders; much of what they do sounds like tape played backwards at a speed that is slower than that at which it was recorded. Well, outside my window there are a couple of birds making a sound like that of dice rattling away in a leather cup and I don't dig it; but maybe if I listen long enough I'll understand they're playing the dirty dozens or quoting the Empson of the birds—upon which feathers will sprout out from behind and I too will learn to fly; sans Pegasus, sans motor, sans rhythm, sans every dam thing.... I've just learned about the fabulous father of a girl who graduated from high school in my class. When a young man he killed a man and escaped to sea, living on board ship for ten years without going ashore out of fear of capture. Later he came to Oklahoma (right after statehood), married and went to work at the packing house. Since then he's raised and educated two families and now, at ninety, he has a young wife and the first child of a third family. They tried to retire the old coot but he refused and works a full day and goes home at the end of the day and starts working on those baby boys he swears he's going to have before he racks up his balls and stands his pool cue in the final rack! I thought I was simply lying when I started creating old Love, but here's a mister who is more fabulous than fiction!

If this goes on any longer it will become more sedatious than a sedative, so now I'll stop it. Take care and rest, none of us can spare you for any serious bit of time and you're my most satisfactory correspondent. In fact I'm going through a phase quite like that I underwent at Tuskegee. I tend to push people away from me and I don't want to waste time with unessentials. You're the only one I really write to and, other than a wild, Russian chick of a girl whose now in the states and who wouldn't write home for eating change, my only friend. So rest, man and sketch out some more of those episodes. Love to lovable Mokable and Miqueable, from Ralphable.

As ever,
Ralph

6 AUGUST 1957

Dear Ralph,
Received yours today & I hope that this is in the mail to you tomorrow. Better news about myself this time. Am now back at work (half day for 2 weeks & then another check up). Had a checkup at the end

of my convalescent leave on Monday and the results were good: my electrocardiogram has returned to normal. In summary things are actually better than my last report probably indicated. They are pretty sure they have got it defined now and it is under control. A mild strain of one of the heart muscles (myocardial infarction), not severe enough to give *me* any indications but enough to throw the EKG off, and of course serious enough to require serious medical attention (rest). The only medicine I took was a mild sedative, but meanwhile, papa, they were running tests on me for everything (they X-rayed everything including my head!). They've taken plenty of time, but they say that I'll be able to return to "normal" activity by the end of September. Went on a diet and hacked off 23 lbs & now I'm back to NYU & Paris weight (how the hell did I let all that fat accumulate?) No restrictions on types of food etc, but from now on I should always keep my weight around 155 or a little below. No other restrictions except to be reasonably moderate about exertion & late hours. Man, I told them I didn't intend to hit a lick at a snake for the next 50 or 60 years.

So it seems that I should be able to get up to Europe in October. Anyway, I'm beginning to make plans again. Maybe I can swing a two-week deal for myself in October and also get back with Moque & Mique during the school break at Xmas.

Feeling pretty good about myself but pretty depressed about that goddamned jury trial victory just scored with the aid of them cowboys and befuddled yankees. How could they let themselves be out maneuvered by Russell and Johnson like that. Goddamnit they KNEW they were coming and they should have been ready. I'm inclined to agree with those who blame the fizzle out on Ike's failure [to] really push the thing. What the hell is the use of having all that charisma if you ain't going to use it for the fundamental things. I still say that old Truman will rank with the very best of them when it comes to the role of the presidency in dealing with fundamentals.

That trip of yours really sounds good, all that and India too. Have been thinking about trying to get to Japan myself, but it would have to be a 36 month deal, so I think I'd better get the gals back home and think about it from there. But now that we're beginning to cut back our troops over there it's strictly a matter of chance. Knock yourself out, man. Wish the hell you'd told me about your film situation earlier. I probably could've got some through the mail to you. Now I don't know whether we can make it in time. I'll see what I can do.

By the way, what the hell are your plans for returning to the US, and how the hell is Fanny?

Albert

ROME, ITALY
AUGUST 17, 1957.

Dear Albert,

Your last letter did a lot to cheer me up and then when Paul[1] blew in with the Plus X and reported that you were up and about I felt even better. I was on my way to get the second of my series of shots and thus had only a few minutes with him and his friend, both of whom wished to yak about Invisible. I was sorry that it had to be so brief but this trip is leaping forward now and any little simple thing becomes enormously complicated here in Rome. And it's all the more compli-cated now that Fanny is back in the States; I'm still getting my own meals and the shopping is the very dregs, you kill most of a morning just getting the stuff from the many small stores among which its scat-tered. I'll be glad to get back to N.Y. and a little simple efficiency; yes, and a little honesty among merchants. Here you can spend loads of lire with a guy and he'll try to short-change you fifty lira. They don't seem to understand that Americans won't accept that crap. The amount of accepted corruption in this society is amazing. Well, it's their world and they deserve it, I'm getting further, I just want some dewy-eyed sonofabitch to tell [me] *now* how superior Europe is.... Anyway Fanny left for home on the 23rd of June and must be up to her neck in getting adjusted because I haven't heard from her as yet. Actually we didn't know where she would make port since she's on a freighter but I expect to hear as soon as the mail starts breaking the log-jam created by the long Italian August festa, as for me, I'm check-

---

[1] Paul Brown, an old Tuskegee classmate of Murray's en route to Rome by way of Casablanca.

ing out of here on the 28th for Japan and I've already started packing to make for home, once I return here. Thanks for the film, I had just bought some medium speed Agfa which I haven't had a chance to try, however I understand it's pretty good and, in bulk it's not too expensive. I loaded my last Anscochrome and discovered that I only had three rolls, so I'm going to pick up some Kodachrome in Japan. This time I'm taking only the Leica and plan to do the best I can with it.... I've been reading about the mess in Alabama and it appears that the crackers have gone a little more mad than usual. As for Ike and the Republicans, I'm afraid that they're playing some rather stupid half-assed politics. I'm getting quite sick of it and whenever I read about these southern senators being such noble characters, à la *Time,* I want to load up a sock with shit and go to work on the editors and publisher. There is something so immoral and rotten in those characters that any attempt to perfume them leads to the corruption of language; and if Russell of Georgia is the most skillful man in the Senate then it's because most of our political leaders don't have the guts to oppose him and are too busy fattening on the swill he's allowed to brew out of democracy. Now I read that Joe MC. is being praised in the Senate!

I've just finished a novel by James Gould Cozzens, *By Love Possessed,* which, except for a certain pompousness in the leading character, is well worth the reading. It hasn't been published yet but it probably will win the National Book Award. Cozzens is a pro and he's grabbed the forms of love and given them an examination that's right down the line, *and* he sees what I've had occasion to point out, that democracy is, or should be, the most disinterested form of love. I've also read Wright Morris' new short novel, *Love Among the Cannibals.* It's a satire and I think he's kidding the "novel-of-manners" boys, and the book isn't to be taken seriously.... I've read several negative reviews of the Newport Jazz shakedown, it seems that they brought in that creep Eartha Kitt and some non-jazz dancers and Louis was wearing his ass instead of his genius. The whole circus sounds as though it was rather limp. I guess you can't throw too many musicians and hep cats manqué together too many times and have it come out listenable. Anyway, Duke wasn't there, I picked up a Columbia recording of his titled *Duke's Mixture,* on which there is a version of Do Nothing, The

Mooch, How High the Moon, & The Hawk Talks. Some are old, some new but all good Duke. Man, you just wait until I get my foot in Sam Goody's door again! Which reminds me, I'm writing for that belt for your turn table and I'll have them mail it directly to you. In the meantime, try washing the one you have; it's nylon. Actually, any piece of ribbon of that width should work until the real thing comes. If you're real desperate have Mokie sew together a piece of ribbon and simply turn the seam to the outside. They've only just gotten the cabinets completed for the set I'm putting together for the academy and I made the mistake of putting the business together temporarily last Sun. so that one of the composers could catch the broadcast of the Hindemith opera. I gave up my evening because I thought the sonofabitch was working and he comes late *and* with several friends. I was annoyed to say the least; but yesterday at lunch I almost threw a plate of spaghetti in the fool's face when he insisted that I put the units together again just for him. I'm working on the thing so that it will be working and out of my hands before I leave for Japan but this punk thinks I'm going too slow—when I've been waiting to complete the thing since I selected the equipment in N.Y. last Oct. I was mad enough to walk the table. When done it will be a fine set but I've got to try to anticipate all the damn fool things such guys are apt to do to it because there are no dealers in Italy and I don't trust the technicians here. These boys are going to wreck this system as quickly as they can but I won't be here to hear about it. My belly fills with acid when I just think about it.... I'll try to write before I take off but if there's anything you want let me know before the 28th. As plans go now I will return here sometime about the middle of Sept. and get off for home as quickly as possible. I don't have the passage yet and I'm trying to save by going freighter, nevertheless I want to be back on the Drive by late Oct at the mostest.

Hi to Mokie and Mique

best,

Ralph

Dear Albert,

I've been back just over a week and have been so busy trying to ship out of here that I haven't had time to write. As it is it looks as though I'll have to stay here until the 3rd of Nov. when I'll ship for Naples. I had been counting on taking a freighter but it didn't pan, so here I am, on the pot but doing no business.... Japan was so exciting that if I could go back tomorrow I'd leap. I spent 14 days there and took in as much of that modern-ancient civilization as I could cram. They're an efficient people—which is always a pleasure to encounter after these slackassed Romans—and dam near everything they touch takes on beautiful form. They've taken the Western way, especially the American, and done something of their own with it. When you visit one of their houses you realize what Mies van der Rohe and Philip Johnson are trying to get at with their frigid designs, but they miss it a mile. A Japanese house is austere but it's also warm; reduced to essentials not by hacking but by blending, brewing, testing until that which is left out is not only the least that is necessary but also the most aesthetically satisfying. I'll have more to say about Japan later, right now it's enough to say that I knocked myself out (traded my Summaron wide-angle for a Nikkor 35 mm fl.8 plus $27.00) and that was the best part of the trip. And, because the smug Indians who make so many moral noises discriminate against writers, I had to skip my trip there except for an 8 hr. wait between planes in Calcutta; and went to Hong Kong. Spent three days there being entertained with two other Congress of Cultural Freedom writers and acting like a hungry dog on a meat wagon over all those beautiful women. I simply didn't know about the Chinese, man; those girls have figures that are the most beautiful I have ever seen, and complexions! Tell Mokie to keep you away from there, they'd drive you nuts. No kidding they *are* lovely and Hong Kong is an exciting international city and I want to return. But as for Calcutta, no sir; too depressing with thousands sleeping on the sidewalks, cows wandering in the downtown sections of a city of 8 million, crowds parading behind the red flag. I was glad to get out of there, even though I was going to lecture in Karachi, which was only a little better, for it too has its refugees from the division between India and Pakistan. I lectured at the University in the late afternoon and returned to my hotel to be introduced to a bunch of white Fullbrighters from 'Bama and had a bitch from Montgomery try to tell me how wonderful things were there until the N.A.A.C.P. and the Supreme Court dropped the shuck. I then had to tell her that I was from down that way and how different the facts of life looked from our side of the line. She didn't like it but she started talking sense, or at least she tried. I won't say too much about Arkansas,[1] I've got a belly full of acid already and it isn't even nine a.m. I ran into it all the way back to Rome and I've been having guys stop me on the street to tell me how bad it is. The communists have used the shot of that girl being jeered and spat upon in a poster which they've plastered about the city. Well, it smoked Ike out and it showed that that mose who put the question of the use of force to Stevenson out there in California was talking about a basic issue. Now I want to see someone charge Russell and those other wild talking motherfuckers with treason because it is exactly the name for what they're playing with. In the end tolerating those guys is as bad as tolerating communist subversion, for they are just as damaging. I flew with two fellows from Pakistan as far as Rome and they simply wouldn't have anything to do with whites—even though they were on their way to London for business. One told me that 'these whites don't like people of our color.' I didn't have the heart to argue with him, the news photos would have made me sound silly.... So that's that. I shot some color in Japan and in Hong Kong which I'll show you when we get together again. Unfortunately it was raining most of the time we were in Kyoto, which is the old capital and most beautiful. Still I shot color there and in Bangkok, where I spent a day. You know, I've been seeing American tourists in Europe for several years now and I agree that some of us can be outrageous, but after traveling with a plane of Frenchmen the Americans rate as gentlemen. I've never been on a nastier flight, the plane disordered and filthy as a

---

[1] Governor Orville Faubus's resistance to the court's desegregation order prompted President Eisenhower, finally, to send federal troops to Little Rock in September 1957.

Macon County outhouse, pushing and shoving at points of boarding and landing; and general rudeness to their hosts. For a while I didn't even want to hear the language spoken again. Then I met Malraux's first wife and became friendly with her and had several conversations with her. She invited me to visit her and their daughter the next time I'm in Paris and introduced me to the Japanese writer at whose home she was staying, and he told me a drink-inspired confidence that he was the original of the character Kyo in *Man's Fate*. Later I was told that there was some truth in this and I wanted to talk to him further about those days but the next time he was sober and reluctant to talk. Clara Malraux is a pleasant woman and I shall look her up, as should you, when I'm in Paris again. She certainly served to remind me of the more pleasant side of France at a time when I was deciding upon which French jaw I would smash with my fist. Cotton field Negroes could teach that crew manners.

Hope things go well with you all. Fanny is fine and back at work with her old firm—and that's all there is to tell just now. Take care of yourself and give my love to the girls.

Ralph Ellison

> *HQ SAMAE*
> *APO # 30*
> *NEW YORK*
> *20 JAN 58*

Dear Ralph,

What the hell's going on over there? Last thing I heard you were heading that way, but as yet we've had no report of your arrival & subsequent doings. Didn't know but what you might've used the old Casa address, which is no longer functional. As for myself, I've been sweating out my new station assignment. The TWX came in this afternoon, and M&M are pretty pleased tonight. We drew just about what they were hoping for: Long Beach, California. Sounds pretty good to me too. I'm to be located at the MUNICIPAL Airport (Not Air Force Base), and I shall be working in the Reserve Training Program. Seems that I shall be specifically concerned with Public Relations. Just the sort of thing I've been wanting to have a try at.

So as things stand now, I expect to leave here by boat on March 3rd and arrive N.Y. about six or seven days later. Name of the boat is the DARBY. It's MSTS (Military Sea Transport) but it'll be listed among the arrivals in the *Times*. Boat is the only way to get back via NY. Air returnees land in Charleston, SC, of all the goddamned places. Shipping the Ford back, so I have to come to NY to pick it up anyway. Decided I ain't putting my money into nobody's new car for a year or so yet. Man, when I think of all that loot this thing looks better & better. And rides better than a Cad—because it's paid for.

Mentioned my October trip to Bavaria, Copenhagen, London, etc. Well, we started '58 with a trip to Wiesbaden and Zurich. We were there for only a few days, but it was definitely worth the money. Hoping to get in one more shopping trip to Gibraltar, and then I'm unassing the area. By the way, if you and Fanny want anything from there or here let me know right away. As I probably mentioned, Gib is the place for clothes: Cashmere sweater sets (women) $32.00; Daks slacks (men) $15 to $18; Daks suits $45. Burberry weatherproofs $32 (top quality); Harris Tweed Sport Coats $18.50; a month or so getting them if I ship them with the furniture, and I want to take them to Tuskegee with me. At the moment I'm just itching to add that new f2.8 Rollei to my operating equipment before I check out. Am also thinking about Braun Hobby electronic flash.

Do you know anybody who writes under the name Ed Lacy. I just finished a whodunit by him. Negro Sam Spade–Phillip Marlowe. Very good pulp. Worth a couple of hours. I definitely do not share the prevailing enthusiasm for James Gould Cozzens. You say he is an old pro, and I say that's all. I'll take Warren, for example, over that bastard, both as a craftsman and as a groping moralist.

But what's with you, man? Start filling me in on the ZI (Zone of the Interior, as they say in Military Personnel). Be seeing you before too much longer, but in the meantime write.

Murray

M/N "GIULIO CESARE"

"ITALIA"   730 RIVERSIDE DRIVE,
SOCIETA DI NAVIGAZIONE   NEW YORK, NY
GENOVA   FEB. 6, 1958

Dear Albert:

Pardon this paper, I'm still trying to get my money's worth out of that lousy trip home on that lousy Italian Line—which I'll never do, because the only way to beat an Italian business man is to kick his nasty ass. But don't let me get started on all that. I arrived on the 14th of Nov., dead tired, broke, and scrambled up inside. My personal life got fairly keyed up last year, which explains some of the scrambling but that must wait until you come here. The rest of it and most of it, has had to do with readjusting, not to my work, but to my place of work; and to a certain modification of conception which returning home has forced upon me. As you can guess, I'm impatient to get through, would like to cut down some of the ambition of this job, but am in so damn deep that I've got to fight it through to the end. It might be an egg but it'll have to be the same egg I conceived two years ago. Otherwise, we're still here at the old stand, doing the best we can. Fanny's well and sassy and keeping busy as hell and I feel pretty good except for the fact that I'm losing that lean look I had when I returned—which isn't all to the good, because I felt much better. I've got to get some exercise.... The news that you landed just where you wanted to go pleases us no end, though I'd hoped that you'd land a little closer to New York. I'll watch out for your arrival and I'm damn sorry that I haven't been able to get the old New Yorker into operation so that I could pick you up, but insurance, battery and licenses are too big a load at the moment because they can't be spread out now that insurance is compulsory. I don't blame you for not investing in a new car, this whole business has gone mad. I've a perfectly good car but I doubt if I could get five hundred dollars for it on today's market; those fins have offended more than my aesthetic sense, they've clobbered my investment. In the meantime ship whatever you wish here and I'll be glad to take care of anything I can. Sorry I can't invest in any of those Gib clothes and it's dam lucky that I picked up a trench coat in Hong

Kong because this wind around the building has no pity. Get the 2.8 Rollei over there, man, because even with all the competition here, they're much too high. I could have bought one with all the attachments from a friend for $200 two months ago but not only did I not have the dough, I'm concentrating on the 35 mm. Haven't been shooting too much here, though; too busy. We spent a weekend with Warren and Eleanor recently and I took a couple of rolls of the crowd of us playing with sleds but have still to have them developed. Actually, I'm waiting to set up a dark room so that I can save the costs. Perhaps I'll set it up at Sarser's, he's got a lot of free space.... I know what you mean about the Cozzens, I was enthusiastic to see a guy bearing down on that particular subject and though I had my reservations about his prissy hero and certain aspects of his style, it wasn't until I started to read the wild shouts of the reviewers that I got down off condescension and looked carefully at the book. He shot off his mouth about Faulkner and Hem. and that made me mad (I could forgive him his opinion of Negroes). He's not in their class and should know by now that anybody can shoot off his mouth but that you have to *write* a novel and after it's written people will know whether you can write or not and who your peers are. Certainly he's no moralist, and I suspect that he doesn't really realize what a shit his hero is even though he's professional enough to know that he had to let the guy undergo a reversal so that the plot could be completed. More about this when you get here. As for Warren I like him better the more I see of him. We spent a very pleasant time with them and I let Eleanor bluff me onto a pair of skis and found that I not only liked it but have a knack for it. I guess the sense of balance developed by hitching on to cars on roller skates, or standing atop moving boxcars remains with me. Anyway, I had enough of it to understand why people are attracted to it, it would be like me to get this old and start messing around with something I should have done ten years ago. Warren's fine and working on another novel. He'll probably win the National Book Award for his last poems.

You know, I'm sticking so close that there's little that I know about the ZI.[1] The crackers are still acting up and Ike and a lot of Republi-

---

[1] "Zone of the Interior," overseas military term for the United States.

cans and Democrats would feel a lot better if they could just forget about Mose, but Mose is still pressing. I've heard that some of the leaders in the struggle are suffering from a lack of ideas of where to go after the legal struggle is won. There's been a let-down, and I suspect that they're really better at counter-punching than at working out broad strategies. But don't get me started in that, the sonsabitches are so provincial that they can't see that we have a hell of a lot of advantages beyond the mere legal. I received Foster's report from Tuskegee the other day, and they're talking of establishing a cultural center but from the sketch of the architecture they propose they haven't realized that they could really change the cultural life of Alabama if they'd forget the cracker bullshit and act like responsible, culturally advanced Americans—Not that many of them are, but they certainly could get people down there who are. Mann[2] just phoned from Idle on his way to Africa. I suggested a few people whom he might see in Rome but I doubt that he'll have time. . . . I was at a *PR* party recently and ran into Kappy,[3] who is now stationed in D.C., family and all. His son is permanently deaf from the fall he had. He sends regards. Bellow is on a ten weeks teaching stint out at Northwestern, and has been rolling smoothly towards the finish of another novel. He and Sandra have an old house up near Bard College and a handsome, intelligent 11 month son, both of which I envy him a slight bit. We were there for a weekend and liked very much the manner in which they're working out their lives. They've been doing some of the work on the old house themselves (it dates from the 17th century) and are making it quite comfortable. Actually there's room for at least two families, and plenty of ground for the kids to play. There is quite a lot of game in that section and when we were there it was lousy for deer hunters. . . . I think Lacy is someone I used to know but I'm not sure but will check. . . .

As for me I'm working hard now both with the novel and on a piece which Hyman feinted me into doing. You'll recall my description on his piece of Negro literature and the folk tradition, well, he sent my letter to *PR* along with his article and I was placed in the position of

[2] William Mann, an architect friend of Albert Murray's from Tuskegee.
[3] H. J. Kaplan, Paris correspondent for *Partisan Review*.

writing a commentary or letting some of his glib confusion go unanswered. For some reason he thought I was furious about his goddam piece and it wasn't until I saw it again after I returned to N.Y. that I understood why: If you label the archetypical role in Negro writing "Darky entertainer" you imply that this is also the symbolic role played by Negro writers. For to an extent a writer's characters are surrogates of his own personal preoccupations, symbols of his own psychological role. Stanley equates the 'darky entertainer' with a 'smart man playing dumb,' which is way the hell off too, and only reveals that he's so fascinated with the machinery of his method that he doesn't bother to see that in my own book at least, the narrator does any[thing] *but* play dumb, either vocally or intellectually. He writes a memoir, he orates, rants and sings for over five hundred pages. So now I am annoyed, not only because this is taking up valuable time, but because I thought this guy knew better. Actually he isn't at all interested in novels but in neat demonstrations that archetypical figures turn up in various places. I think that he's going to be hurt by my essay but I'm just dam tired of guys who are more interested in anthropology monkeying with the novel. These fucks are so impressed that Joyce used myth to organize *Ulysses,* and they miss completely the fact that for all a novelist's interest in folklore or myth, he uses it as a novelist, not as an anthropologist or a teller of folktales…. Hurry home, you all we miss you and it'll be pleasant if Mique and Mokie can hit N.Y. with you. Give them our love.

Ralph

III

LOS ANGELES
AND
NEW YORK
1958-1960

At the end of my two-and-a-half years' tour of duty in Morocco, I was transferred to the Air Reserve Flying Center at Long Beach Municipal Airport in Long Beach, California, where between April 1958 and January 1961 I was officer in charge of personnel services until 1960, and then after returning from a special twelve-week course for Air Force supply officers at Amarillo Air Force Base at Amarillo, Texas, I was made base accountable officer. In this capacity, I became the officer who signed the final document closing the Air Force Reserve Flying Center at Long Beach Municipal Airport in 1961.

I was then transferred to Headquarters Air Base Wing of the Air Force Systems Command at Hanscom Field in Bedford, Massachusetts, my last active-duty station, from which I moved to New York and finally settled into a full-time career as a writer, beginning with the articles and reviews that became *The Omni-Americans* (1970), followed by *South to a Very Old Place* (1971), which grew out of an assignment by *Harper's*. Then I formulated a statement of my conception of the blues as a definitive source of American fiction in *The Hero and the Blues* (1973), which was published by the University of Missouri Press after I presented it in three sessions of the Paul Anthony Brick Lecture Series in 1972.

The fictional material that I refer to from time to time in letters to Ellison was finally worked into the novels *Train Whistle Guitar* (1974), *The Spyglass Tree* (1991), *The Seven League Boots* (1996), and my current novel-in-progress, *The Magic Keys,* a further extension of the same narrative.

When Ralph came back home in the autumn of 1957, he finished writing his response to Stanley Hyman's paper on black American writing, published as "Change the Joke and Slip the Yoke" in *Partisan Review* (Spring 1958), began teaching at Bard College at Annandale-on-Hudson, New York, and also began writing magazine articles about jazz, beginning with a long piece about the origin of bebop, "The Golden Age, Time Past," for a special jazz issue of *Esquire* (Spring 1959). Other jazz pieces written during this period were "The Charlie Christian Story" (about the legendary Oklahoma City guitar player) for *Saturday Review*, May 7, 1958; and "Remembering Jimmy" (about the famous Oklahoma City/Count Basie blues singer) Jimmy Rushing, for *Saturday Review*, July 12, 1958. The appearance of Mahalia Jackson at the Newport Jazz Festival as guest artist with Duke Ellington in July 1958 was the occasion for another article for *Saturday Review* (September 27, 1958). These essays would all appear in Part II of *Shadow and Act* (1964) under the title "Sound and the Mainstream."

Along with all of this, the work on the second novel continued with new characters coming onstage and old characters developing new dimensions. In fact, he was pleased enough with the way the plot was coming into focus that in 1960 he edited several episodes into a long sequence called "And Hickman Arrives," published in *Noble Savage*, a new literary journal edited by Saul Bellow. Until his death in 1994, Ralph continued to write and struggle with the second novel. The parts of the novel grew and multiplied, but it is worth noting that the 1960 sequence formed the heart of the narrative edited into *Juneteenth* (1999) by John Callahan.

When I settled in New York and turned my full attention to the literary material that I had been accumulating over the years, my first published item was a long review of several books that *Life* asked me to do because Ralph had suggested that one of the literary editors get in touch with me. It was also upon his generous recommendation that editor Myron Kolatch asked me to do reviews for *The New Leader*. My collegial relationship with Ralph was also to lead to my personal and professional relationship with Willie Morris, who as editor in chief of *Harper's* not only published an episode from my novel *Train Whistle Guitar* but also gave me the assignment that turned into *South to a Very Old Place*.

A.M.

During these years and over the next two decades Murray and Ellison lived close enough to see each other frequently and be in touch by phone. They last saw each other on Ellison's eightieth birthday, March 1, 1994, at a small dinner hosted by Random House, where through Albert's toast and Ralph's response the two old friends traded twelves for the last time.

J.F.C.

2347ᵀᴴ AIR RESERVE FLYING CENTER
LONG BEACH MUNICIPAL AIRPORT
LONG BEACH, CALIFORNIA

15 MAY 1958

Dear Ralph,

The trip down to Tuskegee was smooth and uneventful. The stay there left me somewhat depressed in spite of the large number of really wonderful friends we spent most of our time with. Foster is a shrinking man, and the school is shriveling up as sure as hell. I couldn't find one encouraging sign anywhere. Even the political situation was somewhat disillusioning. Very very few of them have any idea what they are really doing. I realize of course that you don't just have to have a whole gang of intellectuals to get effective political actions or programs, but you do have to have leaders or a leader, and if they have one nobody knows who the hell it is. Gomillion[1] sure ain't. Naturally Luther ain't. You know very well all of the old elements and different levels of antagonisms always at work there. Well, I couldn't find any evidence that ANYTHING has been transcended. In other words, it looks suspiciously like them Tuskegee Negroes decided to show them moses in Montgomery, and as yet they haven't gotten very much further. Time will tell, but meanwhile all they're doing is counting a very weak cadence. Man, with the situation down there what it is now, they don't really even have to have the offensive. All they needed is a good counterpunch, and they could win on points, what with them crackers swinging not only wild but blind.

---

[1] Charles Gomillion, Tuskegee teacher who brought a significant civil rights suit against the city of Tuskegee, *Gomillion vs. Lightfoot*, and won.

The trip out here was no sweat either. We came by way of OK City & 66. Wonderful weather all the way except for several hours of snow around Flagstaff, Arizona.

We are still temporarily situated in a furnished apt. Our household goods have arrived, but we are not starting to look for a house until school is out. By the way, the month's lay-off seems to have had a positive effect on Miss Mique. Already she is making higher grades than ever before.

So far what I've seen of this part of California has been mostly boomtown stuff, a big shiny supermarket, even the homes & gardens seem to have been bought in a supermarket. Of the places I've seen, prefer Pasadena & several other places farther out, all too far to commute.

The piece on Charlie Christian was very fine. Saw the electronic piece too. You're going good. Wish you would use some of that recent stuff by Jimmy Rushing as a springboard for a background piece on him and that particular aspect of the blues.

What are you doing for the summer? After we find a house and get settled, I hope to get up to San Francisco and down to Mexico. Also keeping on the alert for a chance to get back to the East Coast at Air Force expense.

Love to Fanny from me and the gals.
Albert.

1515 WEST 166ᵀᴴ STREET
COMPTON, CALIFORNIA
22 AUGUST 58

Dear Ralph,

What in the hell are you Ellisons doing these days? We are still in the process of getting settled into a house we invested in last month. We are just about midway between downtown L.A. & Beach front L.B., about 15 minutes one way and 20 the other. We like it out here, but we're not really enthusiastic. There's a lot here. You can't knock production. But ain't much really happening with it, man. When I remember all the poverty I know about, I can't help being impressed with the abundance of material goods. But I must confess that it is also somewhat disturbing to see so many ignorant people with so much.

Certainly we have this same feeling about Texas Millionaires, but I'm talking about average people. I certainly don't wish to imply that they should have less, but I can't help wishing that it all really tended to add up to something. Ralph these sons of bitches are all tangled up in automobiles, lawn mowers, and supermarkets. I'm talking about my impression of L.A. I understand that Frisco is much better. We go there on a visit in a week or so.

Man, you never seen so much "flesh and blood" in all your life. Harlem, sure. But in Harlem it's all stacked up, vertical. Out here it's lateral. Man, you can drive for an hour or so in any number of sections of this town and 90% of what you will see will be flesh and blood. I guess what you saw in Chicago must have been something like this. But this shit is not cubic feet; this is flat square acreage.

I'm sure you remember old Frank D. Godden. Well, here he is out here operating in Real Estate just [like] he used to operate that Special Delivery deal back at Tuskegee, looking just as keen toed, shark skinned, sloped shouldered and shifty eyed as he did when I first saw him back in 1935. Saw old Bill Parker a week or so ago, too. He's in Psychiatric Social work. Says old Sidney is still teaching school in Richmond.

Have been up to my usual tricks of scooting around. Saw Patterson put knots on Harris last week.[1] Free box seats for the military. Harris never acted like he thought he had even the remotest chance to win. What Patterson needs is more "antagonistic cooperation."

I don't have time to finish this, but let's have at least a line from you real soon. Figure you might have lost my other address. Use the one up right.

The gals are OK and send love.

Albert

---

[1] Floyd Patterson knocked out Roy Harris in the thirteenth round to retain his World Heavyweight Championship.

BARD COLLEGE
ANNANDALE-ON-HUDSON, NY
SEPT. 28, 1958.

Dear Albert,

The Ellisons are shookup like everyone else, I suppose, but otherwise we're about the same. I've been intending to write but ran into a busy summer of writing and fighting, of all things I don't need, the hayfever. I finished a long piece on Minton's Playhouse[1] for *Esquire*'s special Jazz issue, which is due in Jan. and that took quite a lot of time running around and trying to talk to those screwedup musicians, drinking beer so that I could listen to their miserable hard-bopping noise (defiance with both hands protecting their heads) and finally realizing that I could write the piece without their help; for after all most of them simply know that they're dissatisfied and that they want fame and glory and to be themselves (or Charlie Parker—which would be even better because most have only that which they've copied from him as miserable, beat and lost as *he* sounded most of the time—but hell, they believe in the witchdoctor's warning: If Bird shits on you, wear it). And anyway they suspect, and rightly, that they *ain't* nobody. Man, I wished for you during the Newport festival. I was asked up to participate in the critics symposium and went up there and put the bad mouth on a lot of the characters. I wouldn't be a jazz critic for love or money, but I discovered that I have quite a number of fans who think that's what I've been doing for the *SRL*. So I had my say the first two days and spent the rest of the time looking and listening and a hell of a lot of it was simply pathetic. I finally saw that Chico Hamilton with his mannerisms and that poor, evil, lost little Miles Davis, who on this occasion sounded like he just couldn't get it together. Nor did Coltrane help with his badly executed velocity exercises. These cats have gotten lost, man. They're trying to get hold to something by fucking up the blues, but some of them don't even know the difference between a blues and a spiritual—as was the case of Horace Silver who went wanging away like a slightly drunken gospel

---

[1] Harlem jazz club that sponsored jam sessions, out of which emerged a new dimension of jazz, bebop.

group after announcing a blues. Monk, who is supposed to be nuts, got up on stage and outplayed most of the modern boys and was gracious and pleasant while doing so. But Bird had crapped on most of the saxophonists, who try to see how many notes they can play in a phrase and how many "changes," as they like to call their chord progressions, they can cram into even the most banal melodic idea. There was even a cat there trying to play Bird on a Tuba. He was spitting like a couple of tom cats fighting over a piece of tail and that poor ole tuba was wobbling like an elephant with a mouse doing a Lindyhop up and down inside his long nose hole. Taste was an item conspicuously missing from most of the performances, and once again I could see that there's simply nothing worse than a half-educated Mose unless it's a Mose jazz-modernist whose convinced himself that he's a genius, maybe the next Beethoven, or at least Bartok, and who's certain that he's the only Mose jazzman who has heard the classics or attended a conservatory. Duke didn't do much up there but it was easy to see why. These little fellows are scrambling around trying to get something new; Duke is *the* master of a bunch of masters and when the little boys hear him come on they know that they'll never be more than a bunch of little masturbators and they don't want to think about it. I was at a party given by Columbia Records at the Plaza recently, where they presented Duke, Miles Davis, Jimmy Rushing and Billie Holiday and it was murder. Duke signified on Davis all through his numbers and his trumpeters and saxophonists went after him like a bunch of hustlers in a Georgia skin game fighting with razors. Only Cannonball Adderley sounded as though he might have some of the human quality which sounds unmistakably in the Ellington band. And no question of numbers was involved. They simply had more to say and a hundred more ways in which to say it. I told Jimmy that I'd hoped to hear him sing with Duke but was afraid it would never happen. It was one of those occasions when the whole band was feeling like playing and they took off behind him and it was like the old Basie band playing the Juneteenth ramble at Forest Park in Okla. City. Duke left for Europe Mon. for the first time in about ten years and invited us to join the mob of fans, writers, and friends who were there to see them off. They served champagne, which helped offset the rainy morning but it didn't stop Duke from talking that gooie bullshit which he feels forced to spread. Great man until he opens his mouth. They did the number he wrote for the Great South Bay festival at the Plaza and it sounded well constructed and generally interesting. Watch out for it.... This business of writing on jazz is quite interesting. Quite a lot of fan mail goes with it and while some of the younger "critics" are friendly, some of the others react as though I'm moving into their special preserve. Old John Wilson of the *Times* won't even acknowledge my presence at the various publicity gatherings—which amuses me to no end, since we aren't playing the same game anyway. At Newport, one of the critic-composers interrupted some remark I made concerning the relationship between Negro dance audiences and jazz bands, to say that he didn't believe that Jazz was connected with the life of any racial group in this country—but when one of his numbers was played by the International Youth band, a Swedish boy stood up and tried to play Bubber Miley on a trumpet and the voicing was something copied from Duke. I really don't have much patience anymore, Albert, and I didn't bite my tongue in telling this guy where he came from and who his daddy was—who his *black* daddy was. I don't fight the race problem in matters of culture but anyone should know the source of their tradition before they start shooting off their mouth about where jazz comes from.

It looks as though I'll have enough pieces before long to form part of a book and in the meantime it gives me a chance to earn a buck. *Esquire* is interested in anything I do, article or story. If you have anything you should send it to Harold Hayes and mention my name. There is a young crowd there these days who are trying to raise its standard and I think they should be encouraged—especially since they're paying dam well. On the ninth they're running a symposium on fiction along with Columbia University and I'm being paid fifty bucks just to be there just in case someone doesn't show—in which case I'll get five hundred and I'm not even bothering to prepare notes.... And what am I doing up here? I'm living in Bellow's house while they are away at Minn. and when I'm not struggling with my novel, I'm working on my notes for that single class in the American novel which I'm teaching at Bard College: I go to campus only once a week, and though it doesn't pay me much it does make it possible for me to stay up here most of the time. It's only two hours away from the city so that I can go down there or Fanny can come up here fairly easily. I'm a little desperate about the book so took this as a way to have the peace to get it over with.... Man, you'll soon have property all over the place, which seems like a good idea at that. Which reminds me that while I'm not yet in the position to send you all your dough outright, I *could* start paying you off at a hundred books a throw. In fact, I've been asked to let *Esquire* see some of the novel which I shall do as soon as I can solve a few problems connected with a certain section, and if they take it I should be able to send you the whole sum.... Had a call from Gwen Mitchell the other morning, she's up there at City College and Juilliard (This was down in New York) and tells me that Mitch is building at Tuskegee. I guess every fox has got a hole but me... What you tell me of L.A. is depressing but the next time you're there I'd appreciated it if you would drop over to 1917 Jefferson and see my brother Herbert and let me know your impressions. He works from 4:30 in the afternoon until late at night so you could reach him during the day. I'll tell him to watch out for you.... I know how depressing it is to see Negroes getting lost in the American junk pile and being satisfied with so little after all the effort to break out of the South. It makes you want to kick their behinds and then go after Roy Wilkins and that crowd who still don't see that Civil rights are only the beginning. Or maybe I should go after myself for not being more productive and for not having more influence upon how we think of ourselves and our relationship to what is truly valuable in the country. I'm trying in this damn book but even if I'm lucky one book can do very little. And wouldn't a damn nutty woman pick King to kill instead of some southern politician? I'm surprised that she wasn't torn to shreds right there on the spot.[2] The New York papers are reporting the gifts of money and letters of well wishers which the crackers are sending this bitch, a further indication of how depraved this southern thing

---

[2] On September 20, 1958, Dr. Martin Luther King, Jr., was stabbed in the side by a mentally ill woman while in New York for a book signing. The injury was nearly fatal, but King recovered in the hospital and at the Brooklyn home of a friend.

can become. And they think we're fighting to become integrated into that insanity! I almost cracked my sides when I heard that baleful voiced hypocrite [Arkansas Senator] John McClellan lecturing Jimmy Hoffa with such high moral tone. Those sonsabitches don't even have a sense of humor. He doesn't see that with his attacks on the Supreme Court he's doing more to undermine the country than Hoffa is or could even if he were stealing a million a day and bribing every so-called respectable official with an itching palm—of which there must be thousands—that he could find in Washington. It would delight me no end if some reporter got to digging into McClellan's background and told the story of how he became such a moral leader, *that* would make interesting reading, because being a southern politician is by definition one of the most corrupt careers to be found anywhere. Everything about this mess breeds sickness, the bastard's lost his sons one right after the other and it's human to feel sorry for such misfortunes and indeed, it's the kind of thing which is apt to touch me most poignantly, since we have no children at all but hell, how can I sympathize with his loss when he's trying to deprive my kids of a chance to realize themselves? No, I hate him and his kind and I believe the world will be a better place when the last of them is put away forever. Certainly this country will have a bit more self-respect.... I saw something of Norman Mailer during the summer and have been discussing Kerouac and that crowd with Bernie Wolfe[3] and I understand something of how far you got underneath that Greenwich Village poet's skin that summer in Paris. These characters are all trying to reduce the world to sex, man, they have strange problems in bed; they keep score à la Reich on the orgasm and try to verbalize what has to be basically warmth, motion, rhythm, timing, affection and technique. I've also talked to Bellow about this and it would seem that puritan restraints are more operative among the bohemians than elsewhere. That's what's behind Mailer's belief in the hipster and the "white Negro" as the new culture hero—he thinks all hipsters are cocksmen possessed of great euphoric orgasms and are out to fuck the world into

[3] Bernard Wolfe, novelist and coauthor of *Really the Blues*, the autobiography of jazzman Mezz Mezzkow.

peace, prosperity and creativity. The same old primitivism crap in a new package. It makes you hesitant to say more than the slightest greetings to their wives lest they think you're out to give them a hot fat injection. What a bore.

Let me know what's happening with you. Are you still shooting? I've been too busy to do much but plan to carry a camera with me when I start hunting the countryside here abouts. How's your health? Mine is weakened more than you'd expect by this damn hayfever but I look fairly well, am a bit more bald and taken to smoking a type of mild Conn. cigar which I discovered in New Milford this summer. Otherwise I haven't slowed much. Got drunk at a party recently and danced a young chick bowlegged, but hell, a rounder never changes. Love to them gals and let me hear what's cooking.

Ralph

1515 WEST 166ᵀᴴ STREET
COMPTON, CALIFORNIA
15 NOVEMBER 1958

Dear Ralph,

Time really gets away. Here it is over two months that I've been trying to make an immediate reply to yours from Bard dated 28 Sept. The piece on Minton's is not just first rate, it sets a new standard for that kind of writing. Man, when those hacks and hustlers that usually clutter up journals with jazz articles read your stuff they must feel as if something they thought they had nailed down just flew loose and stuck them in the ass. They call themselves critics and they're not even good cub reporters. More often than not they turn out to be more interested in conning musicians than in understanding what the musicians are really doing. (I'm convinced that Leonard Feather, for instance, is trying to worm his way in to both the money and the "glory"). Man, you're still just warming up, and already you're clobbering them.

Agree with you on the Duke-Mahalia set. It doesn't do justice to either one of them. Wish Duke would stop messing around and try to pitch a few no-hitters for a change. He still has the stuff, but even when he's going good he doesn't seem to be trying to go the route. On the other hand I'm just about sick of that Count ass Basie. He's got a wonderful band, and he spends most of his time playing warmed over Woody Herman type arrangements! Man, I'm scandalized. At least 75 or 80% of this stuff these days is written by white boys, ofay academicians who would give anything to have been a part of that same KC that produced the old Basie band in the first place. And Barry Ulanov writes on Basie's own abum that he has FINALLY found THE arranger-composer in the person of Neal Hefti. What with the promotion it's getting I'm not even sure that Basie even owns the band anymore. Also share your opinion of the Mose jazz-modernists. And, speaking of Miles Davis, man, naturally Duke's trumpets were after his ass. Clark Terry is a St. Louis boy too, and he's been used to showing Miles what that horn was made for ever since they were kids.

Went by to see Herbert[1] several weeks ago. Spent an hour or so talking. Rest of the family was out. Took several shots, but haven't got around to finishing the roll yet. Appears to be getting along OK. We spent most of the time talking about you. Says your turning out to become a writer was a hell of a surprise. Figured you'd do something, but expected it to be as a conductor and/or composer. Finds it very natural therefore, that you're doing music criticism. Says you had a very good point in that article on Mahalia. Says your stuff is serious. I told him it was not only serious it was also very important and is being recognized as such all over the world.

I've had to interrupt this for a week. My hot water line broke somewhere under the slab, and I had to get me a guy to help me put in a new one. One of those things. Goddamned house is not even four years old. They'd put in copper, which is supposed to be the best, but it turns out that with this Colorado River water galvanized iron is better. Plumbing Company estimated the cost at $150. We did it for less than $45, and they would've left pipes showing in several places. We didn't.

Man, what are we going to do about these fay "hipsters"? Or better still, what are we going to do about these boot hipsters who are so impressed with them? Niggers imitating whitefolks imitating niggers. Goddamn, man, do you reckon Sammy [Davis] Jr and Eartha [Kitt]

[1] Ellison's younger brother.

ever meet themselves coming? As for the hot fat injection, what can you do? It stretches all the way from Faubus to the cult of Marlon Brando (which includes Brando himself) in one form or another.

As for money, I know how you feel, but goddamnit I don't need it yet. So forget it until the book is finished. Meanwhile what did you ever do about your rolling stock? I'm still horsing with the old Ford around. Hope to get one more year out of it if possible. Man, this L.A. is strictly the far west all right. You got to have your own mount or you can't make it. Public trans is downright frontier, and the distances are too great to walk. I remain unimpressed with this town. I'm glad I came, but they can have it when my tour is up. San Francisco on the other hand is something else. We were up there in September, and the difference is amazing. It is really a first rate town by all standards. They've really achieved the kind of urban maturity you associate with European cities, and yet it is not only an American city but a Western city at that. Not the cowboy's west, the tycoon's west. Not just the west of the ranges and deserts and mountains, but also the west of vineyards and olive groves and missions and ships sailing the seven seas, the world-oriented west of Frank Norris and Jack London (both of whom *did* realize how big the world is). Anyway, you'd like that part of California. As for this part, unfortunately, I think it's going to get not better but worse, a goddamn bullfrog or something, killing itself with prosperity!....

28 NOV

Still trying to get this thing out of the typewriter. Finished shooting that roll and am enclosing three attempts at Herbert. Didn't pose him. Just shot him standing there on the front porch in the high afternoon sun talking and looking squinting at the cars passing. Says your interest in photography was another surprise. Told him you were no slouch in that department either. Here is also one of the cat. You remember Kitty-boo. She made the rounds with several of our neighbors while we were abroad and was waiting for us in the Vet School when we got back. Moque sent for her several months ago so now the whole family is back together again.

Love to Fanny, and say the gals are OK.

Albert

1515 WEST 166ᵀᴴ STREET
COMPTON, CALIFORNIA
22 MARCH 59

Dear Ralph,

Maybe if there were not so many things I'd rather talk to you about than anybody else I know, I could do a better job of just keeping in touch. Been having to learn a lot of useful things I hadn't taken time to learn about before (Air Force things, that is); and have also begun to solve some of the more important problems connected with what at long last is beginning to feel like the kind of book I think I ought to be doing. I don't get a chance to get very much down at a time, but the details have been building steadily, and the overall structure is now definite enough to keep me occupied for some time to come. So there you go, the best stuff I ever had in my life; but goddamnit when I had all that time at Tuskegee I never did get anything going like this, so I don't really know whether to complain or not (after all I found a lot of this stuff only by being out here like this). And besides, I'm like the goddamned Buster in your Scalped Indians, I got MYSELF all tangled up in this shit (It may be Stendhal, but it ain't really in the scout manual). It IS a hell of a way to be trying to write about what I'm trying to write about tho.

Actually I like the Air Force less and less everyday, but I like travel more and more, and I still think it's good to be away from the School business for a while longer at least. If they don't start too much crap in handing out these duty assignments (and looks like they just might) I'd like to stick it out and get one more trip overseas and learn another foreign language and finish the first draft of this thing; but if I caint I might just have to cook this tough assed marsh hen at NYU or somewhere.

Very much impressed by Wright Morris' book length version of *The Territory Ahead*. Also read Bellow's latest. Not as good as Augie, but the guy is still growing. Found the Goncourt Journals (Anchor) wonderful. New jazz mag, *The Jazz Review* not too bad in spite of the number of squares connected with it. Another called JAZZ, a quarterly of American Music, published by Berkley, has an interesting second issue out. There is a piece on *Black, Brown, and*

Beige[1] worth discussing. There is also an addled brain piece of music on [André] Hodier. I for one am not at all impressed with Hodier's learning, his "theory" of jazz, or his ability as an arranger. He is obviously a brilliant guy, the only trouble is he doesn't know what the hell he is talking about, and he is another one of these squares who want to legislate the course of jazz.

I cannot understand for the life of me what these guys are finding so *revolutionary* in Gil Evans–Miles Davis's *Miles Ahead* and *Porgy & Bess*. It's nice and pleasant but other than that all I can hear is a bunch of studio musicians playing decadent exercises in orchestration based on Ellington's old pastel period. It is incredible to me that anybody seriously interested in jazz would rave about *Miles Ahead* and pan or pass up *Such Sweet Thunder*. My reservation about *Such Sweet Thunder* is that there could have been so much more of it; but then there could have been more of Saint-Saëns's *Carnival of Animals* & Ibert's *Divertissement* too. Incidentally a guy who seems to have studied Duke to some profit is Robert Prince. I don't know whether he admits it or not, but I enjoyed hearing *N.Y. Export: Opus Jazz* very much, Warner Bros Record B1240. Other side is ballet music from West Side Story. This version is straight out of Duke (*Liberian Suite, Tattooed Bride,* etc). Listen to the Bernstein section called Cool. Gil Evans, my ass. This guy caint even beat Lenny Bernstein.

I see by *Time* that some boot gal named Hansberry[2] has a hit on B'way. Have you seen it and do you know her? I like Poitier's work. Have been hoping that somebody would buy *Invisible* for him. He wouldn't do a bad job, and it might get you out here for a short stay, plus look at the dough in it. What about this Hansberry chick?

I understand that there are serious literary people out here, but I haven't been able to meet any yet. All I know are a few musicians, and it's probably just as well, but I am curious. If you happen to know of anybody I should see let me know, but I fear the entertainment is the word for here. Not much entertainment here however. They live here

---

[1] A Duke Ellington composition.

[2] Playwright Lorraine Hansberry (1930–1965), author of *A Raisin in the Sun,* the first play by a black woman to be produced on Broadway.

and work in Las Vegas. The biggest stars in Vegas are the top of the crust in Hollywood these days. Vegas & TV variety.

Have been trying to find a copy of *They All Played Ragtime* (Knopf). If you run across one or can scrounge one from Harry Ford I'd appreciate it. Have also been looking for things by Wright Morris. Have *Man and Boy, Works of Love, The Home Place, Field of Vision,* and *The Territory Ahead.* If you happen to come across any of the others let me know. By the way, if you haven't, I wish you would take a look at Rudi Blesh's revised edition of *Shining Trumpets.* I think you could do a very fine piece on it that ties in perfectly between your literary pieces leading up to "Minton." Some of Blesh's observations are useful, but all in all he ends up pretty much where Hyman does. Tell me what you think in *SR.*

By the way, what are you doing about stereo. Me, I'm just not willing to put that much more money into this thing yet. I might go stereo when I get around to getting a tape recorder. Am beginning to take the cameras around with me all the time again. Aim to build a good file on this area before I unass it.

Basie has been out here for the last week or so. The book is still more neo-Basie than Basie, but the band as usual is hitting on all sixteen & Joe; and about one-thirty the other night they reached back and got an old Moten Swing that broke the place up.

The gals are OK. Mique is taking Ballet two nights a week in Hollywood. Moque recently started a temporary job which is apt to cost me more than she is likely to make. As for myself, I'm beginning [to] need to visit New York. How is Fanny? We really would like to see you guys. Why the hell don't you hurry up and come on out here for a while before we move again?

Murray

730 RIVERSIDE DRIVE,
NEW YORK 31, N.Y.,
JUNE 27, 1959.

Dear Albert,

I went through my commencement as 'teacher' on last Saturday afternoon and its taken me this long to recover enough to get down to doing what I should have done months ago: write you a letter. It has been a most interesting year, full of irritations and discoveries; progress on the novel and a definite deep[en]ing of my perception of the themes which I so blindly latched on to. I guess old Hickman is trying to make a man out of me—at this late date. I've also been subjecting myself to the discipline of isolation, living alone most of the time doing my own house work and laundry; playing around with French cooking so as not to lapse into eating out of cans and, like a 19th century Englishman living in Africa, have been doing the thing completely, including wines with my meals and desserts which I made for myself. I was also splitting logs for the fireplace and hunting more or less successfully in the snow. Naturally Fanny came up for the weekends but I grew to dread the loss of time in the City and indeed, this is my first trip down in over three months. As soon as I can clean up some of the scenes a bit I'll send them along for your opinion.

For the better part of the year has been the way the novel has been going. I read publicly for the first time before students and teachers there, and at the end of two hours they were still in a trance. Old Hickman had them, man; the few Christians, the Jews and all. You would have laughed your ass off to see that old downhome Moses rhetoric work. It's not too difficult to observe when Mahalia cuts loose at such places as Newport, but most of the jazz fans don't possess the vocabulary to translate it into their own terms—since most have no religion, no sense of literature or art, no way of their own of focusing and coming to grips with profound feeling—but it's more difficult to reduce Hickman's sermons to mere entertainment; that old bastard knows how to get under even so initiated and tough a skin as mine. He preaches gut, and that comes from depths and admits no absolute control. All I can do is ask him hard questions and write down his acts and his answers....

As for the teaching, I guess I'm beginning to learn some of the things you've known for a long time. It went rather well, but I was appalled with how ignorant some of these bright, progressive school products can actually be—not only of literature, but of life. They wear beards and let their unwashed tits bounce around in their low-cut blouses and are still, literally, chewing bubble gum. I'm told that

I'm a popular teacher, but if so I did it the hard way around. They all expect to be entertained but I played the dozens *at* them and signified about them in so many different ways that I don't think they found many places to hide from confronting the connection between their identities, social and personal, and the major concerns of the American novel. I wasn't nice at all. I hit them with their ignorance of the experience and their easy smugness towards the South, then tried to shake some of the shit out of their vague and inflated notions concerning the superiority of European fiction. I must say that they took it well enough—once they found that they couldn't out argue me, and following the last class they caucused at the rear of the room then called my attention to something they'd written on the blackboard: "*YOU WERE RIGHT ABOUT THE DAMNED CIVIL WAR!*" I know Bard is something of a special case but the picture I get of what the American whites who matured during the thirties are doing to their children is frightening. We were, and are, penalized out of the irrationalities of race, but these poor kids are suffering from the excesses of their parents' sentimentality and utter lack of any grasp of the tragic sense. They have little discipline and they think that the world is simply waiting to pat them on the head. At least we got more than that out of Tuskegee, as bad as it was. When I see some of the Negro kids there—interestingly enough none signed for my class or stopped me for a conversation—imitating the whites I wonder where the country will be in thirty years. I signed to teach six hours next year, adding a course in the Russian Novel to the American—so maybe I'll make some contact with the Negroes and try to give them some sense of those things from their backgrounds which they must not lose.

Which reminds me of how right you are about Basie and the sound of his band, doubtlessly his arranger has been selected for him because he sure isn't any hell. I've been listening to jazz from two a.m. to 4, when I find it difficult to sleep and I must say that it's become hard listening. Somebody needs to come along and take the curse of Charlie Parker off the whole crowd because most of it is bird-shit. One of the kids at Bard who plays at being disc jockey came over one afternoon with a pile of records and I thought I'd die before he finished playing that pitiful blat of misplaced ambition and ego. I spent the rest of the evening playing Duke to cleanse the atmosphere. I'm sorry that I don't have your letters here with me so that I could comment on the Jazz mags you referred to, I don't remember which they were, but I have been seeing the *Jazz Review,* in which I've found the interviews of older jazzmen valuable and most of the critical writing more useful for exposing the vapidity of the writers than for any insights it offers into the art. I'm still being asked to do jazz articles but at the moment I'm not at all displeased that I'm too busy to bother. Nevertheless I'm still planning to put together a book of essays. Right now I'm working up a piece on Negroes and Southern fiction, titled *The Seer and the Seen* for an anthology edited by some southern boys and scheduled by Anchor. If this goes well I'll use it along with the other stuff. I've been finding interesting things in Hemingway and Fitzgerald which might well work into a broader piece on the same subject. When you start lifting up that enormous stone, the Civil War, that's kept so much of the meaning of life in the North hidden, you begin to see that Mose is in the center of a junk pile as well as in the center of the cotton boll. All the boys who try to escape this are simply running from the problem of value—Which is why those old Negroes whom I'm trying to make Hickman represent are so confounding, they never left the old original briar patch. You can't understand Lincoln or Jefferson without confronting them. . . .

Mort mailed me some stories by one of the Tuskegee students, but they're mostly in long-hand, which makes me more reluctant than usual to read them. I shall however, and I hope this kid is good enough to take such advantage. If he's not I intend to give him hell. And speaking of Mort reminds me that I've recently been to Hamilton College on two occasions, first to lecture at their art center a couple of months ago—which went so well that when we returned last week to attend the 79th birthday party of a most remarkable woman, the Dean greeted me with "Welcome home." No doubt part of my success there had to do with my speaking of my connection with Hamilton through Sprague *and* Frank Taylor, who is very active there now, and secondarily, through Pound and Woollcott (Alex). Taylor had been the favorite of Grace Root, whose husband's family has been so important in the history of the college (as well as in the government) and through him we've become warm friends. She's one of those alive, tough, independent women who does what she wants to do, whether it's giving land, money, house and guidance for an art center, or going out of the way places in search for new species of primroses to hybridize, she's in her sixties now but last visit we put everyone else to bed while we sat knocking off bottles of red wine and discussing everything from Negro schools to religion. Her husband was Edward Root, the art collector who was so important to American painting, of which the house has excellent examples. We'll have to drive up there when you and Mokie come this way, it's most beautiful and Hamilton is a pocket of wonderful old American types who are amazingly alive as is the old lady I mentioned earlier. She is the first woman to attend Oxford, once taught at Hamilton herself and still uses a couple of the brightest students as readers—her eyes are about gone—who she proceeds to turn into first class scholars. I'm told she knows more about myth than Joe Campbell. Certainly she's one of the most alert and witty women I've ever met. I was placed at her left during the party—which was attended by people from all over the country—and I was never bored a second. Her husband taught chemistry and was the great hybridizer of peonies, a work and business which is still carried on by one of the daughters. It's amazing what you find when you break the confines of the New York literary world; up there some of the old Yankee strength is still expressing itself and thus far I've found none of that embarrassing phoniness which clings to the most authentic white Southern aristocrats. Memory is still alive, both personal and historical, and without the sickness which marks the south. I plan to explore such areas further. Now I know something of the Northern Jews and the Southern Jews of at least two generations, and something of all kinds of Moses so I guess it's time to get some idea of the various New England groups. . . .

Which reminds me that you asked if I knew people on the West coast; unfortunately I don't, but Bellow said to introduce yourself to Gene Fowler[1] as his friend and that you would meet dam near every one worth knowing through him. The same goes for Henry Miller. I'm

---

[1] West Coast journalist and novelist.

still working on this and will send you names as I come to them....
What are you up to this summer? I hope you'll have time to get some
writing done and it's good news that you've worked out certain problems. Why don't you get some of your jazz stuff down? *Esquire* pays
dam well and they need such material. Incidentally, I've been asked to
take part in a seminar on literature which they're running out at Iowa
next fall; I'm part of the fiction faculty at Breadloaf during August.
Bellow has set up something for me at Chicago during the Winter—
and I'm the chief American delegate to the P.E.N. congress at Frankfurt and Heidelberg next month. I'll stay no more than ten days and
then right back and to work. I'm not sure but I think that being away
from the interruptions of N.Y. and under the pressure of weekly lectures at the college I've gotten more writing done. I guess I'm such a
natural bum that if I took a job coal-heaving I'd turn out a master-
piece just so I could goof off. What we must do before too long is
Spain; all of us with enough time to soak in some of it. I had my class
roaring when by making some cultural point I told them about us and
the luggage on the Lido: "Hell, man, we come from a long line of Red
Caps!" which reminds me, if you ever think of teaching again this time
it must be somewhere where you can do some good and everywhere I
go and they like *my* kind I bring you into it. You've got the degrees so
it shouldn't be any trouble at all. I don't know how long I'll work at this
game but I certainly don't wish to get in too far for all the good it's
seemed to have done me. Bellow, who with his family is back in Tivoli,
intends to continue teaching part time and writing the rest. He's very
much sought after as a teacher and Min.[2] has made things very pleasant for him. Respectability is the very devil to escape these days but I
go on outraging quite a number of people just by being me. One of the
fellows in the English dept is married to an Arkansas gal who has been
trying to make it as a jazz singer and who professes to love Negroes,
etc. Well, last winter at a party he flipped when someone shook hands
with him and left him holding an ice cube. Being a Mexican, he
thought his manhood was being questioned and although a small man

[2] University of Minnesota.

he wanted to break up the joint. So I sat on him and talked him almost sober—when his wife told me to sit down and, when I asked her what was wrong, she called me a nigger. No, I didn't kick her butt (he jumped sober as a judge, by the way), but I told her that I could quite calmly kick her all the way to Little Rock but instead I simply wanted her to kiss me. It was something and I'm sure she'd rather I had struck her or at least become angry, and realized later tha[t] I'd been pretty sadistic by remaining calm. It was all so unmotivated, seemingly, that the psychologist at whose home the incident took place, still hasn't figured it out. And oddly enough, I think he distrusts *me* because he doesn't know where I put that provocation. But hell, we grow up at some point and the poor woman wasn't striking primarily at me, she was trying to drag her husband. Poor woman, now every time she sees me she's in trouble.

Well, this shows you how my time has been going. I started this on the 27th and now here it is the 17th and I'm packing to unass the area this evening. In the interim I've been working frantically on the book, trying to complete a section while the emotion was still strong within me. I guess I must be nearing the completion, recently the typewriter has been drawing me like a magnet. Bellow has read book two and is to publish about fifty pages in a new mag which he is editing—THE NOBLE SAVAGE—of all things! I'm a contributing editor and it's paying five cents a word.... I'll keep you posted on this as it develops.... Before breaking this off let me say that I went down to look at the delegates to the N.A.A.C.P. convention yesterday and I must say that the mixture is as before—Only now the clothes are more expensive and there are more young people around. I don't know what I was doing exactly, but it was quite meaningful to simply stand there in the lobby and feel them moving and talking around me. Hell, I know what we want, I just like to hear the idiom. Fifteen minutes in a meeting with some of those studs and I'd want to start a fight, but just seeing them walk and pose and talk and flirt and woof—that's damn pleasant.

Take it easy, man; I'll write you when I return. Love to Mokie and Mique.

as ever,
Ralph

1515 WEST 166TH STREET
COMPTON, CALIFORNIA
17 AUGUST 1959

Dear Ralph,

I've just recently returned from a three month course at Amarillo Air Force Base, Texas. May, June, July. So now I'm in the supply business for a while. I'm now in charge of the Inspection and Inventory section of Base Supply. Goddamnit the Air Force is going to make an organization man out of me yet if I don't keep my personality split wide open enough. I figure I'm still ahead of them, but I'm running scareder & scareder every day.

You seem to have had a very fine year. I'm sure that you are immune to most of the negative effects of the teaching game, crap game, that is, and you've long had one foot in criticism anyway, so you got it made. And if old Hickman is thriving on it.... Doesn't seem to have cut down on your mobility, and that's very important.

I tried to salvage what I could of the three months I had to spend in the Panhandle. Finished one chapter and brought myself face to face with one that I've been putting off for some time. Actually my schedule down there wasn't too bad. Classes in property accounting methods from 0700 to 1400. Rest of the day more or less on my own. Spent a couple of hours in the gym or at the swimming pool trying to recapture some of the old zip. Still seem to have enough of it to get by. (Still trying to figure out how I got so far out of shape that time in Morocco. Must have been busier than I realized and overeating over richly. Am currently qualified for worldwide assignment). Also made use of the base library. Among other things I did some Marquand. Been skipping him for years. Glad I finally got around to him. Kinda sobers you to see an old pro knocking out stuff like that on mostly just intelligence and good journalism. For my money, he is as good if not better than Cozzens, for instance.

Have also been redoing Fitzgerald. Must say it gets better every time I come back to it. It has taken me a long time to cut through some of my own prejudices about "jazz age" ofays (Scott & Zelda, squares on a binge), but I can see that much of the stuff that I once thought was superficial is very valid indeed. And certainly the school theme which runs through most of his work is relevant to some of my own most fundamental preoccupations. Man, this cat was often a very naïve operator in the flesh, but he was far from naïve as a writer. I used to think that he was all tangled up in crap that wasn't worth bothering about. The thirties and Fitzgerald's admirers faked me out on this. Jay Gatsby, Amory Blaine, Anthony Patch, Dick Diver are related to me and you and Invisible and Sandorfra Robinson, Ralph Poe, Sage Hall and all that old stuff including the way we used to feel about *Esquire*. I am finally willing to admit that Fitzgerald really does belong up there with Hemingway & Marse William.

Will probably have another look at Dos Passos before long. Also saw a stack of Van Vechten[1] out in Hollywood the other day, and I can't get him out of my mind. Think I'll do *Peter Whiffle, Parties, Firecrackers* and all that and then *Nigger Heaven* again. Old Van Vechten is probably much more important to an understanding of the twenties than guys like Cowley and even Edmund Wilson have been able to see or admit. If Gertrude Stein was important we certainly caint overlook the very real influence Van Vechten had, much of which still survives today. Man, where did Norman Mailer and them—them—teenagers get that shit from. That goddamned Mailer sounds like a degenerate.

You mentioned that Greenwich Village poet in your other letter. Which reminds me that he got so shook up that he never did realize what I was really trying to tell him. I was trying to tell him that fay boys were making a myth of the Negro "stud" a psychological fact. That all that old talk was turning the Negro man into such a sex object that fay chicks were already half fucked before they even got into bed. I also said something to him about chicks imagining that they were raped, and pointed out that they obviously didn't have to be raped except perhaps on demand. And then I said something about not being able to reconcile my personal knowledge of a tradition of sophisticated sexual technique and barnyard pride in effective coxmanship with the newspaper image of Negroes as frantic snatchers & grabbers.

[1] Carl Van Vechten, American literary critic, novelist, and photographer.

I also pointed out that jazz represented CONTROL not abandon, as did all forms of American Negro dancing. Man, I was mainly trying to destroy the image of the rapist, and I created for him the supercox-man! He began going around asking white women if they had done it with one and was it different! I guess most of them must have thought he was crazy. But some of them said yes and that it WAS different. I told him that his understanding of the exotic should help him to ex-plain that. But by that time penis envy had dam near turned him into a segregationist.

Old Duke is having a good year. The *Jazz Party* record has some very fine spots. The *Anatomy of a Murder* record from the film sound-track stands up even better as an LP than it does in the picture & a col-lection of cocktail lounge pieces, *At the Bal Masque*, comes off very pleasantly indeed. I also hear that he took over Newport and several other "festivals" again this year. Looks like that Jimmy Rushing deal you wrote me about clicked for a lot of other people too. The Curse of Charlie Parker is right. A bunch of birdshit scratchers. Most guys these days are not even passable creative musicians any more. A bunch of studio hacks. These guys are even more dependent on somebody else's clichés than our avante garde literary bores. These guys are con-cerned with fashion, not music. Old Duke is still reaching back, man; and when he hits, the continuity is always there, the newness, individ-uality, and the relevance. . . .

18 AUG

Have just got back from the new LA Sports Arena, where the Air Force detailed me to serve on an inter-service panel of judges for a drill competition put on by the Negro Shriners, who are having a big national get-together out here this week. Man, I was hard put to main-tain a solemn military calm watching some of the old middle-age moses mixing all that old flatfooted, box-ankled, bunnion-toed bell-hopping-headwaitering-pullmanportering stuff in there with West Point. Other judges from Army, Marines & Navy, all born in the idiom. Detroit (Marracci Temple) led by a little hoarse voiced, sharp-eyed, shortstop looking guy whose conception of military bearing is evidently derived from Ray Nance's violin playing, won, with Mecca

10 from D.C., a bunch of softstepping cats in Friendly Fives taking second place.

Something you said in your previous letter gave me the impression that you don't quite place the relationship between Compton and L.A. It is a part of L.A. From my house to Civic Center is about the same distance as from your place to say, Penn Station, and to Hollywood is about the distance to, say, Wall Street from your place. But most of these subsections, unlike Harlem, Greenwich Village, Hell's Kitchen, etc., are postal units. Man, I'm just two blocks off Central Avenue!

The gals are fine. My being out of town didn't cramp them too much, although you have to have rolling stock to do almost anything in this town. Mique took typing in school this summer, is learning to drive, and is taking ballet from a Russian out in Hollywood twice a week. Old Mique will be in the 11th Grade this year. So far she hasn't shown a lot of interest in college as such, but has shown a lot of interest in training in dance, drama, arts, etc. NO success in math. If you or Fanny can send along any information that we might be able to use in picking a school, please do so. I've got to write for catalogues and get current on this prerequisite racket again.

I'm not in very close touch with things at Tuskegee. I did have a letter from Mort this Spring, but otherwise it's been just routine family stuff, neighborhood notes from the Michells.

Wish the hell you and Fanny would come on out here for a visit before we get our next moving papers. I'll never really be an Angeleno, but I'm certainly trying like hell not to miss anything this town has to offer. From the point of view of food, clothing & shelter California as a state must be second to none. I can appreciate more and more why Negroes like it so much, what with the climate too. But, man, I sure hope they hurry up and get used to having enough to eat. At the rate they're stuffing themselves out here now they'll be as shapeless as Mexicans and Hawaiians in another generation or so. They living good, man, and they happy, it just flat takes a little time to stop measuring things by the old days down back yonder. I don't know, but freedom has to remain perhaps even more alert during a time of prosperity than during a time of scarcity. I'm not at all sure that people won't eat and sit themselves into slavery much quicker than they will surrender freedom for food when they are hungry. A hungry man is subject to kick a few asses, tear up things and try a few experiments first. But people given over to bread and circuses are ideal slaves. I like to think that Negroes back east are beginning to learn something about the connection between freedom and power. These folks out here seem too often to confuse freedom with paint (housepaint) and refrigerators. And automobiles. Man, automobiles are an absolute necessity out here, and when there are two people in the family working, as there often is, there must be two cars. Well, it's just expecting too goddamned much to ask people to realize that out here in the west everybody has always had to have his own pony. And I hasten to add that mose is not by himself in any of this. You even hear more moonshine about sunshine from Anglo-Saxons (local phrase! I think it includes Jews, Slavs, Italians etc., excludes Mexicans, us & Orientals) from the Mid-West than barbershop bullshit from Southern Negroes, who after all ARE fairly authentic refugees.

But there is always the news and Faubus, who obviously does not understand how antagonistic cooperation operates.

Albert

the noble savage

published by Meridian Books, Inc., 12 East 22 Street, New York 10, New York

EDITORS ■ EDITORS

Saul Bellow
Keith Botsford
Jack Ludwig

CONTRIBUTING EDITORS

John Berryman
Ralph Ellison
Herbert Gold
Arthur Miller
Wright Morris
Harvey Swados

AUGUST, 1959

This is just to show you that the mag is really in the works. I started this letter on the 17th, but had to stop in order to prepare 50 pages of my m.s. for the first issue. I'll send you a copy when it's ready.

Dear Albert,

Your letter gave me much pleasure. It arrived while I was still up on Breadloaf Mountain exhausting myself with two weeks of alleged teaching of alleged writers and an even larger gang who don't write but who hang around such conferences for the sake of entertainment. Of course they pay their dough and the staff is supposed to do everything to keep them happy. Nothing too demanding, understand. I worked my ass off for less money than I pull down, once in a while at least, for a single lecture; but even though Fanny's expenses were thrown in, the mountain was not bread, but a stone, I came down from there in a fairly sour mood, wondering how I had strayed so far on top of Robert Frost's Kilimanjaro; yes, and wondering why I ever had the idea that a porter's job was so undesirable. Then I found your letter with its fine description of your judging that drill competition. It snatched me back to Oklahoma to the time when that same type of mad drill-master had the kids drilling on the school ground every late spring and summer evening when the weather was good. Sometimes we'd be there marching in the moonlight, and sometimes we'd be there to watch the men dressed in Knights' of Pythan uniforms, going through their maneuvers on nights so dark that you saw hardly more than their plumed hats, their silverex belts, steel scabbards and the gleaming shapes of their swords, which they held blades forward against their shoulders as they moved. They were either members of the Odd Fellows, the Shriners, the Uniformed Ranks(!) of the Elks— here I mean the drill masters who grabbed us kids—it really didn't matter because most of those guys belonged to all the lodges anyway. And quite a number were vets of both the Spanish American and World Wars. As I write I realize why I lost my attraction for things military so early. Hell, by the time I was thirteen I'd had my legs drilled wrong side out and we knew so many fancy formations and had been threatened, cursed and cajoled so often that we might have slipped a West Point squadron on dress parade, and no one would have known the difference—except that we were doing all that swinging you described, even before we had any need to learn the Palmerhouse. Our ankles were still in good condition and only a few had corns (although most could have been called 'Stinky Dog' with justice and precision, since we lived in tennis shoes). Nevertheless, we had all the native movements, including the P.I. limp and the one-butt shuffle. We'd had it all drilled in, like Ivy League boys now have their white buck shoes with the *dirt* machined in. Those old guys were mad for drill, and no kid of a certain height was safe from their enthusiasm. I can see them now on some far distant dead occasion at Slaughter's Hall, dressed in white flannel, going through those pinwheeling formations over the polished dance floor; their canes (phallic rifles, magic wands) exploding against the floor like a fusillade of rifle fire whenever the drill-master turned, eyes closed like a magician disparaging the whole disgusting triumph over the low-down, ignorant, intractable material now transformed by the sheer Joycean mastery of a stud who in a world of justice would have been a five star general at the very least). Come to think of it, I probably embraced the difficult discipline of the trumpet just so that I could escape those cats. I didn't though, because after I joined the school band one or two would come over to the school ground to mess with us on late fall afternoons, teaching us formations we used between the halves of football games. Some of the granny-dodgers were as mad as Capt. Drye, only none had actually reached his rank in the armed forces. Our band used to accompany their drill teams to such battle-and-playing fields as Wichita and Topeka, and once as far as Denver. That time it was with the Elks, who held their Western Convention there and who featured two events, an oratorical contest—which was won by one of my classmates—and the drill contest. There was a woman's auxiliary too, man, and what with the drinking, the sweating and the signifying, it was truly a funky row. They shuffled and ruffled and danced and pranced; some were tight and others were clowning and kidding the whole idea of what they were doing to a military form, discipline, pose, you name it—so that the occasion had everything; comedy and satire as well as the tension of tough competition. I can still see some of those tall, Watusi-looking moses, wearing capes and fezzes and leaning on a pivot like a stage coach taking a sharp curve, their shoulders touching, their faces skimming across a cymbal lightly. Yes, and the enormous hall now so quiet that even a deaf man could hear all that scuffling leather beneath the commands of the drill-master. I suppose there was the usual Negro yearning for ceremony and identification in it, and a feeling of potentiality and a threat—along with the joy in formalized, swinging movement. Whatever, I'm glad I lived through that phase and you brought it all back again. The cream of it was, of course, you and the other judges knowing both idioms, the military and the Negro, and that made it an especially rich juxtaposition. Why don't we do something along this line for publication, perhaps as an exchange of letters? I'm sure it would be taken by someone, especially if we pointed out the relationship to jazz. Think about it anyway.... I wondered where the hell you were, but I wouldn't have guessed the Panhandle in a million years. You want to keep loose, as old Satchel advises, or the AF will gain [on] you. Something always does; I went farting off to Germany for the P.E.N. and simply wasted my working energy; and teaching is a drag even though teaching the Russian novel along with a class in American lit. is rather stimulating. I've been terribly sick with the after effects of hay fever which has left me too tired to even enjoy the hunting season. I can see a flock of about fifty geese going over just now. We've had a very late summer here but with those boys going over in broad daylight, winter isn't far behind them. Anyway, don't let them tie you down too closely.... I agree that Van Vechten is much more present in the fiction of the twenties than we stop to think nowadays and in fact Mailer would be quite surprised to see that the crap he's selling is actually V's leavings.... I missed the *Anatomy of a Murder* records, but we've picked up the others and will soon get it and the newly announced *Back To Back* on which Duke and Rabbit[1] play the blues. He's still the best alright, while that poor Basie flounders around in that big tubby band like a fly trying to take off from a piece of flypaper. And most of the other stuff one hears is teen-age embarrassment and birdshit. When so many musicians can stand up in public and make their horns sound so miserable and self-pitying, castrated and flat, something awful must be happening in the country; something no one has named or even begun to grasp. The stuff sounds gutless and homo—like Lester *looked* that morning I saw him switching down 145th St., but not like he ever sounded. What's most distressing

[1] Johnny Hodges, Duke Ellington's alto sax player.

is that so many of these cats are Negroes who seem as much disorganized by a little acceptance as those L.A. moses are by a little comfort. And just look at the colorphotos on the record sleeves. It's as though Van Vechten has moved out from his photo-castration of a few so-called poets and classical musicians and taken on the whole world of Negro jazz. It looks as though these guys are doing to themselves, out of self hate and a child-like assertion, exactly what all the years of slavery and second-class citizenship couldn't do—they've killed their own rich Negro sense of life and become zombies. Thank God for Old Duke.

I've been thinking hard about getting out to see you and the girls, but thus far I don't see just how we'll do it. I've a lecture offered me at Chicago Uni in May and I might keep flying west at that time, and I've got to be at Iowa during the first week in Dec. for a gabfest by *Esquire*—but none of this would allow for Fanny to come along, nor, since I'll still be teaching, would there be sufficient time. I'll keep working on it because we'd really like to see you before too long and I'd also like to drop in on Herbert. Perhaps we could drive out during the summer, but my car is getting mighty old. We've been promised a larger apartment in our building and if it comes through we'll at least be able to put you up whenever you hit New York again. We've simply outgrown the present place and it has begun to drag me so much that I get depressed everytime I go into the city. I try to have Fanny spend as many weekends up here as possible. Here I simply rattle around in all the space, smoke the endless cigars and talk to myself and the cat. *He* thinks I'm still crazy and by now he plays the dozens better than I do. Saul has offered to let me buy the house because his wife doesn't really like the country but not only do I not have the dough, I'm not so sure that Fanny would want to be this far from the city. So I'm enjoying it while I can. The air is winey now from the apple orchards, the herds of sheep drift into the meadow in front of the house as night falls and I've taken to puttering with house plants. The garden I planted in the spring turned out well under Saul's cultivation during the summer, and even this late I have more squash, eggplant, peppers and tomatoes than I know what to do with. But best of all, I'm able to get some work done. The only thing that's really wrong with it is that there are no moses to keep me tuned in. Speaking of the West coast though, I'm afraid that I'd have the sense that I'd run out of space—unless I took some lessons in walking the water. Because just as a man has to have his own pony I have to have the feeling that I can still take off. Maybe that's what's bothering those L.A. moses, they've run out of psychological running space. Tell Mokie and Mique to watch that stuff because one thing we can't stand is being crowded. By the way, I hear that Archie Moore is playing Nigger Jim, and I saw Althea Gibson playing a slave in the *Horse Soldiers*, so I guess pretty soon somebody will decide to do Faulkner's *The Unvanquished* and cast Wilt-the-Stilt Chamberlain as Ringo—and if that so-and-so, Sugar Ray wasn't so greedy he could have played Pip in the recent *Moby Dick*....

Before I forget, we're asking for information concerning Mique's dance. I can't believe that she's in the 11th grade although the math thing sounds just like me. Next thing we know, she'll have grown beyond all recognition, certainly as far as the little kid we first saw goes. We'd better get out there fast. Take it easy and keep me posted on developments and I'll send you the news from here as it develops. Fanny sends love to you all, as do I,

Ralph

1515 WEST 166TH STREET
COMPTON, CALIFORNIA
29 JANUARY 1960

Dear Ralph,

Since my last note I've been working on a chapter which I think would serve as a pretty good substitute for the letter I couldn't get around to writing during that time, but although I completed it (1st draft) several weeks ago I haven't gotten around to having it typed up yet. Am now all tangled up in another chapter and a special USAF inventory project. So meanwhile this quick memo will have to get 1960 started.

Things are not too bad. The gals are OK. They have ALMOST enough goddamned clothes to be very very happy, but you know how that is. Hey, man, I bought me a FALCON a couple of weeks ago. Well, not really me a Falcon, but US a Falcon. Looks like I'm finally going to have some help with all this driving. Between me and school Mique is just about checked out, and already I've had Moque driving on the FREEWAYS and along Wilshire Blvd. I had 98,000 plus miles on the old Victoria. It was still doing all right with no major repairs, but I figured I'd better quit while I was still ahead, especially in view of the fact that I have been ready to roll by the thousands on a few days notice. So far I'm very happy with the Falcon. I got a white one (California!) fordomatic, padded dash, everything. Still enough room to accommodate all of us on other trips like our 1956 European sweep.

Fanny says you have a bigger place now. Maybe I'll get a chance to see it some time this Spring or Summer. Kinda hate to show my face around New York without at least ¼ of the book, but I've been toying with the idea of making a trip to the Pentagon and trying to find a good overseas assignment to volunteer for, instead of staying out here for four or five years and then getting bundled off to some remote assed island. I'm not supposed to be vulnerable for a year or so yet, but I don't want to wait until I am. So I've been thinking about spending a day or so in Washington and about a week in New York, maybe some time in April. Moque says she's surprised I haven't been back yet.

What's with NOBLE SAVAGE? You never know out here. There are several pretty good news stands in Hollywood which I check two or three times a week, but they are always behind. Haven't been very much impressed with anything I've read recently. Saw *Wild Strawberries* and liked it, also saw *Room at the Top.* Saw a fairly interesting collection of paintings at the Screen Director's Guild a month or so ago. Oh yes, and I went to two RAY CHARLES dance dates, one at the Hollywood Palladium, and one at the FIVE-FOUR BALLROOM. (54th St & B'way, Mose area). Wonderful time. Personally, I think Charles is very good but currently overblown and over rated for the wrong reasons, but, man, that cat operates on these Los Angeles Negroes like Reverend Ravazee at revival time. I don't know how they took that stuff at Newport but these Louisiana, Arkansas, Mississippi, Oklahoma (etc) Negroes at the Five-Four took it like surenuff gospel. Man, they had that shit working both ways just like it's supposed to work. All fucked up like one of them old black pot stews, but goddamn!

That was the Five-Four. And then about two weeks later they followed him into the Hollywood Palladium. Same stuff, same effect. Except this time there were also a slew of various Hollywood types on hand trying their ofay damnedest to be in there with it too. Man, that goddamned Ray ass Charles absorbs everything and uses everything. Absorbs it and assimilates it with all that sanctified, stew meat smelling, mattress stirring, fucked up guilt, touchy violence, jailhouse dodging, second hand American dream shit, and sometimes it comes out like a sermon by one of them spellbinding stem winders in your work-in-progress, and other times he's extending Basie's stuff better than Basie himself. Who knows maybe some of that stuff will help to set a number of people up for old BLISS!

Re: Mique. Mozelle has begun writing for school catalogs. Meanwhile, if you come across anything good, send it along. Thanks to Fanny for the list she sent. Also picked up an American Library Paperback the other day that covers almost every school and college in the US including Tuskegee Institute.

As I said, this memo will have to do for the time being. Meanwhile you drop a line when you get time.

Albert

TIVOLI, N.Y.
APRIL 2, 1960.

Dear Albert,

I had Fanny get off a copy of the *Noble Savage* to you a couple of weeks ago, but have been so busy that only now am I getting around to the follow up letter. I hope it gives you some idea of what we're up to—although I'm not a very active editor at the moment—and I hope you'll let us see something of what you're writing. There is quite an interest in the mag and few detractors have sounded off against the title even before the paper was available. At any rate, we're out to provide a magazine which will make it unnecessary for a good writer to even think about *P.R.* or *Hudson,* or any of the other academic house organs, and any criticism we publish will be by writers, not critics. Best of all, we have a top word rate of 5 cents per—which ain't bad at all.

I'm very glad to hear that you're under way with a book and very anxious to see any thing you wish to send. But never mind about showing your face without ⅘s of a book, most of what's being published shouldn't be, and although I'm damned disgusted with myself because of my failure to finish I know nevertheless that it's better to publish one fairly decent book than five pieces of junk. The work with old Hickman, Bliss and Severn goes on, with Hickman moving more and more into the role of hero and the old guy is so large that I've just about given in to him, some other crazy sonsabitches have been boiling up out of the pot, one who sacrifices a fishtailed caddy on the Senator lawn, and another who discovers that a coffin he'd been saving for 30 years or so had rotted away and decided then and there that the whole American government had fucked up and orders a case of Jack Daniels and a white cooch dancer to come to his house and flip her g-string. He loses his religion and his faith in banks—everything, but the old straight-laced granny dodger is so wild that I'm not sure that he won't blow the book to hell. As you can see, deep down I'm mad as ever—insane, that is, but it seems to be my only way.... I'm also lecturing away. My soph. course in American Lit is the most popular on the campus (!), some forty kids in a school where 14 is about tops; my course in the Russian novel is intense and most useful to me, for I'm learning much more than the kids; a lecture at Rutgers two weeks ago during a blizzard brought an offer of a job—which I rejected—paying 9000—better than a full prof here abouts. I go to Washburn College in Indiana on the 14 & 15—I tell you this so I won't miss you should you make it out this way—and in May I'll be at the University of Chicago for four days. The pay for these is quite good considering, but I'll earn it—what between functioning as a writer-teacher and having to talk about the problem. Which I can't very well refuse to do, now that young Mose is setting the pace for students all over the country. I've been calling attention to the connection between social morality and literature so I can't do one without doing the other. I'm also doing an introduction to a paperback collection of Stephen Crane's work. I hadn't paid much attention to him beyond following Hemingway's recommendation of the *Red Badge,* "The Blue Hotel" and "The Open

Boat"—but I've been reading the neglected stories which haven't been anthologized so often and in which Crane is revealed as not merely the technical link between Twain and Hemingway, and thus the first of the 20th Century American writers, but in which he struggles with Mose just as hard as Mark Twain and which mark him as the last of the 19th century moralists. John Berryman gets some of this in his biography, but he was so busy psychologizing the work that he underplays the fact that Crane was often as indignant over the Negro thing as he was over the slums. More, the little bastard was from a long line of preachers on both sides and when we consider this some of the mystery of how he came to think and feel as he did is dispelled. That damned Methodist fire and brimstone along with all that hockey-assed hypocrisy had the boy running like a puppy with high-life on his balls from a very early age—very much as Henry James's old man's theological interests got to him, or Joyce's Catholicism got to him. The critics have praised Crane for the verbiage he left out, while refusing to see that he wasn't leaving out the religious background of his thought. The other thing which fascinates me [are] the parallels with his own life: not only the Methodism but the resentment of church folks' shittiness at an early age, the early death of the father, and the strict mother. Read the *Monster* and you'll see where Faulkner got part of the idea for Benjy in *The Sound and the Fury*. Dilsey's line to Luster, "Quit projeking with his flower" appears here with Henry Johnson, the Negro hero, telling the little white boy, "I done tol yer many's th' time not to go a-follin' an' a-projeckin with them flowers." When Henry dashes into the burning house to save the boy, his face is destroyed by acid which looks like flowers in the flames. And as you know, Benjy's flower stands for Caddy's maidenhead.... Anyway, I'm having some fun with the thing and at least I won't *ignore* what I always preach—that the literary imagination of the Country (the first class imagination, that is) has to smuggle the black man into its machinery in some form, otherwise it can't function. I wouldn't want to have to prove this in each instance, but for the 19th century boys it's just about true. Beyond this the only news is that I've bought a Labrador pup which I've named Tuckatarby and hope to train for hunting. I still have hopes but as of now it seems that I've got myself a shit machine, but if blood counts he should be a fairly decent dog.... Fanny and I have been talking of coming west this summer, but we've decided nothing since we're still trying to get the apartment in order and there simply isn't money enough for a car.

How about that Falcon! I can just see Mique and Mokie buzzing along all brown in that Hollywood whiteness. My own old wagon is still batting along so I have to look at every new car that passes out of the corner of my eye. You'd better be careful, now that Mique's reaching college age, because the kids here use Falcon's strictly as campus cars. Fanny and I frequently recall the 1956 trip and especially the excitement Mokie and Mique caused in Siena. That's where Mokie was breaking in those nasty-zippered harem pants and the Italians were bug-eyeing all over the streets. I wish we could make another such trip, perhaps in Spain as we'd planned to do that summer. I'm teaching Hemingway and my nostalgia is compounded. Sometimes, in fact, I miss that fucking Rome, where I was anything but happy. I guess the trick in enjoying any part of Europe is to avoid large concentrations of Americans or at least stay cut away from them. I've been turning down trips on the cultural exchange, one which would have gotten me to Russia and the other to Berlin. I lose too much time and there is so much bullshit talked at these conferences that I simply can't bear it. Anyway, I work my ass off and all I get from it is the trip and I've made enough such trips.... I'm pretty pissed off with *Esquire,* which in the publisher's column of the March issue, carried a report on the Iowa conference in which I was described as being 'complacent' concerning foundation grants to writers—this after Mailer launched an attack against them as buying the writer off. My point was that I was more interested in improving my writing than in the possible corruption a gift of a few thousand dollars could do me. I get sick of that childish crap since I see no point in complaining about money you accept on your own free will. *Esquire* missed the irony that with all the grants available I've had only the Rosenwald. I didn't ask to be appointed a Fellow to the American Academy in Rome, that was a prize and if I have any complaint to make, it's that I didn't have the strength to refuse it. The National

Book Award was another prize, for which I received a gold plaque, not the thousand bucks given today. I've never had a Ford, Rockerfeller, or Guggenheim, or any of the lesser gravy. No *Kenyon,* No *Sewanee,* nor *PR,* no *Hudson,* or any of the numerous grants which are doubtlessly designed to aid rather than hinder the writer and which a number of writers who are much less talented continue to receive. But what really angers me is the discovery that the little shit at *Esquire* assumed that because we were paid $500.00 for the time out there I was going to turn myself into a clown like Mailer. I talked seriously and I gave him the opportunity to meet me on my ground but he chose not to tangle. Yet the *Esquire* character is so awed by the phony Mailer image of the outlaw that he couldn't see what was happening. But there's more to it than that. I was asked to do a piece for an issue on New York which should hit the stands soon, and I did one (they guaranteed me two hundred whether they took it or not) in which I started back in Okla, went to Tuskegee and then described what New York meant to one of such a background, and in which I used a switchblade on just about every thing they hold sacred—especially white women—and they dropped it like it was cancer. I could have done the mood piece they wanted and made myself from eight to a thousand but I wanted them to look inside what makes a black Negro black.

Those guys make a man almost sympathetic to a group of boots out in Chicago who presented a film titled *The Cry of Jazz* recently to a Cinema 16 audience and before which I appeared on a panel to discuss it after the showing (Marshall Stearns, Nat Hentoff and Mark Kennedy and Ed. Bland, the script writer and musicologist who made the film, were the other panelists). These guys made a pitifully bad film to advance the idea that whites had killed Jazz, that the American white had no humanity and that they must turn to the Negro to save themselves. The scene was that of an interracial jazz club—no Negro chicks, man, the studs all had white gals—during which one of the Negro intellectuals expounds on the relationship between the Negro environment and jazz and in which he argued that jazz was dead because the Negro community was limited by jimcrow etc, a thesis which he tried to prove by some very questionable musicology. I pointed out that Jazz had the formal characteristics of most American art forms, but they were so busy trying to make a political point that they couldn't deal with it. Nor could they deal with the cinema. I told them that I was very glad to hear them give voice to their disgust and thought it good that the audience could hear what at least one group of Negroes felt, but wished they'd demonstrated their superiority by at least making a competent film. They are some arrogant and most half-educated studs— the same who've done their damnedest to kill off Louis and to make Jazz middle class. They showed scenes of shouting Negro congregations, with women crying and swooning and dancing, but they didn't put it on the sound track, they were too ashamed; they presented it to the sound of some most uninteresting bebop. And when I questioned them about this they answered that jazz and Negro church music was all the same. To which I said even if that were true what about the fact that a Negro church is not a night club or a dance hall? They wanted to cut my throat before it was over, but they were so wide open in their arguments that they were cut to pieces from the floor. The sad thing is that some of their ideas are worthwhile, but they really want jazz to be dead simply so they won't have to deal with it as Negroes while still having the pleasure of beating white folks over the head from having killed it. I wished I had your remarks concerning Ray Charles at hand at the time because he's excellent proof of how vital the old voice remains. He was well liked at Newport, but as much for his blindness as for his musicianship. You still have to be among such groups as you describe out there in order to have any full appreciation of an art that's moving in the deep complex stream of the old American chaos. Just reading your description makes me homesick. On Wednesday nights after I've taught all day, I sometimes go to a local bar to eat and have a few drinks and there I dance from time to time with the students. Once in a while it works up to a mild swing—jukebox—but man, it's a sad substitute for the real thing and a real whiff of downhome funk would explode the joint. Write me.

Ralph

Dear Ralph & Fanny,

We were out to see Stan and Silvia Whitmore last Sunday. I got in touch with them several weeks after I got back out here, and they had just moved. They are just about settled in their new place now. I met him at Allied Artists Studio and had lunch with him one day last week, and last Sunday I took the gals to help him finish christening his swimming pool. They have a nice little place. Nothing fancy, a comfortable, one-story, add-it-yourself affair. They are doing fine, and we'll be seeing more of them.

I am off from now until the end of this month, have some leave time to use up before the new fiscal year. Plan to read and write and take one or two short trips. Have been fairly busy taking over this new job since I got back. Things quiet now, but all hell will be jumping in October when we start phasing out.

Hope you guys can see your way clear to tool on out this way this Summer. During or after the convention is all right with us. Hell, anytime at all is all right with us. By the way, there is no optimum time to visit this part of California. Southern California is unreal any time of the year.

I think Mique is just about set to spend a couple of weeks at the dance workshop at Idyllwild Arts Foundation (San Jacinto Mountains near Palm Springs), last week in July & first week in August. I still don't know what we are going to do about college yet. It's still another year away, but that seems pretty goddamn near, too. Meanwhile she seems to have had a successful prom season. She made two [balls] (No sweat about party dresses because she already had two that she was looking forward to wearing again!) you must get her to tell you about a Japanese hipster who was in their gang at one of the after-parties, who was in there signifying right back at old mose: *Man, don't be calling me no budderhead (Buddha) I'm strictly spook tonight!*

I sent the camera back to NY through a Leica agency out here. It came back the other day. Fifty six dollars worth of work. There was no damage to the lens itself. They repaired the collapsing element and replaced the flange ring on the body. They also installed the preview gismo since they had torn it down anyway. It's like new now. Meanwhile the pictures I made up in the country and in Washington came out fine.

William Styron's book turned out to be a natural dud. I don't know where the hell Granville Hicks got the material for his *SR* notice. *The New Yorker* put bad mouth on it as a false alarm, and I'm afraid I agree 100%. I mention this because I was among those who like many of the things in his first book. This one leaves me cold.

Old Duke is in the area. He was in Las Vegas for three months and here for about a weekend.; is up north now, due back here by the end of the week for a part in a Hollywood Bowl fuck-up, and a stand at the Crescendo. I heard him at three concerts and two dances while they were here week before last, and they were as sharp as they wanted to be when they wanted to be. All in all they were not too happy here however and just might not come back after Frisco and Seattle. Their newest album, *Blues in Orbit*, has some fine moments, a lot seems to be going on in the band. They are in the process of recording Duke's version of the *Nutcracker Suite*, and he's also doing the score for another Otto Preminger movie, *Bunny Lake is Missing*. I heard them play the first part of Nutcracker at a dance one night. Liked it. Lawrence Brown is back with the band. Tizol was back during the Vegas stand and one night here. Told me nothing will ever get him out of L.A. (Las Vegas is considered a part of L.A. or vice versa).

Murray

INDEX